Also by Benoit Denizet-Lewis

America Anonymous: Eight Addicts in Search of a Life

AMERICAN VOYEUR

Dispatches from the Far Reaches of Modern Life

Benoit Denizet-Lewis

For Miguel,
Thanks for coming!
Ben

Simon & Schuster Paperbacks
New York London Toronto Sydney

Simon & Schuster Paperbacks
A Division of Simon & Schuster, Inc.
1230 Avenue of the Americas
New York, NY 10020

First Simon & Schuster trade paperback edition January 2010

Designed by Davina Mock-Maniscalco

Manufactured in the United States of America

1 3 5 7 9 10 8 6 4 2

Library of Congress Cataloging-in-Publication Data
Denizet-Lewis, Benoit.
American voyeur : dispatches from the far reaches of modern life / Benoit Denizet-Lewis.—1st Simon & Schuster trade paperback ed.
p. cm.
1. Interpersonal relations—United States—Anecdotes.
2. United States—Social life and customs—1971—Anecdotes.
3. United States—Civilization. I. Title.
HM1106.D46 2010
306.70973—dc22
2009016589
ISBN 978-1-4165-3915-5
ISBN 978-1-4165-9447-5 (ebook)

Page 295 constitutes an extension of this copyright page.

For my parents,
Dennis Lewis and Benedicte Denizet

Contents

SEX

Introduction

IN A SMALL, DAMP, bloodstained garage on Chicago's South Side, a pit bull named Prince eyed me suspiciously from a specially made dog treadmill. The product of repeated incest, he had lustrous black skin, a strapping upper body, and wild, wrathful eyes that one might expect to find on an angry mountain lion.

"Okay, here's what I want you to do," his owner, David, told me. "Stand right in front of him, put your face to his, and growl at him. Make him mad. That's gonna make him run his ass off!"

Prince did not like it when I moved. No matter where I stood (and at that point I stood as far away from the animal as possible), I seemed to be invading his personal space. "Come on," David said, rolling his eyes. "Don't you see the chain? He can't do anything to you."

I was clearly disappointing David. I must have seemed braver a week earlier, when I had sat by chance near him and his girlfriend at a Chicago restaurant. There, I'd listened intently as he drunkenly bragged about his pit bulls and invited me to meet them sometime. As luck would have it, I needed an idea for a magazine writing class assignment at Northwestern University. David and his pit bulls would surely do.

But what had I gotten myself into? Just the few steps it took me to position myself in front of Prince's treadmill sent the dog into a blistering rage. He started sprinting, tugging at the chain, and gyrating his head back and forth, spraying the garage with saliva.

"Move around or something," David told me. "Do something to make him mad." I waved my left hand meekly at the dog. "Come on," David said, "you can do better than that! Don't be such a *white boy*."

He was right—I was a *white boy* who was scared of killer dogs. But I hadn't come all the way to the South Side to be ridiculed. So I pretended to be brave. I jumped up and down in front of Prince, growled at him, questioned his manhood. "There you go!" David screamed. "Make Prince mad!"

With Prince now beside himself with fury, David promptly lost interest in him and introduced me to another dog, his "top dog," who went by the comparatively pedestrian name of Sam. David opened the door to Sam's crate, making sure to get a firm grip on the dog's collar. Sam was significantly smaller than Prince, but David told me not to read too much into that, because Sam was also significantly meaner than Prince.

"Sam is a *bad* dog," he told me. "He doesn't bother with

all that macho bullshit Prince and others will try to pull. He's all business. He's a *killer*. If I let him go right now, he would either *try* to kill Prince, or he *would* kill you."

IT WAS AN odd time for an epiphany, but as I stood in that garage with David, Prince, and Sam, I realized what I wanted to do when I grew up. I wanted to do this.

No, I didn't want to be a dogfighter. I wanted to combine journalism and sociology, parachuting into different kinds of subcultures, immersing myself in the lives of its members for days, weeks, months, or as long as they could stand me. David, it turned out, didn't want me around for very long. But it didn't matter. There had to be other people doing other interesting things in other American garages.

So I've spent much of the last twelve years looking for them, although I cheated and broadened the search. I've looked in churches, motels, back alleys, retirement communities, nightclubs, schools, Internet chat rooms, skate parks, malls, community centers, fraternity houses, and suburban mansions. I've felt at home in some of these places and astoundingly out of place in others. Either way, once I found people I wanted to write about, I usually hung around for a while, because people are likely to do any number of revealing things when they let their guard down. My job, then, is to wait around for people to be themselves.

In these pages you'll read about teen Christians, lipstick lesbians, homeless youths, "friends with benefits," suicidal brothers, NAMBLA members, "sober" fraternity boys, gay men who hate doing "gay stuff," a seven-year-old professional skateboarder, black men on the Down Low, young pro-life activists, a transgender middle schooler, and Ohioans who live on the road that dare not speak its name.

These stories represent much of my writing about youth culture, sex, and sexual identity. Truth be told, I never expected to write about the things I have. As a young boy, when I realized that I likely wouldn't grow up to be San Francisco 49ers quarterback Joe Montana, I decided that I would be a writer. I assumed that I would write about sports, because then I could go to games for free and sit in the press box, which sounded like a great way to spend my time here on Earth. And although I have written about sports, for the most part I've gravitated toward chronicling the lives of people who are ignored, misunderstood, stereotyped, or outside the mainstream.

A friend once asked me, "Why don't you ever write about *normal* people?" Normal people? Good luck finding those, I told him. As the saying goes, The only normal people are the ones you don't know very well.

I SPENT A good part of my twenties writing about teenagers—and occasionally being mistaken for one. A dear friend once remarked that my "natural dress approximates that of an adolescent."

Looking and dressing young may not have helped me be taken seriously by adults, but it did help me immerse myself in the lives of young people for the stories that make up the first half of this collection. "We thought you'd be some *old guy*," one teen said minutes after meeting me for a story, "but you look cool enough. You can totally hang out with us."

For the most part, the teens I've written about let me into their lives with little prompting. Though it can take weeks or months to navigate through the many protective layers and disingenuous fronts of adults, I've found most adolescents to be remarkably candid. They seemed to relish having someone take interest in them—someone who would listen without judgment.

They could, at times, be a little too trusting, forgetting that I was there with a clear agenda: to write an accurate and revealing story about their lives. I was sure to remind them that if they didn't want to see something embarrassing in print, they needed to tell me that it was "off the record." Some teens quickly got the hang of it, delighting in their journalistic veto rights. "I totally hate my mom," one girl told me as I hung out with her for my *New York Times Magazine* cover story "Whatever Happened to Teen Romance?," about the decline of teen dating. "But, yeah, that's *totally* off the record!"

Though teenagers are a joy to write about, they've also been the subject of some of the most painful stories I've worked on. The most difficult, "Brother's Keeper," which I wrote while a fellow at the Alicia Patterson Foundation, is about two likable and athletic teenage brothers in New Hampshire who committed suicide one year apart. A year after his older brother's suicide, Greg, a high school junior who loved acting, was cast as Conrad—a suicidal teenager dealing with the death of his older brother—in the school production of *Ordinary People.*

Administrators hoped the role would be therapeutic for Greg, but four days before opening night he shot himself in the head with his father's gun—the same gun his older brother, Eric, had used in his suicide. (The boys' father hadn't bothered to get rid of it.)

I'm normally able to keep some psychological distance from the people I profile, but I fell into a deep depression while researching the brothers' lives. Stories of suicide affect me profoundly, probably because my maternal grandfather and two of my mother's siblings also killed themselves. But there was something especially powerful that drew me to these brothers. Their deaths seemed so unreal. I became obsessed with trying to make sense of them, to explain the unexplainable. At one point I considered writing a book about the brothers, but I couldn't imagine spending so much time on a story that made me so sad.

I was also deeply affected by "Trouble in Paradise," about homeless young people in San Francisco's mostly gay Castro District. They came to San Francisco hoping to start a new life, but instead they found homelessness, addiction, and a community that wasn't so sure it wanted them there (except maybe to exploit them sexually).

I grew up only five minutes from the Castro. My parents didn't suspect I was gay in high school, nor would they have thrown me out if they had (I came out to them in college, and they were supportive). But what if the circumstances had been different? As I hung out with the Castro's homeless youths, watching them panhandle and prostitute themselves to support the drug addictions they developed on the streets, I was astonished by their intelligence and creativity. Many of them were good kids who had been abused, abandoned, or rejected by their parents. It didn't take long for me to realize that were it not for chance, they could have been me, and I them.

Of all the stories I've written about young people, "About a Boy Who Isn't"—my 2002 *New York Times Magazine* profile of M., a transgender middle schooler in California—continues to draw the most interest from readers. About once a month, I receive an e-mail from someone wanting to know what's happened to M. in the years since the story was published. Sadly, I don't know. I lost track of him about two years after the article came out, as did the teacher at the school who was helping M. live secretly as a boy. The last the teacher had heard, M. was "running with a gang." I have a hard time picturing the shy thirteen-year-old I'd spent time with doing that, but M. desperately wanted to be seen as a boy—and very little screams "boy" more than gang life.

If M. wasn't your typical boy, I certainly hung out with plenty of those for "The War on Frat Culture," my *Times Magazine* cover story about the movement to ban alcohol in fraternities. Genuinely perplexed by the notion of Greek sobriety, I returned to my fraternity at Northwestern University to see what a dry fraternity might look like. (Hint: still messy.)

I'm often asked if I worry about "kids today." It's not an unreasonable question to ask of someone who has written so much about young people, but the truth is, I'm more worried about some of the adults who raise them. I can't tell you how many teens I've met during the last decade who have suffered neglect or emotional abuse at the hands of their poorly equipped parents. Lonely, disconnected, and desperate for validation and connection, a generation of kids is busy medicating themselves with prescription drugs, video games, Internet chat rooms, pornography, and meaningless hookups.

That's the bad news. The good news is that just as often, I meet teenagers who overwhelm me with their kindness, humor, talent, passion, integrity, and loyalty to their friends and family. Kids don't get much more talented than the prepubescent professional snowboarders and skateboarders in "Kids Inc." And when it comes to passion, I was impressed with the avid teen Christians in "God Is Rad" and the young pro-life activists in "Camp Life." Though I disagreed with them on virtually every issue and politely rebuffed their awkward attempts to convert me, I thoroughly enjoyed the time I spent with them. One of the gifts of writing so often about people radically different from myself is that I can find the humanity in just about anybody. My friends sometimes wonder how I can claim to "enjoy" spending time with avid teen Christians seeking to convert me, NAMBLA members, homophobes, homeless teenage drug addicts, guys on the Down Low, or any other people my friends find distasteful for one reason or another. But it's only by stepping outside of my comfort zone that I can learn something new. For example, after getting to know teen Christians for "God is Rad" (as opposed to relying on my caricature of what an evangelical teen might be like), I couldn't help thinking that if more American teens felt half as passionately about *anything* as these kids did about God, the future would indeed be bright.

That doesn't mean I don't challenge my subjects, or that I'm always comfortable in the subcultures I spend time in. It means that the longer I refrain from judging people, the better I can hope to understand them. And the more honest and revealing my writing will be.

I'm often asked how I get people to open up to me. It's a perfectly reasonable question, and someday I hope to be able to answer it. I don't know why people talk to me. I'm not especially approachable in real life—strangers don't routinely pick me out as their confessor at cocktail parties. If I'm good at getting profile subjects to open up to me, it may be because I'm willing to open up to them. I don't make the time we spend together about me (I still listen far more than I talk), but I also don't play the role of the dispassionate reporter. Immersion journalism requires a degree of emotional intimacy between writer and subject, and I've found that happens with time and with the willingness of both parties to let down their guards and to reveal their shared humanity.

WHEN I WAS twenty-seven, an editor from *The New York Times Magazine* called me with an idea that would eventually become "Double Lives on the Down Low," one of the eight pieces that make up the second half of this collection devoted to sex, gender, and identity. "Black men are contracting HIV at a really high rate," the editor said, "and it looks like a lot of these guys are dating women but secretly having sex with guys. They've created an organized subculture around it called the Down Low. See what you can find out."

"You want a *white guy* to write about the Down Low?" I asked.

"Well, you did a great job on the story about M.," she said. "We know it won't be easy, but if anyone can do this piece, we think it's you."

It was a nice vote of confidence, but it still struck me as preposterous. Many Down Low parties won't even let whites in the door—how could I possibly immerse myself inside a secretive subculture for people of color? But to my surprise, my race wasn't a major obstacle. I spent weeks in Internet chat rooms devoted to guys on the Down Low, and most seemed more interested in whether I was "masculine" than whether I was black. As long as they perceived me as masculine, they could hang out with me without blowing their cover.

When a handful of guys finally agreed to meet in person and show me around the Down Low scenes in Cleveland, Atlanta, and New York, they expressed relief that I didn't look "like a fag," as they put it. They assumed that I would relate to their aversion to "gay culture," and were flummoxed, then, when I told them that I held no similar animosity (in fact, I'm not sure what "gay culture" even means anymore) and am in fact openly gay. Several DL guys couldn't wrap their heads around *that*. They were still living with the belief—as do many men, both black and white—that being masculine and openly gay are mutually exclusive.

(I explore that notion further in "Regular Guys," about a raucous San Francisco social group for "masculine" gay men who hope to debunk the notion that most gays prefer shopping and show tunes to tailgating and action movies. I give "feminine" lesbians similar treatment in "Cosmetically Correct," about a controversial Boston group for self-described lipstick lesbians.)

The Down Low story was my first cover piece for the *Times Magazine,* and I suspected it would make waves. Most Americans hadn't heard of the subculture, and any story at the intersection of race and sexuality is destined to trigger strong emotions—especially when it's on the cover of *The New York Times Magazine*. Still, I wasn't prepared for the hundreds of e-mails I received in the two days after publication.

Some were from black men and women incensed that I, a white man, was writing about this topic at all. Others blamed me for demonizing black men ("Why don't you write about white men in the closet?" was a typical criticism), while still others said I was too forgiving and didn't demonize DL guys nearly enough (for denying their sexuality and sometimes infecting their wives and girlfriends with HIV).

Outside my inbox, bigger things were happening. Panicked black women all across the country grilled their husbands and boyfriends about their sexual behavior. Oprah devoted an hour to the Down Low; *Law & Order* produced a Down Low storyline; and newspapers all across the country ran Down Low articles.

This all served to create a kind of Down Low backlash, where some of the same experts who had hyped the DL phenomenon to me and others were now backtracking, claiming that there weren't as many guys on the Down Low as the press was claiming, and that DL guys were being unnecessarily scapegoated for the HIV epidemic among black women. I understood their concern, but their backpedaling—and the endless efforts by some journalists to "debunk" the Down Low, claiming that the subculture is either tiny or nonexistent—doesn't change the reality that an *increasing* number of black and Hispanic men are claiming the Down Low identity. And in a sure sign that the world has gone completely mad (and that there is no part of black culture that white men won't brazenly co-opt), some white guys—apparently unsatisfied with the comforts of "the closet"—are now claiming to be "on the Down Low," too. (You can read about that in "Get Out of My Closet!")

As stigmatized as men on the Down Low are, they can point to one group of men who have it worse: the North American Man/Boy Love Association (or NAMBLA). For "Boy Crazy," my lengthy *Boston Magazine* piece about one of the most despised and ridiculed organizations in America, I spent time with self-described "boy-lovers" in Boston and in cities across the country.

In this decade of sexual "predators" and televised Internet sex stings, it's a challenge to write unsensationally about an organization advocating man-boy relationships. I decided early in my reporting that I didn't want to write the typical NAMBLA piece, with its barely concealed presumption that NAMBLA members are incorrigible perverts who should all burn in Hell. What interested me was why the organization, which was founded in the late 1970s and fully expected a seat on the sexual revolution bus (and a place in modern gay culture), failed to achieve any of its political and social objectives and has become little more than a loose-knit coalition of lonely, paranoid members. (It took me months to gain the trust of NAMBLA members, some of whom insisted on communicating by encryption.)

While NAMBLA members are ridiculed for their fixation on youth, one man who has made millions off our cultural obsession with sex and young people is Mike Jeffries, the eccentric then-sixty-one-year-old CEO of Abercrombie & Fitch and the subject of "Abercrombie Nation." A cartoonish physical specimen (dyed blond hair, golden tan, bulging biceps, torn Abercrombie jeans), Jeffries granted me a rare interview in his secluded corporate compound in Ohio, where painfully attractive young employees in Abercrombie clothes traversed the campus on playground scooters and worked hard to impress their demanding boss, who has, through his own peculiar obsessions, made over himself and the world in his image.

Sweating profusely and fidgeting in his chair, Jeffries defended himself against what he called the "cynicism" of the outside world and soon grew tired of my questions (Does he regret making thongs for middle school girls with "Eye Candy" and "Wink Wink" printed on the front? Is his advertising purposefully homoerotic?), pulling his cooperation from the story. But I wrote it anyway, and it made news with Jeffries's admission that he would prefer it if the world's unpopular, overweight, or otherwise undesirable teens would shop elsewhere. "A lot of people don't belong [in our clothes]," he told me, "and they can't belong. Are we exclusionary? Absolutely."

Speaking of exclusivity, one of my favorite stories in this collection is "What's in a Street Name?," about the residents of a rural Ohio road who changed their street name from Gay Road to Green Apple Road. Not only was the Gay Road sign a magnet for persistent, mysterious thieves, but nineteen residents of the road signed a petition claiming that "the repercussions of living on a road called 'GAY' are not pleasant. The snide remarks and thoughtless comments about one's address being 'GAY' are intolerable." I spent a day talking to the folks on the road formerly known as Gay, and I left convinced of two things: first, I was in arguably the gayest neighborhood in America. Second, as much progress as we've made in combating homophobia, we still live in a country where nineteen people on one road signed a petition to avoid the "stigma" of living on a road called Gay.

But we also live in a country where, in at least one state, gay people can have more than their own road—they can get married! *The New York Times Magazine* cover story "The Newlywed Gays!" is my look inside the lives of the first generation of young gay married men in Massachusetts. While the story ponders serious questions (How will they fashion their unions? What will they use as a model?), some of the couples I profiled had more practical concerns. After picking up their marriage license at City Hall in Boston, twenty-four-year-old Vassili Shields stopped, grabbed his husband by the arm, and with great fanfare asked, "Will you still love me if I'm fat?"

I hope to check in with these couples periodically over the next five or ten years. Will they succeed where so many heterosexual marriages have failed, and—as the sex columnist Dan Savage posited to me—will they "teach the straights a thing or two about how marriage is done?"

Stay tuned, and happy reading.

YOUTH

About a Boy Who Isn't

At a California middle school, M. is a popular 13-year-old boy. Only a few of his teachers know what he's precariously hiding: he's a girl.

STANDING IN A CIRCLE under the shade of a tall, skinny palm tree, five boys smile in unison as they recount a particularly absurd scene in the teenage comedy *Don't Be a Menace to South Central While Drinking Your Juice in the Hood.* The boys—who've watched it countless times on video—agree that it's a comedy classic, but they can't seem to settle on its funniest scene. "Man, the whole movie is dope," says the tallest of the five, who wears a heavy Starter jacket even though it's seventy degrees outside.

It's a bright, sunny California morning, and this middle school recess is humming along lazily. Packs of twelve-year-olds in dark pants and white-collared shirts (the school uniform) meander about, looking for something, anything, to do. Next to the palm tree, three haughty girls with pocket mirrors gossip as they reapply their makeup. A hundred yards away, groups of loud, cocky boys play basketball on outdoor courts. And surveying it all are smiling faculty members with walkie-talkies who easily negotiate this sea of mostly Hispanic students.

An openly gay male teacher leans against a table in the outdoor lunch area, the quietest spot in this expansive courtyard. When he isn't teaching English or theater, he facilitates the school's discreet weekly support group for gay, lesbian, and transgender students. Not far from him is one of the group's regulars, a strikingly beautiful thirteen-year-old girl with piercing brown eyes and long black hair. This morning, as on most mornings, she's being trailed by a group of fawning boys, who can't seem to get enough of the bisexual eighth-grader in the tight white shirt, black pants, and rainbow-colored belt.

If she is the darling of the school's boys, one of her male counterparts stands under the palm tree with his friends, who are still talking about movies. A well-liked and attractive thirteen-year-old, he has short-cropped black hair, brown eyes, and a clear, soft complexion. His backpack is tied loosely around his thin frame, and his stylish, oversize gray sweater falls nearly to his knees.

None of his friends know that he's a member of the discreet school group for gay students. They have no reason to suspect it, either. He likes girls. He has a girlfriend (a *high school* girlfriend, no less), and there are countless other girls willing to date him should he ever want another.

So although his friends assume he is one of them, the

support group members presume—though they don't know for sure, because he doesn't say much during meetings—that he's probably secretly gay or bisexual, or maybe just confused. But they all have it wrong. He isn't gay. He isn't confused. Biologically, he isn't even a boy.

FOR THE LAST four years, M., who was born a girl, has secretly lived as a boy. (As is his preference, I will refer to M. as a "he.") Though most transgender teenagers are unwilling or unable to cross-live, M. finds himself in a nearly unheard-of position: with the support of his family and a few teachers at his middle school, he lives as a boy.

The seventh child in a close-knit family of seven girls and two boys, M. showed early signs of gender identity disorder (GID), the controversial American Psychiatric Association diagnosis for people who repeatedly show, or feel, a strong desire to be the opposite sex and are uncomfortable with their birth sex. By age five, M. refused to wear girls' clothing. Though many children with GID don't continue their cross-gender identification into their teens, M. only became more boy-identified with age.

"We always thought she would grow out of it," M.'s twenty-year-old sister tells me, sitting upright on the couch in her sparsely furnished one-story home, where she lives with her husband and infant son near a busy freeway in a working-class Hispanic neighborhood. "We would try to get her to wear dresses, but she would cry and cry and cry."

M. lounges deep into the couch across from his sister, his

legs spread wide and his small head resting against the back of the couch. He's wearing baggy black jeans and a hooded black sweatshirt, and he's cradling a small pillow on his lap. In his left hand, he holds his pager.

Except for his exceeding civility (particularly toward adults), everything about M. screams thirteen-year-old boy: His clothes are too big. His voice is boyish and uninterested. He bosses his younger sisters around. He answers multipart questions with one-word answers. He spends hours each night on the phone with his girlfriend. And he has only one real hobby to speak of: watching action and comedy movies with his friends.

"When I look at her now, I see a boy," says M.'s twenty-three-year-old sister, who sits next to M.'s twenty-year-old sister on the couch. "I used to think she was just going to be a lesbian, but she doesn't want to be a girl with another girl. She wants to be a boy with another girl. I know she is a girl, but I see a boy."

"We used to ask her all the time: 'How come you want to be a boy? You're a *girl*,'" recalls the twenty-year-old sister. "People would stop my mother on the street and say, 'Oh, your son is so beautiful.' And she would correct them and say, 'No, this is my *daughter*.'"

M.'s mother still can't bring herself to refer to M. as "he." "I accept my daughter because she is my daughter and I love her," she says in Spanish, sitting next to her eldest daughters. A slender, delicate woman, she works as a housecleaner and speaks little English. "But I don't understand it. Sometimes it makes me cry."

Several family members broke down after seeing the film

Boys Don't Cry, which tells the true story of Brandon Teena, a female-to-male transgender twenty-one-year-old who was raped and murdered when her biological sex was discovered. "We all say, 'Look, what happened in that movie can happen to you, too,'" the twenty-year-old sister says. "We always try to get her to tell the truth to people, because what would students at her school do if they found out she was lying to them?"

There is a long pause, during which M. glances down at his vibrating pager. M. is paged about every fifteen minutes, usually by his girlfriend, who tells him she loves him in pager code. I ask M. if many girls at school like him. "Girls flirt with me," he says matter-of-factly, "but I tell them I have a girlfriend."

M. hasn't told her about his secret. All they've done is kissed. "When she wants to do more, I just say, 'No, I'm not ready,'" M. says. "I want to touch her, but then she would want to touch me back. So we just kiss. I want to tell her the truth so bad, but every time I try, I can't."

Few transgender teenagers face M.'s unusual predicament. While he's part of his school's elite social group, most self-identified transgender teenagers can't hide their biological gender and face daily harassment and ridicule at school. M. says he feels safe everywhere, but as his female body develops, he knows it will become increasingly difficult to keep his secret.

ON HIS FIRST day of fifth grade at a new school, M. stood sheepishly in the classroom doorway. His hair was cut short, and he wore baggy clothes. M. was then living as a girl, but to the teacher M. looked like any other boy. "Show the gentleman to his seat," the teacher instructed another student.

The *gentleman*? Too embarrassed to correct him, M.—who at the time went by his birth name, which though primarily a girl's name is occasionally a boy's—shuffled to his seat and sat down. Minutes later, he grasped the significance of that moment. "That's when I realized I could live as a boy, without anyone knowing," he says. "People just assumed I was a boy."

M. didn't tell his family what happened at school, and that year he lived a double life: at home he was a girl, at school he was a boy. (Because of his gender-neutral first name, teachers and students didn't suspect anything.) Although he can be painfully shy around new people, M. soon made friends with both boys and girls.

M. had to change schools again the next year for middle school, but he continued living as a boy and started dating girls, who were drawn to his good looks and sweet, calm demeanor. M. even took gym class with boys—the school didn't require students to shower, and he never had to get fully naked in the locker room. The more M. lived as a boy, the less he worried about being discovered. "I would go weeks without thinking about it," he says.

That changed last year, when a counselor at the school discovered his secret during a routine call to his mother. The counselor referred to M. as "your son," but his mother—unaware that M. was passing as a boy—corrected the counselor. "She's not my son," his mother said. "She's my daughter." The counselor was shocked. "She's your *what*?"

M. says the school told him that he would have to take gym class with the other girls the following year when he went into eighth grade. M. wasn't about to go back to living as a girl, so in the fall he transferred to his current school. And finally aware that M. was passing as a boy, his mother insisted that M. tell the school's administrators.

On his first day, M., his mother, and the school dean walked to the classroom of the openly gay teacher who runs the support group. He was in the middle of a lecture about Kabuki theater when the dean knocked on the classroom door and took the teacher aside.

"You need to talk to this young . . . this young . . ." The nervous-looking dean leaned in and whispered in the teacher's ear, "This is a *girl,* and this is her mother."

And so began the highly unusual transgender experiment at this California middle school. As far as the teacher knew, the school hadn't dealt with a transgender student before, let alone one who wanted to cross-live. The teacher consulted with the principal, a counselor, a nurse, and a representative from the school district.

"I needed to tell the nurse, because I wanted M. to be able to use the private bathroom in her office," says the teacher, a powerful personality who is renowned at the school for getting what he wants. "People were smart enough to get out of my way and let me handle it. M. has the right to be safe in school, no matter what his gender identification."

Most concerned with the prospect of M. in the locker room for gym class, the teacher approached the school's dance instructor about instead enrolling M. in dance. The class doesn't require students to wear tight outfits, and M.

could change in the teachers' private bathroom, which is near the dance rehearsal space. (Because the school is so big, no one seems to notice that M. doesn't change with the rest of the class.)

"I briefly explained the situation and told the instructor that he needed to trust me and do me this favor," the teacher says. "I don't think he had ever met an openly gay person before me, so this was a lot for him to digest. Finally he said, 'Okay, but if there is any problem with this, I'm coming to you.'"

The teacher then hand-selected M.'s other teachers, choosing those he thought would be sensitive to M.'s situation. He reminded them not to call M. by his given name, which legally has to be in the roll book, but to use the name that M. and the teacher had come up with. "Even though his given name can be a boy's name, many people in the Latino community know it as a girl's name," the teacher says. "We didn't want to take any chances."

"When he told me about M., all I could do was picture *Boys Don't Cry,*" says one of the teachers he approached. "Was this child going to be safe? I went home and had a long talk with myself. I wanted to make sure I didn't do anything stupid to jeopardize this."

Helping M. live as a boy may seem compassionate, but there are some—even some sympathetic to M.'s predicament—who think the school should be handling his situation differently. Ken Zucker, head of the Child and Adolescent Gender Identity Clinic in Toronto, says that M.'s well-meaning teachers are bordering on unethical conduct.

"They're perpetuating a deception," Zucker tells me

after I explain M.'s situation to him. "What if M. starts dating a girl at school, and she finds out and is traumatized? The school is potentially liable, because they have actively perpetuated a deception. I would advocate that this youngster be encouraged to 'come out' as a transgender youth, so that everyone knows the score. But whatever decision is made, this kid needs to be evaluated by a local expert in gender identity—not by a well-meaning teacher."

The teacher insists he's only doing what's necessary to keep M. safe, and other transgender youth experts say that having M. "come out" as transgender could be dangerous. "The consequences are too great," says Gerald Mallon, an associate professor at the Hunter College School of Social Work and editor of the book *Social Services with Transgendered Youth*. "If M. gets found out at school, he will probably be beaten or raped."

The teacher agrees: "In a more understanding and accepting world, my preference would be for this child to be able to be honest. But M. wishes to live as a boy, and it is my responsibility to protect him. According to the laws in this state, I am in compliance. If we didn't take the basic steps, it would be impossible to protect his safety, short of hiring an armed guard to escort him from class to class."

M. says he doesn't worry about being discovered at school, where he walks around confidently with his friends. But he acknowledges that he's less sure about next year, when he'll attend one of two area high schools. "I don't know if the teachers there would want to lie for me," he says.

The teacher doesn't know, either, but he's already spoken with a counselor at one of the schools who runs a similar support group and plans to meet with someone at the other. "I have to find someone who will look after him," the teacher tells me.

M. PULLS AT his apartment's courtyard gate and is surprised to find it locked. "They never lock this," he says, tugging at it a second time. "Hey, kid!" he shouts toward a boy dribbling a basketball inside the courtyard. "Open the door!" The boy—who looks younger but is bigger than M.—bows his head slightly, apparently hurt to have been labeled a kid by another kid. He eventually dribbles the ball over to the gate and opens it, for which M. mumbles a quick "Thanks."

M. lives in this subsidized housing community, in a small, two-bedroom apartment he shares with his mother, stepfather, and two younger sisters. (M.'s father is a mechanic who lives nearby and is a regular and supportive presence in his son's life.) M.'s family has moved several times in the last few years, so his neighbors know him only as a boy. "There are always kids everywhere around here," M. says near the steps to his apartment, stopping to avoid a speeding shopping cart with a crazed boy at the controls.

The door to M.'s apartment is open. His mother is in the kitchen, and his six-year-old sister is running around the carpeted living room in overalls. M.'s ten-year-old sister—with whom he shares a small room with a bunk bed, television, and no posters on the walls—is at a friend's house. "Normally she's cool," M. says of his sister and bunkmate, "but when she gets mad at me, she calls me names, like 'lesbian' or 'boy-girl.' I tell my mom, and my mom gets mad at her."

M. plops himself down on the living room couch and takes off his black hooded sweatshirt, under which he wears three layers of shirts. His small breasts, which began developing last year, are barely noticeable. "I don't want anyone to see them," he says. "When they first started growing last year, I just hoped that they wouldn't grow that big." In addition to wearing layers, M. often stands with his shoulders slightly hunched, making it nearly impossible to see his chest from a profile position.

As M.'s mother brings him a glass of juice, I ask him if he's thought about someday taking hormones and having gender reassignment surgery, which for female-to-male transgenders can include breast reduction, the construction of male genitalia, and the ablation of the uterus and the ovaries. "If I could do surgery right now, I would," M. says without hesitation. "But I don't think they can do it at this age."

"Why would you want to take away what God gave you?" his mother says in Spanish, her voice soft and loving. "Why would you want to do that?"

It's clear that this is the first time the subject of surgery has come up, and M. doesn't have an answer prepared. There is a long pause, during which M.—who often pauses before answering a complicated question, visibly collecting his thoughts—takes a sip of juice, leans forward, and scratches the side of his head. "I want to live as a boy," he says finally. "I want to do it because I want to be a guy."

I ask M. if he wants a penis as an adult, and he nods his head. I ask his mother if she would be supportive of that.

"They can attach a penis?" she says in Spanish, unbelieving. She looks at M. "I don't know. Why would you want to do *that?*"

To M., the answer is obvious: he is a boy, and he wants a boy's body. In that pursuit, hormonal therapy could drastically change his physical development, stopping menstruation and bringing about the onset of male puberty. (M. started getting his period two years ago.) But according to the Harry Benjamin International Gender Dysphoria Association's Standards of Care, the widely recognized blueprint for management of gender-identity disorders, hormonal treatment shouldn't begin before age sixteen. In the United States, transgender teenagers under eighteen need parental consent and psychological and physical evaluations before receiving hormones from a doctor.

"Hormones before puberty would be very hard to defend," says Kenneth Demsky, a psychologist and gender specialist in Boston, when I tell him about M. "When working with someone who is young, you want to delay irreversible physical intervention as long as clinically appropriate." But it's a dilemma, Demsky says, because "the earlier people get hormones, the better the effects."

One of the best arguments for delaying hormone treatment is that gender identity, like sexual preference, can be changing and fluid, particularly during childhood and adolescence. Does M., at age thirteen, truly know what he will want in five or ten years?

"Most likely, yes," says Zucker from the Child and Adolescent Gender Identity Clinic in Toronto. "The chance that M. could change his mind at this point is close to zero. If he has been so consistently boy-identified from an early age and is reasonably psychologically stable, he seems like a possible candidate for puberty-blocking medication. But to find that out, he needs to be evaluated by an expert. And he needs to be seeing a therapist who can help him in talking about all this, planning ahead, and in learning how to negotiate disclosure to his romantic partners."

M. has never seen a therapist (he has never asked to see one, although he says he would like to), and it is very unlikely his family could afford regular visits to a gender identity specialist. Still, Zucker says it's only through therapy that M. and his family can better understand how and why M. chose to cross-live and how he should best navigate the next four years of high school.

"I would be interested in understanding more about how he came to this very early and conscious choice," Zucker says. "Did he ever think about the possibility of being a lesbian, and was that abhorrent to him? And was that abhorrent to his family? Do they see him as more normal living as a boy and liking girls, as opposed to being a girl and liking other girls?"

When I pose the questions to M., he's initially confused. He eventually says that he never felt like a lesbian because he always felt like a boy. But he suspects that his family prefers him as a boy rather than as a lesbian. "I don't know for sure, but they might think it was nasty if I was a girl into other girls," he tells me.

• • •

"HEY, FAGGOT!"

M. and I look to our left, where a male voice comes from a passing car. We're walking down a busy boulevard toward M.'s apartment, and the loud taunt—which was more mocking than threatening and probably aimed at the young man behind us—lingers in the muggy air.

M. seems unfazed (he doesn't consider himself gay, after all) and continues talking about his girlfriend, who's just paged him for the fifth time in thirty minutes. When I ask him if there's any chance she might know his secret, M. recounts a recent phone call between them that did manage to faze him.

"Out of the blue, my girlfriend said, 'What would you do if I was a guy?'" M. says. "I didn't know what to say. I just said, 'I don't know.' Then a minute later I asked her, 'What would you do if I was a girl?' She said, 'I would be mad at you, but I would still love you.' Sometimes I think she might know about me, because why would she have asked me that? Does she know I'm a girl?"

That's just one of the many questions M. is pondering today. He says his mind is a muddled sea of thoughts—about his girlfriend, high school, and his developing female body. I ask him what he would do if his friends discovered his secret this year or in high school. Would he transfer? "No, I don't think I would," he says. "I would just deal with it."

Though M. seems aware, on some level, that his life would change drastically if people discovered his secret, he plays down the consequences. Does he worry about being beaten up? "No, not really," he says. Would people make fun of him? "Maybe, yeah," he says. Does he think his friends would understand? "I don't know," he says. "I would try to explain to them that I feel like a guy and that I always have."

Finally, as we approach his apartment complex, I ask him if he's happy. He takes a few steps and tightens his face in thought. He scratches his head. He starts to open his mouth and then closes it, mulling over the question for some ten seconds. Just when I suspect he's given up on answering it, he speaks.

"Yeah, I'm happy, but I always think, Why did God make me like this?" he says, staring off into the distance. "Why couldn't he have just made me one way, either a guy or girl? Because I don't feel like a girl at all, but I have a girl's body. I don't understand why God would do that."

God Is Rad

Inside the coolest, weirdest, fastest-growing teen Christian movement in America.

THERE IS AN EXPLOSION of pyrotechnics onstage, causing a large, scary ball of fire to leap toward the audience. People jump. People cheer. A tall, attractive teenager with waist-length blond hair stands on her chair, then jumps high in the air, singing as she elevates, oblivious to the potential catastrophe awaiting her return to Earth. Beneath her, three teenage boys, all wearing baggy pants and sideways baseball hats, are sobbing in one another's arms. They do not see the girl descending.

It's a minor miracle, really: she doesn't decapitate the boys. She glances off them, landing on the cement. She props herself up on her hands. She leans on her bony elbows, bows her head, and prays. Randy McClellan, a baby-faced seventeen-year-old with big ears, steps on her hair. He didn't mean to, he says breathlessly, but he can hardly stand up under his own power.

"I got up near the stage to recommit my life to God," he tells me, "and when I went up, my friend started praying for me, and that's when it really hit me. I started getting hot, and it felt like I was tingling, and my whole body went numb. I didn't feel heavy anymore. Have you ever felt like that? Ever felt like a completely *new person*?"

There is another explosion, causing another large ball of fire to leap toward the thousands of teenagers who've assembled at Teen Mania's Acquire the Fire Convention in San Bernardino, California. A thunderbolt soars through outer space on two mammoth video screens, and some extremely loud drum 'n' bass blasts from a set of large speaker towers. "They're, like, totally pyrotechnic-crazy!" says eighteen-year-old Yanni Vera, who is attending his first Teen Mania convention. "It's like the WWE, only with God!"

Gabe Bahlhorn, a nineteen-year-old Teen Mania volunteer who repeatedly asks me if I want to run up to the stage to "give God a chance," looks relieved. "You never know when those pyrotechnics aren't going to work," he says. "You hope that the fire does what it's supposed to do, because it would suck if we killed people."

A short girl in a blue beanie and tight jeans jumps off her chair, dropping her Bible. Everyone, it seems, has a Bible. The jocks have them. The punks have them. The kids who look like Rod and Todd Flanders *never* forget their Bibles. The ravers, they keep their Bibles in the back pockets of their baggy pants, where they fit perfectly. "Coincidence?" asks sixteen-year-old raver Noah Price. "I think not."

I see a tall, thin, red-haired boy wielding a walkie-talkie walking toward me, gaining speed as he approaches, and I wonder if I am in some sort of trouble. He stops in front of me, smiles, sticks out his right hand, and says, "Hey, bro, my name's Rich! Rich with Jesus! How are you feeling? You feeling good? I'm feeling good! I'm high with the Lord!"

MEET THE MODERN Christian army that plans to save you, me, and every young person in America. Its enemy is a society that long ago ceased to love. Its weapons are modern, surprising, and controversial. Its goal is a spiritual revolution that will feel, more than anything, like one big party. Its soldiers are junior high and high school kids with spiky hair and braces. Its commander is God, and its role model is Jesus Christ—neither of whom, regrettably, could be here in person today.

In their places, a thirty-nine-year-old Italian American named Ron Luce is pacing the auditorium stage, a bundle of unfettered Christian momentum. "We're gonna celebrate Jesus together!" Luce screams. "How many of you would like to see God do something huge with your generation? I'd like to see God do something with your generation that makes the sixties look like a *tea party*! Guys, we haven't even taken off yet! We're on the runway! Are you ready to take off? Are you ready to devote your lives to God? Are you ready to live *for* him?"

The tall blond girl with the waist-length hair is ready. She jumps to her feet and springs back on her chair, only to leap up again, high in the air. As she rises, she sings, "The Lord is my life and my salvation, who shall I fear?" She lands on her feet, then hurls herself over a row of chairs. She sprints down the aisle and runs past the Teen Mania vending booths, past the four boys playing Hacky Sack in the dark, past the girl who used to believe more in aliens than in God, past the former drug user, past the former drug dealer, past the former gang member, and past the current high school baseball star.

She runs past all that, arriving near the front of the stage, crying and shaking. When Ron Luce asks the crowd who would like to know God, when he asks who would like to join Teen Mania's growing army, when he asks who would like to be saved this fine November evening, she raises both hands toward the heavens and screams, "Me!"

THOUGH MANY CHRISTIANS have spent the past decade trying to update Christianity's image (see Christian rock, Christian video games, Christian karate), Teen Mania Ministries is taking the concept to brazen, controversial extremes. In the pursuit of the American teenager, Teen Mania, a nonprofit ministry founded in 1986 and based in Garden Valley, Texas, is marketing God in radical ways, borrowing tactics from the very cultures it hopes to change and/or eradicate: professional wrestling, raves, MTV, the Internet, Hollywood, Las Vegas. At the same time, Teen Mania is holding dearly to a strict biblical and moralistic approach to Christianity, challenging teens to live disciplined lives of sexual purity, honor, and a rigid moral code.

There is no telling whether God approves of Teen Mania's unique packaging, but there is no denying the results: Teen Mania is by most accounts the hottest teen Christian ministry in America, succeeding because it is smart, inspired, modern, well financed, and has thrown out the old Christian playbook, the one that amounted mostly to scaring teens into submission.

The new game plan is complex and multifaceted, but at its core, its philosophy is simple: Teen Mania wants to make a relationship with God seem, well, rad. Teen Mania isn't opposed to using words like *rad,* because it wants—more than anything—to speak the language of American teenagers. It wants to *relate*. If it relates, it figures it will entertain. And if American teenagers are entertained, there is no telling what they might give their lives to.

This is Teen Mania's game plan. It is working. It has turned a small, two-person operation into a $22 million organization that reaches a quarter-million teens each year at its twenty-six Acquire the Fire conventions and thousands more with its weekly television show.

Later this year, about seventy thousand American teenagers from all fifty states will gather in the Pontiac Silverdome in Pontiac, Michigan, for Teen Mania's Stand Up!, which it dubs a "National Gathering of the Unashamed." It will be a loud, dazzling, and emotional show of fire, electronic music, and Christian rock. People will be lowered dramatically from the ceiling by cables. There will be explosions. There will be fire. There will be synchronized montages on the giant video screens. There will be contemplative moments of prayer and thought, followed immediately by more explosions, more fire, more people dropping from the ceiling. Ron Luce will scream a lot, and he will say things like "We need to come out of the closet as Christians! We need to go back to our schools and start a revolution!"

BEFORE THE ALCOHOL, the marijuana, the mushrooms, the acid, the crack, the heroin, the lying, the stealing, and the generally disrespectful attitude, Teen Mania Honor Academy intern Joey Ortega was a good little Christian boy. He was a regular churchgoer, a talented volleyball player, a straight-A student. Overall he was a boy who made his Christian mother, Linda Sitton, proud.

But all this changed during Ortega's freshman year of high school, when Ortega—plagued by a bad relationship with his father—became angry at the world. "And that's exactly when the devil set in," he says. The devil started with alcohol, which wasn't so bad, but then the Devil introduced Ortega to marijuana. When that got boring, the Devil welcomed Ortega to the colorful world of mushrooms and acid, which eventually led to the less colorful world of heroin, which Ortega would inject up to five times daily, often at school.

One day, Linda Sitton got on her knees and prayed harder than she had ever prayed before. About thirty minutes later, the phone rang. The man on the line was from a local church group planning to attend the Acquire the Fire convention in Denver, and he was calling to see whether one of the boys in the group was still planning to come. It was a wrong number—or was it? Sitton wondered if maybe it wasn't a sign from God. Sitton started talking to the man and told him to call back if the other boy couldn't make it.

It turned out that the boy couldn't go, so Sitton drove to her son's school, where she had the principal pull Ortega out of class. When he got in the car, Ortega asked his mother what the fuck her problem was. He tried to unlock the door and jump out, but she locked the doors and kept driving. They arrived at the local church moments before the group's van was leaving. Sitton pushed her son into the van and threw his bag in behind him, saying only "Take him, and may God be with him."

When the group arrived in Denver, Ortega sat in his seat that Friday night at the Acquire the Fire convention. He expected the whole thing to be pretty lame, but before long he was jumping during the pyrotechnics explosions and dancing to the Christian rock.

Ortega couldn't sleep that night in the hotel, and the next day, he sat in his chair and did not think about heroin once. That night, during the final altar call, he felt something drawing him toward the stage. "God was pulling me to the stage," Ortega says. "He was pulling on my heart." Ortega rose from his seat and walked to the front, where he got on his knees and started to cry. He says he felt intense warmth. He says he called out to God, and he says God answered.

"I was a different person after that," Ortega tells me. "It's impossible to explain what happens, and people can't understand how it can happen, but the second you really give your life to God, the second you ask for his help and guidance, you're a new person. The next day I didn't want any of the drugs. My withdrawals from heroin were gone. It was all gone. And I'm not saying my life has been perfect since then, because there are always struggles, but God saved me. Acquire the Fire saved me."

EACH YEAR, TEEN Mania welcomes thousands of teens to its summer camps and five hundred to its Honor Academy, a yearlong internship program designed to develop what Luce calls "future leaders made of honor, courage, leadership, and character."

Honor Academy interns work eight-hour days for free at Teen Mania's corporate headquarters. The organization relies on strong relationships with churches across the country, which in turn bring their youth groups to Acquire the Fire conventions. There, Teen Mania heavily cross-promotes its summer camps, summer mission trips, and Honor Academy, urging teens to return to their schools and communities as missionaries.

Teens choose to do this in any number of ways, from talking to their friends about God to approaching strangers at Disneyland, raves, parties, bowling alleys, and anywhere kids congregate. Most say they aren't looking for one particular kind of teen, because, as Joey Ortega says, "*everyone* needs to know."

"Many young people in this country are tired of fake religion, of hypocritical Christianity, and consequently they aren't giving God a chance," Luce tells me, sitting at his desk at Teen Mania headquarters. Luce looks nondescriptly all-American: parted black hair; medium build; black slacks; button-down shirt. "For too long, pseudo-Christianity has inflicted hurt on people, and the only way to change the perception that many people have is to go out and show them what a real Christian is all about. And when those people see someone who is full, who has something real, that makes them want that." He pauses almost imperceptibly to give a very modern interpretation of the effects of covetousness. "What we do is make people jealous for what we have."

While Ron Luce credits much of Teen Mania's growth to the faith of teenagers and the power of God, there may be a more tangible explanation. "In 1990, Ron looked at the way Madison Avenue was courting teenagers, throwing a lot of money at them, marketing themselves brilliantly, and he asked, 'Why can't we be just as aggressive and smart in reaching teens?'" says Jon Tryggestad, Teen Mania's director of marketing. "That's how it all started. That's why you see the pyrotechnics, the music, the videos, and all the modern tools at our conventions. Since then, our goal has been to keep looking for ways we can push the envelope. We want to be 'out there' and 'crazy' but still have a professional taste and world-class flavor, to create a real, entertaining experience for teens where they look back and say, 'Hey, that was cool!'"

Teen Mania wants desperately to be cool. In fact, its success depends upon it. From its Acquire the Fire conventions to its weekly television program, the organization's goal is to be everything that teens think organized religion is not: hip, progressive, modern, fun. To that end, Luce—who holds a master's in counseling psychology from the

University of Tulsa and has published twelve books—spends much of his time observing and copying popular culture. In his free time, he sits in on teen chat rooms on the Internet, reads young secular magazines, and watches MTV. When in Hollywood or Las Vegas, Luce takes notes on what he likes, often incorporating that into Acquire the Fire conventions.

The end results are conventions that look like a bizarre fusion of a circus, an electronic music concert, a professional wrestling event, and a classic religious revival. It's clearly struck a chord with many teenagers, though some traditional Christians are wary of Teen Mania's flirtations with modernity.

"I like Teen Mania a lot, but they use propaganda sometimes, and I don't really believe in that," says Michael Jelensky, a sixteen-year-old from Anaheim Hills who attended the San Bernardino convention and is considering attending the Honor Academy. "I think Acquire the Fire should just focus more on the word of God and not try to get kids to accept it because of lights and music. I think they should just show people God, because that's all that matters."

But Luce argues that the modern tactics are essential to keeping a teenager's attention, and many Acquire the Fire attendees agree. "If it had just been your average boring Christian event, or if they had just preached at me, I never would have trusted them, and I never would have listened," Ortega says. "Teenagers are easily impressionable, but they have to trust you first. All the lights and music and pyrotechnics are there to relate to teens and to gain their trust. What I learned from how I reacted at Acquire the Fire is the importance in using any possible tactic to spread the word of the gospel. Whatever works, you use."

Teen Mania produces a weekly television program, which runs on local Christian cable channels in most states. A recent program, titled "Defending Your Lifestyle—Why Live With Honor?," opens with techno music, then cuts to a colorful set with video screens, couches, and a trippy pink-and-blue background. Produced at Teen Mania headquarters and hosted by Luce, the show features academy interns as the guests and studio audience.

Teen Mania also works to be hip with its commercials and infomercials, which it usually airs in specific markets several weeks before an Acquire the Fire convention. Developed by independent creative consultants (and tested for "hipness" by academy interns), the commercials feature footage from conventions, mostly pyrotechnic explosions and bands.

When Teen Mania strays from explosions and bands, the end result can be nothing short of surreal. In one infomercial, a man is saved by a flying thunderbolt, leading to an unintentionally hysterical scene in Satan's high-tech command center, which looks like a submarine. There, the Devil's right-hand man screams, "I'm not going to let a bunch of God-loving kids wipe out the world I perfect! These kids still eat what I feed them! Double the propaganda! We've got the press, late-night cable. Cater to their *addictions*!"

In an effort to reach all kinds of teenagers, Teen Mania caters to those same addictions. One is MTV, where Teen Mania—in an effort to reach non-Christians, now a main goal of the organization—placed an ad three years ago, marketing itself to teens who felt something missing in their lives.

Among Christian teens, the goal is to impress what Tryggestad calls "the influencer in the group. We want to reach the cool, well-liked kid who is listened to and admired, the kid who is going to bring the rest. To reach that kid, we have to be hip and cool."

> I know that some people think we're a cult. People think that because we're close to Waco and because we give up a year of our lives to come to this random place in Texas, that we must all be brainwashed or really insane. But the thing is, we *want* to be here.
>
> Nobody made us come here. We want to become better people.
>
> —Honor Academy intern Norman Aubrey Sanchez

WHEN JOEY ORTEGA arrived at the Teen Mania Honor Academy last August, he knew there would be rules. A few rules, he thought. Obvious rules, like no swearing, no staying out until 3 a.m. on weeknights, no courting anyone's daughter (or, worse yet, *son*). But Ortega was surprised to learn that he had vastly underestimated the scope of Teen Mania's structural vision: not only would Ortega not be allowed to do those things, but he would not be able to listen to any non-Christian music, the Internet would be severely restricted, and he would be spending time with girls who must abide by the "one-fist" rule: in a kneeling position, a girl's skirt must be no higher than one fist from the floor, front and back.

"I got here and I was like, 'What are these people talking about?'" Ortega says. "It was just a big shock. But then I really started thinking about it, and it became clear that they were necessary to help us focus on God and to keep us from temptation. If we are to live like Jesus did, we have to live by the standards he set."

The Teen Mania headquarters and Honor Academy is located in Garden Valley, Texas, a mostly agricultural and blue-collar community seventy-five miles east of Dallas. The 464-acre campus features four two-story dorms, a cafeteria, an administration building, basketball and tennis courts, and a rec room.

In addition to working in one of Teen Mania's administrative offices, the five hundred Honor Academy interns—who fork over $4,500 to spend a year here—take a few hours of class each week on character development, leadership, and theology. Interns must also exercise at least four times a week, attend a mandatory chapel service each week on campus and another service at a local church, and fulfill a number of other on-campus and off-campus requirements.

The majority of the interns are white and were raised in Christian homes. Some are high school athletes who turned down college scholarships to attend the academy. Others are lifelong Christians who battled drugs and alcohol in high school. A few are former ravers who now believe that raves are the "Devil's playground." Though some interns plan to go into full-time ministry, more hope the academy will give them the tools needed to succeed in business, secular pursuits, and life.

Still, the leadership training is secondary to the real reason the interns chose to delay college for a year to come here: to develop a deep, passionate, loving relationship with God.

"All *nonsexual*, of course," jokes a nineteen-year-old intern, Bill Ranahan, who gets up at 3:45 each morning (most interns get up at 6 a.m.) to have a three-hour talk with God.

Everything at the Honor Academy is designed with the platonic in mind, and male interns are told often to view the female interns as "sisters." Dating is forbidden. While preaching hipness and modernism, Teen Mania is a mostly conservative, by-the-book Christian ministry. This is most evident when it comes to issues of sexual purity: the interns are told that masturbation is sinful and that homosexuality is a sinful choice that is curable with prayer and God's love.

The academy's many rules and regulations are detailed in *The Saber,* a twenty-six-page policy handbook. The interns must follow a long list of rules, including no R-rated movies; no cross-gender wrestling; no sitting in the same seat with the opposite gender on buses after dark; and no male viewing of the Internet without another male present. "All the rules are designed to guard our hearts, to keep us from temptation," Ortega says. "At the academy, we learn all these things in theory, but it's when you go home to the real world that you actually have to put them into practice."

Most interns seem to take the academy's lessons quite seriously. While a fierce afternoon rain pounded Teen Mania's Honor Academy auditorium room, I listened as a lawyer and Christian speaker, John Graves, used a vehicular metaphor to make a very serious point about potential wives. Teen Mania's male academy interns sat on folding chairs, taking copious notes.

"People say, 'Oh, I need to go test-drive a woman before I marry her,' and that is a lie straight from the pit of Hell!"

shouted Graves, who later told the interns that he had waited until his wedding day to kiss his wife. "If I get in a Lamborghini and I know what the Lamborghini will do, and I put it in first gear and I put my foot on the gas and it goes fifty miles per hour, I do not need to take it to 140 to know that it will do that after I buy it. Do I? That's ridiculous. You don't need to *test-drive it*!"

The boys laughed. A short, overweight intern in a white sweatshirt scribbled a long, thin car and a big-breasted woman in his notebook. Between the car and the woman, he put an equals sign.

THE HIGHLAND HILLS Church in Highland, California, is sandwiched among a doughnut shop, a dentist's office, a pizza joint, a real estate agency, and a Mexican restaurant in a small strip mall. The beige, one-story structure (it used to be a grocery store) has wall-to-wall carpeting. There are no stained-glass windows, no pews, no wooden crosses, no confessional booths.

But at 11:45 on this Friday night in November, the church is bustling with thirty teens who've just returned from day one of Teen Mania's Acquire the Fire convention in San Bernardino. In a far corner, two teenage boys are playing Sega on a big-screen TV, simultaneously plotting to bleach the hair of their youth pastor, John Diaz, while he sleeps. On the makeshift stage, which doubles as an altar during church services, sit seventeen-year-old Brian Pierce and Nick Zendejas. A first-time Acquire the Fire attendee, Zendejas tells me he's bored. "Hey, man, can I leave when you leave?" he asks me. "This whole Christian thing isn't really my scene."

Zendejas came to the Acquire the Fire convention an atheist, and he left an atheist. "Teen Mania knows how to push all the right emotional buttons, and they're dealing with kids who are really impressionable," he says, reclining on the church floor, using his sleeping bag to prop his head up. "A couple of flashy lights, some cool music, and lots of talk about loving each other, and kids are *sold*. I just didn't like how much conformity I saw. Everyone was acting like a bunch of clones, doing the same things. It didn't work on me."

Zendejas saw the pyrotechnic explosions, he listened to the Christian rock, and he watched the boys and girls crying and feeling powerful warmth they attributed to God. He heard Luce say, "Maybe you are tired of just crying yourself to sleep, of having people stomp on you or let you down, and some of you tough guys have been acting like, 'Oh, everything is fine.' Well, everything is *not* fine!"

But when it really mattered, when Luce told the teens that God is the only answer, when he called for them to join his growing army, Zendejas sat firmly in his chair. "God is not my answer," he says, shaking my hand to say good-bye.

He leaves the church, flanked by the woman who will drive him home. He gets into the car and closes the door. The car pulls out of the parking lot, slowly gaining speed as it turns onto Church Street, carrying Zendejas exactly where he wants to go, which is away from the Highland Hills Church, away from Teen Mania, away from the God he does not believe exists.

When he gets home, Zendejas will turn off the lights and lie in his bed. He will not say his prayers. Teen Mania, though, will pray for him, because if it believes one thing to be true, that thing is this: pyrotechnics might get him into the building, but pyrotechnics will not save his soul.

Whatever Happened to Teen Romance?

And what is a friend with benefits, anyway?

JESSE WANTS TO MEET at Hooters. "It's forty minutes from where I live," he says, "but trust me, it's worth the drive."

Surprisingly, there is no age requirement to dine at Hooters. When I call the restaurant to make sure I'm not aiding and abetting teen delinquency (Jesse is fifteen), the woman who picks up seems annoyed I would even ask. "No, we're a *family restaurant,*" she says snootily. So, amid the bronzed, scantily clad waitresses and a boisterous bachelor party, I find Jesse, a smart and outgoing high school sophomore with broad shoulders and messy brown hair underneath his baseball cap. Jesse is there with four of his close friends, whom he has arranged for me to meet.

Among them is Caity, a slender fourteen-year-old freshman with long blond hair and braces. Caity tells me that she's a virgin but that she occasionally "hooks up" with guys, although she doesn't make clear what she means by "hooking up." The term itself is vague—covering everything from kissing to intercourse—though it's sometimes a euphemism for oral sex, usually performed by the girl.

Sitting next to Caity is her best friend, Kate, also fourteen, whom everyone affectionately refers to as "the prude." Cute and outgoing, she's had a boyfriend for a couple of months, but they haven't even kissed yet. In her New England exurban world, where oral sex is common by eighth or ninth grade and where hookups may skip kissing altogether, Kate's predicament strikes her friends, and even herself, as bizarre. "It's retarded," she says, burying her head in Caity's shoulder. "Even my mom thinks it's weird!"

Just a few weeks ago, Caity and Kate met a cute boy at the mall. "Me and Kate walked into this store," Caity tells me, "and this boy saw the shirt Kate was wearing that says, KISS ME, I'M AN AMOEBA. So he was, like, 'That's an awesome shirt.' And she was, like, 'Want me to make you one?' So he went and got Sharpies, and she went and got T-shirts, we met back there, and then he said to me, 'You want my screen name?' So he wrote it on my arm. He just got his license, so he came up, and we hooked up."

I ask Caity if that's it or if her hookup might lead to something more. "We might date," she tells me. "I don't know. It's just that guys can get *so* annoying when you start dating them." Adam, a sixteen-year-old sophomore at the end of the table, breaks in, adding that girls can get equally annoying when you start dating *them*. A soccer player with a muscular body and shaggy blond hair, he likes to lift his shirt at inappropriate times (like now, to the Hooters waitress) and scream, "I've had sex!"

Adam has had the most hookups of the group—about ten, he estimates. When he lived in Florida last year, he lost his virginity to a friend who threw a condom at him and ordered him to put it on. "Down in Key West, high school girls are crazy," Adam said. "Girls were making out with each other on the beach!"

Though Adam and Caity denied it, a thick fog of sexual intrigue surrounded their friendship—and a few weeks after our dinner at Hooters, Jesse sent me an online message notifying me of a hookup in the making between the pair. They were planning to go over to Jesse's house and "mess around." As Jesse explained it, Adam told Caity he didn't want a relationship, which was fine with Caity. She said she didn't want one, either.

According to Jesse, Caity set the ground rules. "Caity told me, 'Adam knows he's not going to get in my pants, but I might get into his.' For now they might just make out, but Caity said that if they hang out a lot more, maybe they'll do more." The next day, Jesse messaged me online to say that the hookup never materialized. "Everyone got busy. But I'm guessing it still might happen."

• • •

I FIRST MET Jesse on facethejury.com, one of many Internet sites popular with high school and college students, where teenagers can post profiles, exchange e-mail, and arrange to hook up. (Though facethejury.com, like many such sites, requires members to be eighteen, younger teenagers routinely lie about their age.) Over the course of several months spent hanging out in person and communicating online with nearly one hundred high school students (mostly white, middle- and upper-middle-class suburban and exurban teenagers from the Northeast and Midwest), I heard the same thing: hooking up is more common than dating.

Most of the teenagers I spoke to could think of only a handful of serious couples at their school. One senior in Chicago, who'd been dating the same girl since sophomore year, told me that none of his friends has a girlfriend and that he's made to feel like a "loser" because he's in a relationship. Searching for reassurance, he turned to me and asked, "Do you think I'm a loser?"

The decline in dating and romantic relationships on college campuses has been deplored often enough. By 2001, it had become so pronounced that a conservative group, the Independent Women's Forum, took out ads in college papers on the East Coast and in the Midwest pleading with students to "Take Back the Date." But their efforts don't seem to have paid off, and the trend toward "hooking up" and "friends with benefits" (basically, a friend you hook up with regularly) has trickled down from campuses into high schools and junior highs—and not just in large urban centers.

Cell phones and the Internet, which offer teenagers an unparalleled level of privacy, make hooking up that much easier. Dating isn't completely dead, of course, but teens today tend to date in ways that would be unrecognizable to their parents or even to their older siblings. A "formal date" might be a trip to the mall with a date and some friends. Teenagers regularly flirt online first and then decide whether to do so in real life. Dating someone from your school is considered by many to be risky, akin to seeing someone from the office, so teenagers tend to look to nearby schools or towns, whether they're hoping to date or just to hook up.

It's not that teenagers have given up on love altogether. Most of the high school students I spent time with said they expected to meet the right person, fall in love, and marry—eventually. But high school, they say, isn't the place to worry about that. High school is about keeping your options open. Relationships are about closing them. As these teenagers see it, marriage and monogamy will seamlessly replace their youthful hookup careers sometime in their mid- to late twenties—or, as one high school boy from Rhode Island told me online, when "we turn thirty and no one hot wants us anymore."

Brian, a sixteen-year-old friend of Jesse's, put it this way: "Being in a real relationship just complicates everything. You feel obligated to be all, like, *couply*. And that gets really boring after a while. When you're friends with benefits, you go over, hook up, then play video games or something. It rocks!"

DATING PRACTICES AND sexual behavior still vary along racial and economic lines, but some common assumptions, particularly about suburban versus urban kids, no longer hold true. Parents often think that teens who grow up in cities are more prone to promiscuous sexual behavior than those in the suburbs, but according to a comprehensive study sponsored by the National Institute of Child Health and Development, slightly more suburban twelfth-graders than urban ones have had sex outside of a romantic relationship (43 percent, compared with 39 percent).

It's unclear just how many teenagers choose hookups or friends with benefits over dating. Many, in fact, go back and forth, and if the distinction between hooking up and dating can seem slippery, that's because one sometimes does lead to the other. But just as often, hooking up is nothing more than what it's advertised to be: a no-strings sexual encounter.

A 2001 survey conducted by Bowling Green State University found that of the 55 percent of local eleventh-graders who engaged in intercourse, 60 percent said they'd had sex with a partner who was no more than a friend. (That number would likely be much higher if the study had asked about oral sex.) Though the teen intercourse rate has declined, from 54 percent in 1991 to 47 percent in 2003, many teenagers have simply replaced intercourse with oral sex.

To a generation raised on AIDS, Britney Spears, Monica Lewinsky, and Internet porn, oral sex is definitely not sex (it's just "oral"), and hooking up is definitely not a big deal. The teenagers I spoke to talk about hookups as matter-of-factly as they might discuss what's on the cafeteria lunch menu—and they look at you funny if you go on for too long about the "emotional" components of sex.

But coupled with this apparent disconnection is a remarkable frankness about sex, even among friends of the opposite gender. Many teenagers spend a lot of time hanging out in mixed-gender groups (at the mall, at one another's houses), and when they can't hang out in person, they hang out online, asking the questions they might not dare to in real life. While this means that some friendships become sexually charged and lead to "friends with benefits" (one senior from Illinois told me that most of her friends have hooked up with one another), a good number remain platonic.

On Valentine's Day, I was invited to spend the evening with twelve junior and senior friends in an upper-middle-class suburb of Chicago. They were hanging out, eating pizza, and watching TV. Not one had a Valentine, and most said they wouldn't have it any other way. Several pointed out that having close friends of the opposite sex makes romantic relationships less essential. Besides, if you feel like something more, there's no need to feign interest in dinner and a movie. You can just hook up or call one of your friends with benefits.

"It would be so weird if a guy came up to me and said, 'Irene, I'd like to take you out on a *date,*'" said Irene, a tall, outgoing senior. "I'd probably laugh at him. It would be sweet, but it would be so weird!"

Irene and her friends are not outcasts. They are popular, and most have had at least one romantic relationship. If that experience taught them anything, they say, it's that high school is no place for romantic relationships. They're complicated, messy, and invariably painful. Hooking up, when done "right," is exciting, sexually validating, and efficient.

"I mean, sometimes you'll go out with a group of friends and meet someone cool, and maybe you'll hang out and hook up, but that's about it," said Irene's friend Marie (who asked me to identify her by her middle name). "There's a few people I know who date, but most of us are like, 'There's no one good to date, we don't need to date, so why date?'"

THE LAST TIME American teenagers seemed this uninterested in monogamous, long-term relationships was the 1930s and early 1940s, when high school popularity was largely equated with social (but not sexual) promiscuity: the "cool kids" had lots of dates with lots of different people, while the "losers" settled down with one person or didn't date at all. This the-more-the-merrier philosophy played itself out most notably on the dance floor, where there was nothing more embarrassing for a young woman than to be stuck with the same boy all night.

In her book *From Front Porch to Back Seat: Courtship in 20th-Century America,* Beth Bailey points out that magazine advice columns at the time urged teenagers to keep their options open—and, most important, to appear to be always in demand. Dating was seen as a competition that must never be lost. The advice column in *Senior Scholastic*, a current events magazine for high school students, told girls never to reject any boy outright, because "he may come in handy for an off night." And *Ladies Home Journal* urged teenagers to be open to blind dates: they "help keep you in circulation. They're good press agents. They even add to your collection."

Bailey found that "going steady," when it was discussed

at all before World War II, was often ridiculed by teenagers and the media. Dating a variety of people simultaneously was the key to a good social standing in high school. "These dates had to be highly visible, and with many different people, or they didn't count," Bailey writes.

But the war changed everything. Suddenly, women outnumbered men, and popular women's magazines and advice books scared American girls with dire warnings such as "Male shortage . . . It's worse than ever" and "Baldly stated, many girls of your generation will never marry." Young women apparently took up the challenge, because by 1959, 47 percent of brides were under nineteen, and those who weren't would often report that they had gone to college solely to find a husband.

With marriage occurring at a younger and younger age, teenagers started dating earlier, too. It wasn't uncommon for thirteen-year-olds to go steady. Bailey cites one 1961 study of a middle-class district in Pennsylvania, in which 40 percent of fifth-graders were already dating (for many, this meant holding hands and kissing). One frustrated high school boy wrote a letter to *Senior Scholastic* complaining that everyone he knew went steady and that he was labeled a "playboy" for wanting to date different girls.

By the late 1960s and early '70s, the rituals of high school dating had taken on an almost prehistoric cast. The "rules"—boy calls girl, boy asks girl out, boy drives to girl's house, boy talks to girl's dad, boy takes girl to movies, boy has her home by eleven (or else)—were viewed as restrictive and old-fashioned, not to mention sexist. And that's pretty much how things stood until the Reagan era, when dating made a serious comeback. Many teenagers settled down into a mix of serial dating and going steady—being "popular" often meant having a highly coveted boyfriend or girlfriend.

And though parents may have felt, as they typically do, that they didn't always understand teenage culture, most still thought they had a pretty good idea of whom their kids were talking to regularly. "Teens still had to call the home to reach the person they were interested in," Bailey says. "But then came cell phones and the Internet."

IT'S NO COINCIDENCE that hooking up has become popular with teenagers just as the Internet has become an integral part of their social lives. In the mid-'90s, teen personals sites and Internet chat rooms were mostly the domain of young gays and lesbians looking for love, sex, or someone to talk to.

Today, many heterosexual teenagers place personal profiles on meeting sites, usually without their parents' knowledge, and spend hours in chat rooms. (Two of the more popular sites—hotornot.com, with 4.3 million members, and facethejury.com, with 1.2 million—were both launched in late 2000.) And while gay high school boys frequently advertise that they "don't do hookups" and are looking only for relationships, fewer straight teenagers make that claim—and many make it clear that they're looking for anything but commitment.

"Straight teens have abandoned the rituals of dating, while gay teens have taken them on," says Peter Ian Cummings, the editor of *XY*, a national magazine for young gay men. The Internet, Cummings says, has made it possible for heterosexual teenagers to act the way "most of straight society assumes gay men act."

The day I spent with Haris and Emcho, two varsity soccer players at a high school in the Chicago area, would seem to bear that out. I'd met Emcho (he asked me to use his nickname) on facethejury.com, where he typically receives high ratings. Visitors to the site judge personal photos on a scale from 1 to 10, with anything under a five meaning, as one teenager told me, "that you should crawl into a hole and die."

Tall and lanky, with brown hair and a broad smile, Emcho said there are benefits to being highly rated on a site like facethejury. First, there was the college girl online who invited Emcho and a friend over to a party at her apartment. "I was online writing my senior paper," Emcho said, "and this girl instant-messages me and says, 'Hey, I saw your picture on facethejury.'" She invited Emcho over that night. They had sex in her bathroom, Emcho told me, and met up a few more times, but he says he cut it off when she started talking about wanting to date him.

Emcho and Haris said they're both partial to "preppy suburban girls." As Haris put it, "City girls are cool, but suburban girls are crazy cool!" (Meaning, Haris explains, that suburban girls are *easier*.) Recently, he and Emcho met up with two high school girls. One girl sneaked them all into her house, where she and Emcho hooked up on the floor, while Haris and her friend used the closet.

With so many teenagers online willing to hook up, Emcho and Haris say there's no need to rush into a relationship. "A lot of guys get in relationships just so they can get steady ass," Haris told me. "But now that it's easy to get sex outside of relationships, guys don't need relationships."

Last year, there was one girl Emcho really liked who also liked him, but he decided to wait a year or two before beginning a relationship with her. "He's waiting until the well runs dry," Haris said with a smile.

James Hong, cofounder of hotornot.com, knows that much of his demographic thinks like Emcho and Haris. He says his site purposefully doesn't advertise itself as a dating service (most of its members are under twenty-four). "You'll never see the word 'dating' on our site, because that's much too serious for our demographic," he says. "There are obviously relationships that come from the site, but mostly I think it's a lot of hanging out and hooking up. This demographic doesn't want to appear like they're needy and looking for a relationship."

But the neediness comes through in other ways. Many teenagers are obsessed with how complete strangers view them, and they often check their online ratings several times an hour. You have to show enough of your body to entice—washboard abs and cleavage are popular—but not enough to have your photo rejected by the site moderators. If your ratings climb high enough, the sites will often feature your profile in their "top girls" or "hottest guys" sections, making some high school students feel like superstars.

Once there, you're likely to receive hundreds of adoring e-mail messages from teenagers around the country and many local offers to hang out and hook up. For teenagers who already consider themselves attractive, the sites can be an ego boost. And for teenagers who aren't sure, the sites offer a chance—with the right picture—to feel wanted, too.

But if your ratings are only average, it can be tough. I spoke to several boys with low ratings who tried hard to sound unfazed, but underneath their nonchalance was an obvious hurt. One pouty, brown-haired sophomore in Boston with an average rating called facethejury.com a "whorehouse for people who hate themselves and the way they look, and search for affirmation from the outside." So why is he on it? "Boredom," he told me. "It's also entertaining in a perverse kind of way. I've had four highly overweight women in their late twenties ask to meet me."

There's something surreal about thirteen-year-olds with online personal profiles, but that's some of what you'll find on buddypic.com. Out of some fifty thousand profiles, more than four thousand are from baby-faced kids around the country. Some lift their shirts in their pictures, showing off their stomachs. Others make it clear what they aren't looking for. "LOTS of piercings, ugly . . . chicks, snitches, teacher's pets, stinky . . . chicks" reads one thirteen-year-old's "Dislikes" column. His "Likes" column is simpler: "Sexy body, Blonde, Blue eyes . . . good personality, willing to go out of their way to be with me."

Buddypic.com is careful to advertise itself as "fun, clean, and real." But on facethejury, "adult" meeting sites are just a click away. The links are advertised alongside teenage profiles, which makes for some eerie echoes between the self-styled photos of teenage members—suggestively posed and airbrushed—and the long-standing conventions of adult erotica. For many teenage boys and some teenage girls, Internet porn, cybersex, and real-time cam-to-cam connections exert a strong pull. As one Boston teenager told me, "Who needs the hassle of dating when I've got online porn?"

Most of the boys I spoke to said they have access to Internet porn, and many said they started watching it regularly in middle school. Some experts maintain that this kind of exposure is a lot more damaging than sneaking a peek at your dad's *Playboy* collection. "The Internet gives teen boys the idea that girls are interchangeable sexual objects at their disposal," says Lynn Ponton, a professor of psychiatry at the University of California at San Francisco and the author of *The Sex Lives of Teenagers*.

YET FOR ALL the resemblance of teenage hookup culture to a '70s singles bar, the old stigmas and prejudices haven't disappeared altogether. Most teenagers who engage in hookups still worry about being discreet. "If you're not careful, by lunch the next day at school, everyone will know," says Irene, the senior from the Chicago suburb. "Some people won't care, but others will, and if it happens too often, it will hurt your reputation."

Girls aren't the only ones who are worried. David, a boyish eighteen-year-old varsity basketball player at an all-boys high school in Chicago, said the same thing when I spent time with him. Like many male varsity athletes I spoke to, David says he isn't lacking for hookup possibilities. But he tries to be cautious. After all, too much hooking up can ruin any chances for a future relationship—and, like many teenagers, he holds out the possibility of dating if the "perfect" person comes along.

"I've got, like, five girls in my phone book I can call or text-message who will give it up to me," he says. "But I don't just hook up with *anyone*. You have to be careful. I have this huge crush on this girl who knows a lot of the girls I know, and I don't want her to find out I hook up a lot and think I'm dirty."

David isn't the only teenager who used the word "dirty" to describe hookups. Inherent in the thinking of many teenagers is the belief that hooking up, while definitely a mainstream activity, is still one that's best kept quiet. And underneath the teenage bravado I heard so often are mixed feelings about an activity that can leave them feeling depressed, confused, and guilty. As much as teens like to talk a good game, hooking up isn't nearly as seamless as they'd like it to be, and there are many ways it can go wrong.

At the Valentine's Day gathering, Irene and her friends laid out the unwritten etiquette of teenage hookups: If you want it to be a hookup relationship, then you don't call the person for anything except plans to hook up. You don't invite them out with you. You don't call just to say hi. You don't confuse the matter. You just keep it purely sexual, and that way people don't have mixed expectations and no one gets hurt.

But people invariably do. Many teenagers told me they had been hurt by hookups—usually because they had expected or hoped for more. But they often blamed themselves for letting their emotions get the best of them. The hookups weren't the problem. *They* were the problem. When Irene was fifteen, she hooked up for a while with a boy ("We basically became friends with benefits," she says) who never came around to asking her out officially, as Irene secretly hoped he would. In the end, she was devastated. "Since then, I've become really good at keeping my emotions in check," she says. "I can hook up with a guy and not fall for him."

In fact, many teenagers opt for hookups after a romantic relationship has soured. Boys are less likely to admit this, although Jesse, from New England, isn't afraid to. "I'd usually hook up because I got my heart broken by a girl, and I didn't want to feel like I had lost everything," he said. "So I'd hear that a girl was interested in me, I'd get a ride to her house, we'd hang out and mess around some, and I'd leave. Afterward I'd feel dumb, like it wasn't needed. But before you do it, you feel like it's definitely needed."

Melissa, a senior in a high school north of Boston, confessed she'd never had a good relationship. "Dating causes pain," she told me when I first communicated with her online. "It's easier not to get attached. And I realized that if it's O.K. for guys to play the field and have sex with twenty-eight thousand people, I should be able to, also."

The day we met in person, Melissa was in a foul mood. Her "friend with benefits" had just broken up with her. "How is that even possible?" she asked, slumped in a booth at a diner. "The point of having a friend with benefits is that you won't get broken up with, you won't get hurt. He told me online that he met a girl that he really likes, so now, of course, we can't hook up anymore."

Melissa and the boy used to meet up about once a week. "To be honest, we don't even really like hanging out together," she told me. They met only to have sex. "I go to his house, we sit there and talk for two minutes, then we go at it. Then we sit there again for about ten minutes, and I go home." (Clearly, for some teenagers, "friends with benefits" is a misnomer. Take away the sex, and they probably wouldn't hang out at all.)

Melissa forwarded me one of her online conversations with the boy:

Boy: What are you doing other than not talking to me?

Melissa: Nothing at all. . . .

Boy: Wow, you're as bored as I am?!? . . .

Melissa: Boooooooooored.

Boy: lol. Yup. Life is good. lol.

Melissa: Freakin' fantastic. Lemme tell ya.

Boy: I wish you lived like next door. . . . It would be so much easier . . . . Like I don't know about you, but I wanna fuck.

Melissa: U always wanna fuck.

Boy: True.

Melissa: Haha.

Boy: But that's cuz we've been talking

ABOUT IT AND HAVEN'T DONE IT. IT'S BUILT UP.

MELISSA: THAT'S BC U HAVEN'T PICKED ME UP YET SILLY. . . . WELL I'M GONNA GO LAY DOWN. U KNOW MY NUMBER AND WHERE I LIVE IF THINGS WORK OUT SOON.

BOY: HEY WAIT. IF I CAN DO YOU WANNA COME OVER

MELISSA: SURE. SO JUST CALL ME.

BOY: DO YOU HAVE CONDOMS?

MELISSA: YES DEAR.

BOY: HOLD ON.

MELISSA: I'M HOLDING.

BOY: I CAN COME GET YOU RIGHT NOW IF YOU WANT.

MELISSA: UM GIMME A SEC. . . .

BOY: O.K.?? I'LL COME GET YOU NOW IF YOU'RE READY. . . .

MELISSA: BUT I'M GONNA BE BORING TONITE . . . AND I'M JUST TELLING U I'M NOT IN THE MOOD FOR NETHING BUT STR8-UP SEX.

"I have my friends for my emotional needs, so I don't need that from the guy I'm having sex with," Melissa explained at the time, sounding very much like the *Sex and the City* character Samantha Jones. So why, now that the boy had "broken up" with her, was she feeling so depressed? "It's really stupid, I know," she said, shaking her head. "It's kind of ironic, isn't it? I try to set up a situation where I won't get hurt, and I still manage to get hurt!"

On the plus side, there's a new boy who's interested in her. "Problem is, he's annoying," Melissa said. "I liked him before we hooked up. Now I can't stand him. He's so *needy*, and he won't stop calling." Melissa said she was going to wait until after Valentine's Day to tell him she wasn't interested. "I want a Valentine's Day present," she said. "After that, I'm just not going to answer my phone."

Like other high school girls I talked to, Melissa says she doesn't see why boys get to have "all the fun," although during the few months we communicated, it was clear that Melissa's hookups rarely brought her joy. She complained often about being depressed, and her hookups, which she hoped would make her feel better, usually left her feeling worse. But a few days after a hookup, she would have forgotten that they tended to make her miserable and would tell me excitedly about a new boy she was planning to meet. When that boy failed to show or called to say he was running an hour late, Melissa's spirits would sink—again.

But when I asked Melissa whether she thought hookups worked equally well for girls and boys, she surprised me with her answer. "It's equal," she said. "Everyone is using each other. That's fair."

• • •

ASHLEY, AN OUTGOING junior who is friends with Jesse, met her current boyfriend at a concert in her hometown. Her parents initially balked at the age difference (she's seventeen, he's twenty-one), but she was quick to reassure them. "People assume that if the guy's older, he's the one making all the moves and using the girl," Ashley told me. "But trust me, I was definitely the aggressor. I got into his pants. He didn't get into mine."

The question of who's in control and who is getting the short end of the stick—whether in dating or hookups—kept cropping up. "Guys who are sixteen, seventeen, eighteen, they're just totally clueless," said Irene, the seventeen-year-old from the upper-middle-class Chicago suburb. "They'll be, like, 'I kind of want you, but now that I have you, I don't really want you anymore, so maybe I should break up with you and have you as a friend with benefits.'"

Like many of her high school friends, Irene has no problem meeting boys who are in college—and the implication is that maybe they offer something high school boys don't. So who's hooking up with guys in high school? Freshmen and sophomore girls. "Some senior girls won't even look at us," said one high school senior from Glenview, another suburb of Chicago. "But underclassmen, they look at us like we're gods. Which, of course, we are, so it works out well!" He told me that he regularly hooks up with a sophomore from another school, but he doesn't take her out with his friends. "Until I find someone special, I'm playing the ball field."

While many girls insist that they receive sexual attention during hookups, just as many boys say hookups are mostly about pleasing the guy. Michael Milburn, a coauthor of the book *Sexual Intelligence,* an examination of sexual beliefs and behaviors in America, says that the boys' take is more accurate. "Most of the time, it's the younger girl performing fellatio on the older boy, with the boy doing very little to pleasure the girl," Milburn says.

Some girls told me that guys think it's "nasty" to perform oral sex on a girl. So a lot of girls will just perform oral sex on the guy "and not expect anything in return, because she'll know that he probably thinks it's gross," Irene told me. But her friend Andi pointed out that many girls are themselves insecure about receiving oral sex; they'd rather just have intercourse.

There's a firm belief among many experts on teenage sex that girls, however much they protest to the contrary, are not getting as much pleasure out of hookups as they claim. I was invited to a high school in Boston, where I met with a group of seniors who were debating this very issue. I relayed a conversation I'd had with Marline Pearson, a sociologist who has developed a school curriculum for teenagers called "Love U2: Getting Smarter About Relationships, Sex, Babies, and Marriage."

"In some ways," Pearson told me, "I think girls had more power in the 1960s, when they said: "Okay, you want to get to first base? This is what you have to do.' Today it's: "Okay, you want to get to third base? Come over.' I'm a feminist, but I think we've put girls back in the dark ages, with very little power."

One girl, a brown-haired senior who says she sometimes hooks up with guys she meets through friends, doesn't feel that she's in the dark ages, or that she's powerless. "If I ask a guy to come over to my house and hook up," she said, "I'm the one benefiting, because I'm the one who wants to. It's not just about pleasing the guy."

Her friend, a well-spoken senior with shaggy brown hair, faded jeans, and a T-shirt with the sleeves rolled up to her shoulders, listened quietly as her friends defended a woman's right to hook up. Finally, and with some hesitation, she voiced an unpopular opinion among her friends. "I feel like women have less power today," she said. "It's not just that the guy often doesn't respect the girl or the girl's sexuality, but the girl sometimes doesn't really respect and validate herself. I have a friend who's twenty, and he goes on the Internet and meets sixteen-year-old girls from the suburbs." He drives out there, she performs oral sex on him, and he drives home. "Who has the power there? I think that a lot of the times girls are really self-destructive."

"Well," the first girl said, slightly annoyed, "I don't see why a guy can have a random hookup with a girl and no one questions his motives, but when a girl does it, there's this assumption that she's a girl, so she automatically wants more out of a hookup. When I hook up, I don't want more, and it's not self-destructive. And I enjoy it."

Dr. Drew Pinsky, a cohost of *Loveline,* a nationally syndicated radio program about sex and relationships, doesn't buy it. "It's all bravado," he tells me. "Teens are unwittingly swept up in the social mores of the moment, and it's certainly not some alternative they're choosing to keep from getting hurt emotionally. The fact is, girls don't enjoy hookups nearly as much as boys, no matter what they say at the time. They're only doing it because that's what the boys want."

Wendy Shalit, whose book *A Return to Modesty* embodies what has been termed "the new chastity," also says she believes that girls are being manipulated, but by a society that tries to convince them that they should act like boys, turning sexual modesty into a sign of weakness or repression—something young women are taught to be embarrassed about. "In the age of the hookup," Shalit writes, "young women confess their romantic hopes in hushed tones, as if harboring some terrible secret."

Those who embrace an abstinence-only sex education program try to influence teenage behavior by explaining that sexual pleasure requires mutual respect and security. Sarah LaBella works for CareFirst Prevention Services, a group that has taught in junior high and high schools since 1998. One gray, frigid February afternoon, I sat in on a class she was giving to teenage girls in an unremarkable suburban Illinois high school with a view of a Dunkin' Donuts.

"Do you want to know the difference between girls and guys?" LaBella asked. Some of the girls listened intently; others doodled or stared blankly out the window. "Guys are like microwaves. You hit the right button, and they're ready to go. We, on the other hand, are ovens. It takes a little while for us to get heated up. You have to *preheat* us."

Most of the girls smiled, and several laughed. LaBella smiled, too, because if you can make teenagers laugh (with you, not at you), you might get them to actually listen. LaBella, who typically delivers her message to coed classes, knows that some teenagers tune her out between the sexually transmitted diseases slide show and the claim that "the best sex" happens only within marriage. But she says that many teenagers listen intently, as if hearing some life-altering news.

"We know that most teenagers are never really taught what's involved in making a healthy relationship," she told me after class. "They're trying to build relationships out of hookups or casual sex, and those relationships do not tend to be fruitful ones."

But are teenagers—and teenage girls in particular—*always* ill served by choosing hookups over relationships? Jeanette May, a cofounder of the Coalition for Positive Sexuality, a grassroots advocacy and educational organization based in Washington that argues that teenagers should be supported in making their own decisions about safe sex and their sexuality, is one of the few adults I spoke to who doesn't think so. "Often, I think girls, if they are getting as much out of it as the guys, are better served by having sex for their pleasure, without a lot of emotional attachment," she says. "Because they would feel more empowered to practice safe sex, use birth control and avoid sexual interactions that would not benefit them. When girls think they are in love or in a relationship that will lead to love, they're more easily manipulated."

Few adults would take that line. Regardless of which end of the political spectrum they find themselves on, parents and teen sexuality experts tend to agree on one thing: hooking up is a bad thing for teenagers. They insist that it's bad emotionally and potentially bad physically. Female adolescents ages fifteen to nineteen have the highest incidence of both gonorrhea and chlamydia, and according to the latest figures from the Centers for Disease Control and Prevention (CDC), 48 percent of new STD cases reported in 2000 occurred among fifteen- to twenty-four-year-olds. Many of the teenagers I talked to told me that no one they know uses condoms during oral sex, only during intercourse.

"Both conservatives and liberals have their respective blinders on when talking about teen sexuality," says Michael Milburn. "I can think of nothing more important than getting in schools and talking about sexual intelligence and healthy relationships, but most conservatives don't want an open and honest discussion about teen sexuality, and they oppose any conversation that doesn't focus on abstinence until marriage. And many liberals will resist any discussion that might touch on the negative consequences of unbridled sexuality. The conversation we need to have with teens is 'What's the role that sexuality should play in an emotionally healthy person's life? What are the different ways that people can be sexual? What are the potential dangers?'"

FOR ALL THE efforts to make teenagers aware of the dangers of hookups, many of the high school students I spoke to shrugged off the idea that hooking up is ultimately a bad thing. As they see it, if they're not going to marry for another ten years, why not focus on other things (friendships, schoolwork, sports) in high school? And if they're not hurting anyone and not getting anyone pregnant, where is the harm in a little casual fun?

The truth is, teenagers may spend less of their time hooking up than adults think they do; for many of them, friendships have become the most important part of their social lives. Kate, Caity, and Adam (the group I first met at Hooters with Jesse) often spend weekend nights hanging out together and talking about sex in ways many adults would find difficult to do themselves.

I met up with them again one Saturday evening, as they lounged around a friend's living room. No one was paying much attention to the music video playing on the big-screen TV. Instead, they spent the night talking about music, soccer, their town (and why it's better than the next town over), oral sex (why some people can't do it well), masturbation (whether girls do it and whether they do it in the shower), and anything else that sprang to mind.

But the big news was that Kate *still* hadn't kissed her boyfriend. "We talk about it all the time, but it's like whenever we get to a point when we're going to, we don't," Kate said. "I feel like I'm going to have to make the first move, and I don't do first moves!"

"Why don't girls make first moves more often?" asked Brian, Jesse's sixteen-year-old friend. "It's really annoying."

"Oh, they do if they're drunk!" said Adam (the boy who likes to lift his shirt), sitting on the couch and strumming a guitar.

A lot had happened since I first met Jesse. Through a friend, Adam met a girl he would actually date, except she lives too far away. The biggest development, though, was that Caity and Adam had made out at a concert in front of all their friends. "It was really disgusting!" Jesse said. "They did it right in front of everybody. And it was *long*." Both Adam and Caity dismissed it as a momentary lapse. "It just happened," Caity told me. "Nothing serious," Adam said.

The two got only to first base (kissing), which is about the only base that anyone can agree on anymore. "I don't understand the base system at all," Jesse said, lying on his back on the floor and staring at the ceiling. "If making out is first base, what's second base?"

"We need to establish an *international base system*," Brian said. "Because right now, frankly, no one knows what's up with the bases. And that's a problem."

Jesse nodded in agreement. "First base is obviously kissing," Brian said.

"Obviously," Jesse said.

"But here's the twist," Brian said. "Historically, second base was breasts. But I don't think second base is breasts anymore. I think that's just a given part of first base. I mean, how can you make out without copping a feel?"

"True," Jesse said. "And if third base is oral, what's second base?"

"How does this work for girls?" asked Ashley, the seventeen-year-old junior. "I mean, are the bases what's been done to you, or what you've done?"

"If it's what base you've gone to with a girl, you go by whoever had more done," Jesse told her.

"But we're *girls,*" Ashley said. "So we've got on bases with guys?"

"Right, but it doesn't matter," Jesse said. "It's not what base you've had done to you, it's what bases you get to."

Kate shook her head. "I'm totally lost!"

"See how complicated this is?" Brian said, turning to me. "Now, if someone asks you, 'So, how far did you get with her?' you have to say, 'Well, how do *your* bases go?'"

Brother's Keeper

The Kochman brothers were inseparable.
Even in death.

ON THE AFTERNOON OF Saturday, May 4, 2001, the nine-person cast of the Monadnock Regional High school production of *Ordinary People* gathered in the school auditorium in Swanzey, New Hampshire, for their first dress rehearsal. Opening night was only four days away, and the cast's five boys and four girls were starting to feel the pressure. The mood was strained and occasionally hostile. The problem, most everyone agreed, was the angry Greg Kochman, who played the lead role of Conrad, a suicidal teenager coping with the death of his older brother.

Then a junior at Monadnock, Greg was in one of his moods. "He was so angry that week, and that day was the worst of it," recalls Kristen Arrow, who played Conrad's mother in the play. "He would just lash out at people for no reason. It was the first day that I had gotten really irritated at Greg."

Still, there was no denying that Greg could act. And on Saturday, the broad-shouldered, brown-haired seventeen-year-old was acting even better than usual. "Then I sit down and think about—things," Greg, playing the role of Conrad, said. "Everything that hurts. And I cry. Inside, I'm burning up. Outside—all I can feel is the cold tile floor. And my chest feels so tight—it hurts—everything hurts—so I hold out my hand and close my eyes—and I slice, one quick cut, deep cut."

Katharine DePew, who played Conrad's therapist in the play, had never heard Greg say the lines so well. "He said it static, monotone, and it was the best he had ever done," says DePew. "It was eerie."

That's because *Ordinary People*—based on the novel by Judith Guest, which was later made into an Academy Award-winning movie directed by Robert Redford—was supposed to be therapeutic for Greg. After all, Greg was, like Conrad, deeply depressed over the death of his popular and well-liked older brother. Like Conrad, Greg was seeing a therapist. Like Conrad, Greg had already tried to kill himself.

Theater, it seemed, was going to save him. "Greg loved the role of Conrad," recalls Casey Gallagher, a friendly, demonstrative Monadnock senior who considered Greg his best friend. "He needed that role. He was acting out what he felt for his brother."

Still, the play didn't make Greg any less sad. The day before Saturday's dress rehearsal, he broke down crying in the school auditorium. Saturday wasn't much better. "By the end of rehearsal," recalls DePew, who is tall and gangly with long brown hair, "I just wanted to go somewhere a little more positive."

That was nothing new for DePew, who was increasingly trying to build boundaries in a rocky relationship that had become exhausting. Their close friendship started because DePew had a crush on Greg, and though she says their relationship never included a serious romantic element, friends say they saw never-ending sexual tension between the two. DePew—who is funny, emotionally intense, and brutally sarcastic—essentially became Greg's unofficial therapist. "Greg expected me to be there twenty-four hours a day for him," she says. "And I tried to be, but I also had to live my life, too."

As she left the auditorium that Saturday, Greg, who was sitting in the first row, told her he loved her. "He had never said that to me before," she says. "But I was so frustrated with everything, I just said 'Bye' and went to the parking lot to get my car." She drove her Honda Accord toward the auditorium's entrance, where she intended to wait for cast member Kristen Arrow. Greg put his hands up for her to stop. When she did, he asked if he could call her.

"I told him that I probably wouldn't be home, that I was going out and wouldn't be back until late," recalls DePew. "He said, 'Please, can I just call you?' I said, 'I probably won't be home, but sure, you can call.' I was just pissed off."

DePew and Arrow went to dinner by themselves, where they spent most of the meal complaining about Greg. Jordan Self and Gallagher, Greg's best friends that year, thought about inviting Greg out with them but decided against it. "It was, like, 'Okay, this is leave-Greg-alone time for a little while,'" says Self.

The boys went to a friend's house, where they spent the night playing video games and doing doughnuts in their friend's truck in a nearby field. As the boys headed back to Self's house, they almost called Greg. "But we were both tired," recalls Self. "We wanted to go home and make nachos."

DePew dropped Arrow off at home at about ten, then headed north on Route 12. When she reached Monadnock Regional High School, she had a choice to make: she could go left, which would bring her to Greg's house, or she could turn right and drive to her house in nearby Troy. "I put my blinker on and was about to go to Greg's, but then I thought, 'It's kind of late—maybe I shouldn't,'" she says. "I just drove home."

Greg's father, David, and his wife, Sandy, got home from dinner with friends at about 8:30. Greg's 1994 Ford Escort wagon was in the driveway, but he wasn't home. Greg was scheduled to work at 6 a.m. the next morning at the Colony Mill, a marketplace in Keene. When David went into Greg's room to wake him up the next morning, he found an empty bed. David walked downstairs and was about to call Jordan Self's mother when he looked out the window and saw Greg sitting in a plastic lawn chair by the pool.

What David couldn't see from the window—but what he would discover when he walked out back—was that this younger son, like his older son a year before, had fatally shot himself in the head.

• • •

DAVID KOCHMAN IS a short, athletic, forty-five-year-old man with curly black hair and a mustache. He is punctual, polite, friendly, and disciplined. When he laughs, which he does often and unexpectedly, his face scrunches up, his shoulders bob up and down, and his mouth emits rapid-fire chuckles. Until Eric's death two years ago, he had never cried as an adult.

A man of habit, David rises early most mornings to exercise at Gold's Gym, after which he works eight-hour days as a premium audit manager at Peerless Insurance in Keene, a ten-minute drive from his spacious home in a quiet, wooded area of Swanzey.

When his boys were young, David spent much of his free time shuttling them to and from soccer games, baseball games, and weight-lifting events. Both Eric and Greg loved sports, and they seemed intent on making their father proud. "Eric would always call me at work and tell me to hurry home because he had a new soccer move to show me," recalls David. "And when Greg was nine, I coached his soccer team, and I remember at one practice some of the other kids weren't paying as much attention to me as they should. Greg, who was already pretty intense at that age, turned to the kids and said, 'If my father tells you to run through a wall, your only question should be, *which wall*?'"

When David and his boys weren't talking about sports, it's a good bet they were discussing politics. David, Greg, and, to a lesser extent, Eric, were regulars at New Hampshire Republican fund-raisers and political dinners. "Eric and Greg were always busy doing something," says the boys' mother, Rose, who lived with them until 1997, when she and David divorced. "It was nonstop."

As the boys grew older, Rose—a forty-six-year-old saleswoman at a Honda dealership in Keene—watched her role in their lives diminish. "David was really involved with them," she says, "and it came to a point when I felt like I wasn't needed as much anymore."

In September 1997, Rose and David told the boys (then fifteen and thirteen, respectively) that they were separating. The brothers seemed unfazed by the announcement, and even their friends were unsure how it affected them. David sold the family house and he and the boys moved into a three-bedroom condo. Rose moved into a one-bedroom apartment two miles away.

It was about this time that the brothers, already talented soccer players, became local celebrities of sorts in power lifting. In an article about the brothers in the local *Star Spangled Banner*, Greg said he was shooting for Eric's state record. "He's never going to do it," Eric countered. "Although I can't imagine losing the record to any better guy."

The quote was typical Eric: cocky but respectful of Greg. One of the most popular students in school, Eric—tan and well built, with long eyelashes, curly black hair, and a crush-inducing smile—had many friends, but none meant more to him than his younger brother. "Their favorite song was 'Siamese Twins' by the Smashing Pumpkins, and in many ways that's the way they saw themselves," says David. "They were inseparable." They were also different. Eric was a classic extrovert—outgoing, popular, funny, emotional, and, at least on the surface, sure of himself. Greg was studious, disciplined, and not as gregarious, although he shared

Eric's ability to make people laugh. (Greg's imitation of Austin Powers could bring people to their knees.)

"The boys were very different, but I tried to instill in them a strong loyalty to each other," says Rose. "I told Eric, 'This is your brother, and no matter what happens, you are loyal to him.' I told Greg the same thing. And they were. I remember I was upstairs at David's condo after the divorce, and Eric had two friends over. I could hear that [the friends] were basically ridiculing Greg, and Eric joined in for a second. Greg got really hurt, and Eric told his friends to knock it off. But they kept going, and Greg ran up to his room. Then I heard Eric tell them, 'If you ever fucking mess with my brother again, I'll kill both of you!' And that's when I knew that what I had told Eric flowed through him. The boys were normal brothers, but they were not normal brothers."

And it was clear early on that Greg was not a normal student. He was a voracious reader and had finished all of John Grisham's books by the sixth grade. While Greg was two years behind Eric in school, it was Greg who would help Eric with his homework. After reading *The Long Gray Line* in eighth grade, Greg became obsessed with attending West Point. "Eric always bragged to everybody that Greg would be president someday," says Chad Wellington, a soccer teammate and friend of both the boys.

Eric was not particularly interested in academic success. Though also an avid reader, he was a B and C student prone to skipping school or sleeping through a morning class if the mood struck him. Eric's focus was always on sports (soccer, baseball, weight lifting) and friends, whom he never lacked.

Eric opened social doors for Greg, and many of Eric's friends became Greg's friends, too. "We'd take Greg with us to parties, and Eric was always protective of Greg," says Kris Kesney, a close friend of Eric in the ninth and tenth grades. "Greg was the innocent little child. He was shy and seemed insecure a lot. Eric was the partier. We used to drink a lot. Like most people around here, Eric liked to get fucked up."

According to several Monadnock students, a majority of the school's students smoke marijuana by the time they graduate. Eric was no exception. According to friends, he started drinking and smoking weed late in junior high. In eighth grade, the school reprimanded him after he was caught drinking from a hair spray bottle that a fellow student had filled with alcohol. In ninth grade, Eric was suspended for two months when a fellow student's parents complained that Eric had helped their child get marijuana.

Still, Eric was one of the most popular and best-liked students at Monadnock. "Everyone liked him, because he was nice to you whether you were popular or not," says a Monadnock senior, Tim Wilder. "He was in the group with the snobs, but he wasn't a snob at all."

At home, Eric and Greg were polite and respectful. The family usually ate dinner together, and the boys had a deep respect for David, whom they called "a genius." Still, friends said the boys' relationship with their father was superficial. "David isn't comfortable talking about feelings," says a friend of the brothers, "and I guess Eric and Greg just followed his lead."

The boys differed greatly in their relationship with their mother. Though Greg didn't get along well with Rose, particularly in the last year of his life, Eric routinely stopped by Rose's work to talk. "And he would always give me a big hug and say, 'I love you, Mom,' right in front of everybody," recalls Rose. "And people were flabbergasted. Other mothers would say, 'My God, if my son would only say that to me!'"

THE MONADNOCK VIEW Cemetery in Keene is well kept, with narrow, circular paved roads that intersect islands of tombstones. Visitors drive slowly through the cemetery, often parking their cars with two wheels on the road and two on the grass, so as to avoid blocking traffic. Not that there is much of that, which makes this a safe place for the meandering bike rides of elderly women from two nearby retirement complexes.

On a drizzly, overcast Sunday afternoon, the area around Eric's tombstone is cluttered with flowers, engraved rocks, a small container with poems inside, a ticket to the school production of *Ordinary People,* and glow sticks (both boys liked to dance with them). Kris Kesney, a good friend of Eric's, and Denene Groat, Eric's best friend and on-and-off girlfriend, are here to pay a visit.

"After Eric died, I would come here and lie on his grave for hours," Kesney says, lighting a cigarette. "At first I was so angry at Eric. Suicide is the most selfish thing you can do to a group of people who love you."

"I used to come here every day, too," Groat says as she brushes dirt off of the container with poems. "After Eric died, I would be driving to school, and somehow I just ended up here instead. I was suicidal. I don't know how I'm even alive. I would lie here for hours every day. I would talk to Eric. And I would ask myself over and over again how I couldn't have known that he was depressed. How can you know someone so well and not know *that*?"

Eric Kochman didn't look depressed. He made his first and only plea for help in late July 1999, as he walked along Hampton Beach with his mother. "Eric looked at me and said, 'Mom, I have a chemical imbalance,'" recalls Rose. Knowing little about mental illness or clinical depression, she assumed Eric was talking about his hormones. Eric shook his head. "Mom, it's not that."

Rose says she pressed him for details, but Eric was reluctant. They agreed that he should see a therapist, and Eric told Rose that he didn't want anyone, including his father or brother, to know. The next week, Rose accompanied Eric to the offices of Monadnock Family Services, a community mental health agency in Keene. It was there, David would later claim in a wrongful death lawsuit against the facility, that Eric was grossly misdiagnosed. (The agency and doctors denied any wrongdoing.)

The case never made it to trial and was settled out of court, and one of the provisions of the settlement bars the parties from discussing it. But according to court documents, Eric was evaluated by Monadnock Family Services psychologist Richard Slammon, who took the following notes: "Eric reports suicidal ideation that has been fairly chronic for close to one-and-a-half years. This ideation has included some degree of planning but no intent. Eric adamantly denies that he would ever or has ever acted on his suicidal feelings, primarily because he is aware of the impact that such an act would have on his family, whom he reports to love very much. Eric's risk for causing harm to himself is considered to be moderate, but not acutely at risk at present."

Slammon then referred Eric to the psychiatrist Richard Stein, who met with Eric six days later. According to the allegations, Dr. Stein prescribed Eric several drugs without his parents' consent: Prozac and Paxil, the powerful antianxiety medications Klonopin and Lorazepam, and the sleep-inducing drug Trazadone.

"After that first visit, Eric just shut me out," recalls Rose. "I didn't know anything. Eric didn't want to talk about it. [Monadnock Family Services] didn't tell me anything about any drugs. I just thought he was going to see a therapist to talk about whatever he was feeling. I had never seen a therapist. Depression doesn't run in my family, and I don't even know if anyone in my family has ever seen a therapist. I was just completely clueless. I just thought a therapist was someone you go to see for a few sessions, and then you feel better."

Eric wasn't feeling better. He saw Dr. Stein again twice more the next month. According to court documents summarizing the expected expert witness testimony of psychiatrist Allen Shwartzberg, of the Psychiatric Institute of Washington, Dr. Stein's notes "clearly indicate a severe and life-threatening deterioration of Eric's condition. Dr. Stein completely failed to recognize and/or treat this condition. . . . Dr. Stein's notes document self-destructive behavior of drinking glasses of undiluted liquor, mixing alcohol with drugs against the doctor's advice, and over-medicating himself with the prescribed medication. . . . The drug regimen prescribed was inappropriate, particularly in light of Eric's abuse of the drugs and his use of alcohol." According to press reports, Dr. Stein was prepared to call expert witnesses to demonstrate that he met an appropriate standard of care.

Like many suicidal teenagers, Eric was drinking heavily in the last few months of his life. (When he died, his blood alcohol level was at .41 percent). David says he never saw Eric drinking and that the liquor wasn't coming from home. But alcohol isn't hard to get in Swanzey ("I could make one call and have whatever I need on my doorstep in twenty minutes," a Monadnock senior told me).

Still, Eric didn't exhibit many of the characteristics of a depressed or suicidal teenager: He didn't seem sad. He didn't have mood swings. He didn't express self-hatred. He didn't harass others. He didn't gain weight, lose weight, or withdraw noticeably from friends and family. And he didn't talk about death.

Until the end, Eric looked just fine. When Rose told David in mid-August about what Eric had told her on Hampton Beach, David was stunned. "The whole thing was just so off the wall," he recalls. "I spoke to Eric for about thirty minutes that night, and he blew the whole thing off. He said he was a little bit stressed, but now he was fine. I just accepted what he said on face value. I didn't know about any drugs. He was still always smiling."

But in the week before Eric died, Monadnock soccer coach Chana Robbins didn't see Eric's smile as often as he would have liked. In fact, Robbins and Eric were frequently in disagreement, with coach wanting more hustle from his best player and player wanting less lip from his vocal coach.

On September 27, 1999, four days before his death, Eric knew it would take more than a smile to convince Robbins to let Denene Groat ride on the team bus to an away game in Lebanon, New Hampshire. Eric would have to rely on another of his talents: "his *incredible* ability to bullshit," says friend Kris Kesney.

Eric told Robbins that Groat had to ride on the team bus, because the pair needed to work on a photography project for school. (Eric was a remarkably talented photographer.) Groat was going to take pictures of the game, Eric told Robbins. Never mind that there was no film in the camera or that Groat didn't know how to work it.

In Lebanon, Groat stood on the sidelines and pretended to take pictures of Eric, who played his usual brand of garish, aggressive, trash-talking soccer. Groat also pretended to take pictures of Greg, then a sophomore, who patrolled the Monadnock defense with physical, no-nonsense intensity.

Robbins felt Eric's mind was elsewhere on that day, and Robbins was furious when Eric drew a yellow card for roughly tripping an opposing player in the open field. He pulled Eric from the game, and Monadnock went on to lose 2–0. On the bus trip home, Eric rested his head in Groat's lap. "I'm so depressed," he told her. Groat assumed he was talking about soccer.

Three days later, Eric quit the team after Robbins took away Eric's captain status for two games. The next day, Eric left school early with no explanation. Worried, Groat drove to the condo Eric then shared with his brother and father. David was at work, Greg was at school, and the door to Eric's room was locked.

She walked downstairs, where she found a single-page, handwritten note signed by Eric: "I can no longer watch depression win me over and destroy my opportunities. . . . Soccer plays no part in this. . . . I am sorry you cannot fully comprehend my situation for just one second. . . . I was not chemically meant for this world."

Depression? Chemically meant for this world? Groat didn't understand a word of it. "Eric was the happiest kid in the world; this made no sense," she says. "Going up to his room again, I was just telling myself that he was sleeping or playing a joke or anything." She grabbed a coat hanger from Greg's room and unlocked Eric's door, using the technique Eric—prone to doing absent-minded things, like locking himself out of his room—had taught her.

When Groat opened the door, she found Eric dead on the floor, his father's .44 Ruger by his head. Hysterical, she yelled at him. She tried to call the police, but Eric had disconnected the phone. She ran outside and knocked on every door in the complex, but no one was home. She fell to the ground, unable to speak or walk. She crawled across the street to a neighbor's house, where someone finally opened the door.

At Monadnock, the soccer team was midway through practice when David came sprinting down the hill and called Greg off the field. "By the way David came running, we knew something had happened," says Josh Tong, the team's senior goalie and a friend of Greg's. "We thought that maybe Eric had gotten into a car accident. They rushed us all over to the side of the field, and you could see David and Greg talking. Then Greg just dropped to his knees."

• • •

MONADNOCK REGIONAL HIGH School serves eight nearly all-white, mostly working- and middle-class rural communities. The school made national news in 1991 when a sixteen-year-old former student, wielding a rifle and wearing a trench coat, took fifteen students hostage in a classroom just as morning classes began. As frightened teens ran for the exits, the principal, Daniel Stockwell, followed the boy to room 73, knocked on the door, slowly entered, and sat on the desk. While the boy pointed the rifle at Stockwell's head, the principal convinced him to let the students go. Police later entered the classroom and subdued the student, and Stockwell was labeled a hero.

There were no similar scares at Monadnock last year, although there was a real concern that Greg might kill himself. Three weeks after Eric's death, Greg told a friend, Lindsey Jernberg, that he was going to overdose on pills. "Greg and I had talked every night since Eric's death, usually about Eric," recalls Jernberg, a popular Monadnock senior who plays softball, field hockey, and basketball. "So I called him at about eight the night of his last soccer game, and he wasn't himself. He wasn't talking at all. I knew something was wrong. I kept hounding him, asking him what was wrong. Finally he just lost it. He started yelling at me and swearing at me. He said, 'I can't believe you fucking called me! You ruined all my fucking plans! I had everything fucking planned!'"

Greg was hospitalized for ten days and started seeing a therapist and a psychiatrist, who prescribed him Paxil. Greg told friends he got little out of his therapy sessions and didn't like taking his medication. "He joked a lot that he couldn't get an erection on Paxil," says friend and Monadnock senior Tim Wilder.

To everyone who knew him, Greg was a different person after Eric died. "Part of me knew on some level that Greg would probably end up killing himself," says Josh Tong, a good friend of Greg's. "I had never seen someone so sad and angry."

Much of Greg's anger was aimed at his mother, whom he never forgave for not telling him that Eric was depressed. They often fought on the phone, and the last conversation they had before Greg died ended when Rose hung up on him. Greg also expressed constant disappointment in fellow students, whom he said were shallow and superficial (often to their face).

"He was so angry at the world, at students, at his family, at himself for not doing better," says Katharine DePew. "When Eric was alive, Greg didn't care where he was, or what he was doing, or anything, because he could live in Eric's shadow, which is where he felt comfortable. When Eric died, Greg was just so lost."

Still, not every day was bad, and Greg's two closest male friends that year—Jordan Self, then fourteen, and Casey Gallagher, then sixteen—said they never consciously feared that Greg would commit suicide (Greg assured them several times that he wouldn't). "I think he liked hanging out with us because unlike a lot of other people, we didn't treat him like a dangerous person after Eric died," says Gallagher.

The three boys spent most of their free time joking

around and bonding over their difficulties with girls, which were endless. For whatever reason, Greg—who had a body that turned heads—had been rejected by several girls he had crushes on. "He would always say, 'Girls don't go for nice, romantic guys like me,'" says Greg's friend, Kristen. "And he was right. In high school, most girls go for the cocky jerks. But I think a lot of people also got weirded out by Greg toward the end. He was a lot different than he was before."

For one thing, he started to look eerily like his brother. He wore Eric's soccer uniform during games, sometimes wore Eric's clothes to school, and grew his hair out long like Eric's. "It spooked people out," says friend Kris Kesney. Greg also became obsessed with studying suicide: he read books about suicide, depression, and bipolar disorder, and he even wrote a paper for English class entitled "The Social Enigma of Suicide."

"Even with all of the opportunities to identify and prevent suicide," Greg wrote, "teenagers still complete suicides and throw their friends and family into turmoil and an endless void of 'What ifs?'"

When David learned that Greg had also landed the part of Conrad in *Ordinary People,* he considered forbidding Greg to take it. "Greg had become a student of suicide," says David. "He knew everything about the means to do it, the reasons behind it, statistics on who does it most and in what circumstances. The play, the paper, it bothered me a lot on some level. I think it was way too much suicide so soon after Eric killed himself. But I didn't stop it. The play seemed so important to him."

School officials say they carefully considered letting Greg

play the role of Conrad. "Greg's therapist felt strongly that the play was going to be therapeutic," says Principal Daniel Stockwell. "His parents had been consulted. In my mind, I'm thinking 'Greg's out there, he's able to express himself, don't take that away from him.' Keep in mind that the ending of the play is the surviving boy coming out mentally strong. This could have been a very positive story—if it had stayed to script."

There were countless signs that it wouldn't: Greg was hospitalized a second time by his therapist, who considered him dangerously suicidal. Then, a week before his death, Greg cut his wrists, but David and Rose say they didn't know about it. "When I saw the marks and confronted Greg," recalls David, "he said he had gotten cut at work. We didn't find the truth out until after he died."

Greg later told Katharine DePew that he was living for the play and that once it was over, he would kill himself. "Everyone was so worried about the week after the play," says DePew. "No one expected he would do it *before*." Greg also told several friends that he didn't want to live to be older than his brother.

True to his word, he lived one week less.

LIKE THE NEWS of Eric's suicide fourteen months before, news of Greg's suicide spread through Swanzey in a matter of hours. "People couldn't believe it," says the mother of one Monadnock student. "And people were so angry. Everyone wanted to find something to blame."

There were two main targets. The first was *Ordinary People*. Angry students and parents—most of whom didn't know Greg was playing the role until after he died—wanted to know why a suicidal student was playing a suicidal teenager in the school play. "The first few days of school after Greg died, I talked to so many people who said, 'I can't believe they did that play! They shouldn't have done the play!'" recalls Kristen Arrow. "I couldn't believe people were blaming his death on that."

But people did, and David Kochman added to the anti-play sentiment when he spoke to *The Boston Globe* two days after Greg's death. "When I heard about the play, I thought it was a sick joke," he told the paper. "I couldn't believe it. I blame myself for not stopping it outright." David says he regrets making that statement. "The reporter talked to me as I was going to my son's funeral," David says now. "I don't blame the play for what happened."

Neither do most of Greg's close friends, many of whom angrily defend Greg's role in *Ordinary People*. "I am so sick and tired of all these people who didn't even know Greg saying that the play killed him," says Katharine DePew. "The fact is, if they had canceled the play or told Greg he couldn't act in it, he would have killed himself the next day."

But though many of Greg's friends refuse to blame the play, they express anger and astonishment that David kept a gun in the house after Eric's death. David insists there was no ammunition in the house and that the gun—which he bought in 1988 as a security device and occasionally used for target shooting—was locked in the attic and had a trigger lock, but it's an explanation that Greg's friends say falls short.

"Who the fuck keeps a gun in the house after your first kid kills himself with it?" says a close friend of Eric and Greg. "When I heard the way Greg died, I was like, 'Are you fucking kidding me?' Why would David do that? Why would he even take that chance? What purpose did it serve? It's not like the gun is a *memento*. I guess my question is, does he still have it?"

David says he doesn't. "With twenty-twenty hindsight, I would have removed the gun, but I am quite sure that the result would have been the same," he says. "Greg stressed many times how easy it was to commit suicide, and he was an expert on various methods. Greg believed in personal responsibility and liked the saying 'Blame the finger, not the trigger.' I understand that people want to blame one thing so they can say to themselves, 'This can't happen in my life because I don't own a gun or because my kid isn't in a play about suicide.' The truth is, I'm not sure anyone could have stopped what happened. Eric died because he didn't think he could live with his illness, which none of us knew about. And Greg? Greg died because he couldn't live without his older brother."

THE DEATHS OF Eric and Greg Kochman left several of their friends suicidal. And three years later, the brothers' deaths still invade their friends' dreams. Kris Kesney has a recurring dream involving Eric: In it, he and a friend, Travis Smith, are relaxing in front of an old ski cabin on a cold, dark, quiet winter night. Slowly, a police car pulls up.

"Shit, what did we do *now*?" Kesney thinks to himself. Nothing, it turns out. Out of the cruiser's driver seat steps Eric Kochman, beer in hand and a grin on his face. "I can't stay long," Eric says, lighting a cigarette.

The boys drink a beer together, after which Eric says he'd better be going. "I feel okay now," he tells them. "I'm all right." As Eric walks back to the cruiser, he stops, pivots, and looks at Kesney. "Kris, you better do your goddamn schoolwork," Eric says. "You be well with yourself. I don't want to see you fail." With a beer in one hand and a cigarette in the other, Eric steps into the driver's seat. He sits down, shuts the door, smiles, and drives into the black night.

Greg Kochman also had a dream after Eric died. Greg's dream, according to a suicide note he wrote before he was hospitalized, went like this: "In my dream, I had killed myself but had come back to Earth as an observer. Eric and I were reunited and it was the happiest dream I have ever had. We talked with people, talked to each other about things we had done, and my death seemed almost like an unreal inside joke between the two of us."

Kids Inc.

Prepubescent skateboarders and snowboarders are making millions—and rewriting the rules of sports marketing.

ON WARM, DRIZZLY SUMMER afternoons in southern Vermont, when heavy fog blankets a nearly deserted Stratton Mountain, professional snowboarder Luke Mitrani does what many snowboarders do when there is no snow: he skateboards. "Basically, Luke's happy any time he's going *sideways*," explains his father, Al, who stands next to the large green skateboard ramp near the garage in their 10,000-square-foot mountain home.

Right now, though, the ramp—emblazoned with two giant Mountain Dew stickers, courtesy of Mountain Dew—is wet and perilous. "Don't break your head," Al tells Luke, at which Luke grabs a mop and begins mopping. "I should be a professional mopper," Luke tells me, outfitted in a black T-shirt, baggy shorts, and a green Mountain Dew wristband.

Luke says he likes Mountain Dew a lot. As luck would have it, Mountain Dew trucks come to the house often with free crates of soda. And a few times a year, Mountain Dew sends big checks in the mail.

Mountain Dew is one of Luke's many snowboarding sponsors. Sometimes, Luke, who is thirteen, can't remember all his sponsors. "Let me think," he says, taking a deep, ponderous breath. "There's Burton, Oakley, Stratton, Wendells, Power Bar, Mountain Dew, LEGO, Independent, Hurley, and"—he pauses and looks toward the sky, counting sponsors on his fingers—"um, I think that's it. Oh, and I might be getting sponsored by a candy company soon. That would be so cool! I think that's like nine sponsors, right? Did I say Wendells? Whatever, it's nine or ten sponsors."

Luke Mitrani doesn't look like the future of American snowboarding. He's short, shaggy-haired, skinny, and hyper. At four-foot-seven and seventy pounds, he looks like the kid who gets picked on at school. But in the age of extreme sports, it's best not to judge a kid by its cover: last year, Luke made six figures in endorsement deals.

FOUR DAYS LATER and 2,563 miles away, a seven-year-old named Mitchie Brusco skates at the Renton Skate Park east of Seattle. It's a clear, warm day, and Mitchie, a skateboarder who has eleven sponsors and his own Web site, sits on the ground sipping a Slurpee to keep himself cool. He's decked out in what his mother, Jennifer, calls his "warrior gear"—helmet, elbow pads, and knee pads. He looks serious and determined, which is how he gets when he's considering a move he's never landed. The trick in question requires that Mitchie skate through bushes and over rocks, landing a six-foot drop onto cement.

"Hey, Mitch, I'll tell you what," says his father, Mick, a former college baseball player. "You land this, and you can light the barbecue when we get home."

"Really?" Mitchie says, his face lighting up at the bribe.

"He's a total pyromaniac," Mick says, laughing. "Mitchie's very cautious, and he won't do anything he doesn't want to do," Jennifer interjects, perhaps fearing that motivational bribes could be used as evidence of controlling and overzealous sports parents. But Jennifer's right. On a skateboard, Mitchie, who has fallen enough to know that falling hurts, has a serious, self-protective nature.

And now Mitchie is ready. Or at least he was. He scampers over to his mother. He stands on his toes (she bends down to meet him). He whispers something in her ear. "He wanted us to say a prayer for him," she tells me once he's back on his skateboard. "I think he's realizing that not too many other kids have his talent. We definitely think there's a purpose for this talent."

And with that, the future of skateboarding is off, speeding toward the bushes, the rocks, the six-foot drop, and the unqualified respect of every skater in this skate park. Mitchie goes flying through the bushes and over the rocks, his little body landing cleanly and dramatically on the cement. Jaws drop.

"Holy shit," says a skinny teenage skater with no shirt and sagging jeans.

• • •

WHILE YOUR KID is trying valiantly to make the soccer team, young extreme-sport athletes are making a living. Unencumbered by NCAA regulations barring everything from free shoes to lucrative endorsement deals, snowboarders, skateboarders, BMX riders, and other extreme-sport athletes are promoting everything from skateboards and snowboards to LEGOs. In the process, they're rewriting the rules of sports marketing.

The new rule is that there are no rules, except maybe an unwritten one about not sponsoring unborn babies. The last five years have seen an explosion of interest in extreme sports—a survey of twelve- to seventeen-year-olds found that they preferred extreme sports to professional football, basketball, and baseball—and a predictable interest from mainstream advertisers trying desperately to reach Gen Y. For marketers, that means sponsoring young, talented extreme-sport athletes. And sometimes that means sponsoring kids.

Three years ago, Mitchie's mother decided that Mitchie needed representation. He was four. "I was just worried that we would sign his life away without knowing what we were doing," says Jennifer, a former college basketball player and professional baseball player for the Silver Bullets, a women's team that operated out of Colorado in the mid-'90s. "People were just like, 'Sign this, sign that.'"

So she called Peter Carlisle, the director of Olympic and action sports at Octagon. "My first reaction was 'No, that's too young,'" recalls Carlisle, who represents numerous Olympic and extreme-sport athletes. "I couldn't imagine that

Mitchie would need representation at that age or that he would be receiving contract offers so young. I told her, 'As long as you aren't signing anything, you're okay.' Then she said, 'Okay, well then, what do I do with these contracts that came in by fax?' To my surprise, Mitchie was talented enough and compelling enough to skateboard companies that they wanted to sponsor him."

Jennifer and Mick said they had no idea what to do with their skateboarding prodigy of a son. "Mick and I had never been on skateboards," she says. "People always ask us, 'Where did you get him lessons? What did you guys do to make him this good?' Well, we haven't done anything except drive him to the skate park. He's done the rest."

It all started at Target, when Mitchie was shopping with his mom and spotted a little Tasmanian Devil skateboard. It was only nine dollars, so Jennifer bought it. "I knew he liked Tasmanian cartoons, but I just figured this was another toy going in the toy box," she says. "But we got home and it was just unbelievable. He spent hours trying to kick-flip it, and he hasn't stopped since."

When Mitchie was five, he competed in the Amateur Challenge at the Gravity Games in Cleveland, one of extreme sports' two major events (the other is the X Games). Mitchie placed second to last, but the next youngest competitor was twelve. "Mitchie can do things on a skateboard that no one has ever done at his age," says Carlisle. "That doesn't mean he'll automatically become the best skateboarder ever, because he has to continue to love doing it, and he has to continue to improve. But if you look at the athletes who truly elevate their sports, you've got athletes like Tiger Woods, who is a prodigy much in the same way Mitchie is. Andre Agassi is the same thing. Guys like that somehow get to the top of their profession at a ridiculously young age."

For his part, Mitchie seems unfazed by his sudden fame. On the *Today* show last year, he charmed Matt Lauer when he decided, after some deliberation, that he preferred Popsicles to his big brother. On *The John Walsh Show,* Mitchie showed just the right combination of concern and amusement when Walsh tried to skateboard and broke his ankle in three places.

On a car ride from the skate park to the family's modest home, I ask Mitchie if he has any idea why he's so good at skateboarding. "Maybe they don't practice as much?" he says, half statement and half question. "Or maybe I started before them?"

Or maybe there is just *something* about Mitchie. Sponsors certainly think so. In addition to free-product arrangements with numerous companies ("A lot of big FedEx packages arrive at the house," Jennifer says), Mitchie has cash deals with LEGO and Termite Skateboards.

"Because of his age, there was a little bit of a shock in the action sports world when Mitchie signed his deals," says Bill Carter, the president of Fuse, an action sports and youth culture marketing agency. "But there are twelve million skateboarders in America, and a huge portion of those are very young kids. Young action sports athletes like Mitchie, Luke, and others speak directly to the consumer. These kids are the same age as the target consumer, and they live essentially the same lifestyle. It's a near-perfect fit. Even in a successful marketing campaign like Michael Jordan and

Gatorade, Jordan wasn't speaking directly to his peers. These kids do that."

LEGO sponsors only four athletes, all of them in extreme sports: Mitchie, Luke, the snowboarder Ross Powers, and the skateboarder Bob Burnquist. Why not sponsor conventional team-sport athletes? "Part of it is their availability," says Melinda Carter, a marketing manager at LEGO. "In general, you can go to a skate park and skate right next to Mitchie or end up next to Luke on a chair lift somewhere. It's less likely you'll bump into Shaquille O'Neal or Jason Kidd on the street. The athletes we sponsor are people you could conceivably meet walking down the street. These athletes are accessible. They're just like other kids."

And that, LEGO knows, is part of the problem. Should LEGO be sponsoring *kids*? LEGO officials say they had long internal discussions before deciding to do it. "There was a lot of us sitting around saying 'Is five years old too young? Is this going to be misconstrued?'" recalls Carter.

Other companies hoping to reach Gen Y have similar concerns. "They worry that they're going to look like a big bad corporate entity using a kid," says Fuse's Carter. "In the end that's only going to do harm to the kid and the brand. So companies like Mountain Dew structure the contracts in a very relaxed, no-pressure way. With Luke, for example, you're not going to ask him to do twenty appearances at different events. You have to treat him like he's a thirteen-year-old."

But can you do that when you're paying him more than his parents earn? Eric Anderson, a sports sociologist at University of California—Irvine, doubts it. "Even in the best-case scenario, one with great and well-meaning parents, it's still highly problematic," Anderson says. "With other young athletes and child actors, we've seen the real dangers of adultifying children. With sports, it's teaching the child to take risks with his body for the sake of the maintenance of his or her endorsement deals. Kids certainly have an idea of expectations, and even if the parents attempt to remove expectations, kids are intuitive, and they want to please. If that's the best-case scenario, the worst-case scenario is a kid who is literally exploited by his parents."

Carlisle says that's much less of a concern in action sports. "People's perception is based on the sports that we grew up seeing," says Carlisle, who now represents Luke and Mitchie. "When we think of young athletes, what comes to mind? Figure skating. Gymnastics. Tennis. And what we've seen of young athletes in those sports is a nightmare. But the structure of action sports is different. For one thing, many of the parents never played the sport, and this is really their kids' passion, not theirs. Also, what it means to turn pro in action sports is different. You don't have NCAA eligibility issues or Olympic issues. It's not some big decision to turn pro. Basically, these kids are pro the minute they receive a free sticker from a skate company."

For many companies, associating with young extreme-sport stars is safer than trying to market to them directly through conventional ads. "Companies are so intimidated by Gen Y," Carlisle says. "Ten years ago, Nike marketed with skateboards, and the company did such a poor job that it took five years before any athlete would even associate with them. So now many companies have cleverly concluded that one way to reach Gen Y is to effectively associate with someone in that space. They say, 'Let's not market. Let's just associate.'"

There's a long list of companies hoping to "associate" with Mitchie, but Jennifer says that the family is careful not to sign every deal that comes along. "After all, he's a kid, and it's about him having fun," she says. "If we had signed with Jones Soda, we couldn't have any other soda in our fridge. We're not going to sign any deal that would mean he could only wear certain clothes. I mean, he's seven, so if he wants to wear a Superman T-shirt, he's going to wear a Superman T-shirt."

LUKE MITRANI WANTS his friend Chris to come over. But being thirteen means there are hurdles to overcome. First, Luke must get permission from his parents, which is eventually granted. Then he has to convince Chris's parents, who must drive Chris over. Luke dials Chris's number and plops himself into a big chair next to the family's two huge dogs, an Akita and an English mastiff.

"Wattup?" Luke says into the phone. "Chris, you gotta come over for a night sess." (Translation: "You have to come over for a night session of skating.") Chris tells Luke that he's still sick. "Dude, you're not sick," Luke says. "You've *been* sick. You're not sick anymore. Come on, you have to come over." Chris still isn't convinced his parents will let him. "Tell your parents I just got something brand new and you *have* to see it," Luke says. When that doesn't work, Luke tries another tactic. "Dude, let me talk to your mom or dad," he says, sounding very much like an adult. "I'll convince them."

An hour later, the boys are in Luke's basement, where they spend the night practicing skate moves on a treadmill and crank-calling friends. Observing Luke for a day, it's clear that he often gets what he wants. He knows how to reason with adults, mostly because he spends so much time in the adult world of sponsors, marketers, and professional athletes. But he's equally comfortable hanging around his friends. Although Chris is two years older than Luke, Luke is the decision maker in the relationship. He's the "star," so to speak, and while he's humble about his snowboarding ability ("I'm not that good," he often says), he clearly loves the attention that comes from being a famous thirteen-year-old.

When he calls friends of friends with Chris (using the speaker on the fax machine), there are several boys on the other end of the line who've never spoken to Luke before, and though they try to sound cool, it's clear that they're starstruck. After all, they're talking to one of the most famous young snowboarders in America. Chris sits patiently on the sidelines while the boys pepper Luke with questions: "How many sponsors do you have?" "When did you turn pro?" "Do you think you could come over sometime and hang out?"

Luke deflects most of the questions (answering them could be perceived as bragging), but he clearly loves having so many kids want to be his friend. With that comes power, which Luke uses subtly. When a particularly adoring boy asks Luke to name his sponsors, Luke toys with him for a while by alternating his sponsors with icons on the computer desktop next to the fax machine. "Oakley, Netscape, Mountain Dew, Internet Explorer, Java," Luke says, laughing. It's not a mean laugh. It's the laugh of a thirteen-year-old who doesn't quite know what to do with his celebrity.

Upstairs, Al and Cindy marvel at how humble Luke is. "He's careful not to brag about anything to anyone, especially his brother and sister," Cindy says. Luke hasn't changed since the family (Al, Cindy, older brother Jack, and older sister Liza) commuted most weekends from Long Island to Stratton Mountain. "He's always been a little midget with a lot of energy," Al says. Luke quickly focused his energy on snowboarding. "One day, when I was, like, seven, I saw a group of snowboarders and I was, like, 'Wow, that's cool, I want to do that,'" Luke says. "I rented a snowboard. That first day I wasn't good at all. But then I bought a snowboard. So did my brother and sister."

Before long, all three excelled, but Luke seemed particularly gifted. Luke was also determined to be sponsored. "When I was eight, I was at the US Open, and I kept bugging the people at the Burton Snowboards booth," recalls Luke. "I was, like, 'Will you sponsor me? Will you sponsor me? Will you sponsor me?' They got so annoyed that they just gave me a helmet to shut me up. I still wear it, because it's the only helmet that fits."

That year, Luke went to Ross Powers's snowboarding camp, where it didn't take long for the Olympic snowboarding champion to notice the fearless kid. "It was an icy cold day," recalls Powers, "and I was telling the kids to take it easy. But Luke was out there doing flips. It was unbelievable."

Powers told Burton, and Burton officially sponsored Luke. At that point it was just a "flow" arrangement—the company provided Luke with free snowboarding equipment. In the last few years, though, Luke has signed money deals with Mountain Dew, LEGO, and Oakley (eyewear). "And there's a long list of companies dying to work with Luke," says Carlisle, who notes that Luke's marketability skyrocketed last year when he made the U.S. snowboarding team. "There's a chance he could make the Olympic team at fifteen, and there are many companies that would kill to sign him in the off chance that happens. Luke is a complete and utter standout. He's a marketer's dream."

Cindy says that Luke is aware of many of the details of his sponsorship deals. "At first we weren't going to tell him, but he's not an idiot, and he knows what's going on," she says. "Now I tell him what I think he can handle. He's proud of the deals. He also has to sign them, so he knows. And he knows we're saving up for his future, his education, a house, whatever."

A real estate developer, Al takes time off to travel with Luke. "Basically, I'm a secretary for a kid," Al jokes. Luke is a sophomore at the Stratton Mountain School, a ski and snowboard academy where he snowboards every morning and attends academic classes until 5 p.m. Luke spends much of the winter and spring traveling to competitions.

"The snowboarding, the travel, the sponsors, all of that he can handle easily," Cindy says. "But then to focus on school is hard. To be honest, it's even hard for me. If we're all traveling and suddenly he has to open a book, he has no mind-set to do it. But you have to do it."

In many ways, Cindy says that Luke is at the perfect age to focus on snowboarding. "When I first heard he made the U.S. team, I thought, 'He's twelve, what do they want a twelve-year-old on the team for?'" Cindy says. "But when you think about it, it makes perfect sense to take him now. There is no one more eager and earnest than him. He's totally focused on snowboarding. He's not distracted by the things that most teenage boys are distracted by."

MITCHIE BRUSCO IS distracted by many things. They include Popsicles, Slurpees, trampolines, and anything on a grill. The latter two are in play on a Saturday afternoon in August as the Brusco family gathers in the backyard with some friends. On the trampoline, Mitchie divides his time between perfecting a back flip and trying new skateboarding moves on a board without wheels (it's a common technique for trying new moves, because the trampoline softens any fall). When he senses that it's time for a hamburger to be flipped on the grill, he sprints over and tries to grab the spatula from his dad.

Inside the house, Jennifer shows me the room Mitchie shares with his four-year-old sister. The bedroom is a shrine to Mitchie's success: the walls are covered with countless framed newspaper and magazine articles about Mitchie. Jennifer says she doesn't approach media outlets. "They just hear about Mitchie and call," she says.

I ask her again about sponsorship deals. Does part of her wonder whether any of this (the fame, the money, the expectations) could hurt him? She's been asked this question before. "When I was nine, Nike wanted to sponsor me and send me free shoes and stuff once in a while," Jennifer says. "But I wasn't allowed to accept it because of all the NCAA rules. I look back now and say, What would that have affected in my life?"

But Mitchie is getting more than shoes, I tell her. She smiles. "It's easy for people to criticize the way parents handle it when they're not directly involved," she says. "But I'd like to meet one parent who would tell their kid, 'I know you're an incredible skateboarder and this is what you love to do, but you're not allowed to compete, you're not allowed to accept free skateboards, free LEGOs, or any compensation for this incredible talent that God gave you and that you work hard every day to nurture.' I'd like to meet that parent, because I don't think that parent exists."

Camp Life

One long, occasionally successful day in the life of the next generation of pro-life activists.

THE TWENTY-SIX CAMPERS AT Survivors Summer 2000—a pro-life activist camp for teenagers—emerge groggy-eyed from their gender-segregated tents at the Leo Carrillo State Park in Los Angeles. As the boys and girls wash their faces and down exceptionally bad coffee, talk turns to the unmitigated success that was the previous night. That's when a screwy valet parking scheme outside a ritzy Democratic fund-raiser allowed the campers (and their big posters of aborted fetuses) within twenty feet of the politicians and celebrities leaving the party. "You can't *buy* access like that," one of the teens tells me.

The highlight of the evening was an encounter with Cher, who wasn't pleased when the camp's founder, Jeff White, screamed, "Your party is killing babies!"

Pirouetting to face her accuser, Cher allegedly yelled

back, "You need to shut up, because you don't have a fucking vagina!"

The campers giggle as they recount the story, although they do so without using the words "fucking" or "vagina" (they let the camp's leaders fill in that part). These are Christian campers, after all, who have come here to learn pro-life activist tactics and to fight for the reversal of *Roe v. Wade*. For the past few years, White, a cofounder of Operation Rescue, has focused his time and resources on these camps for teenagers. The idea is to groom a future generation of dedicated, politically savvy pro-life activists.

Later that morning, an energized White shows the campers the front page of the *Los Angeles Times,* which features a picture of a dump truck pouring manure in front of the Staples Center, home this week to the Democratic National Convention. "This is a classic piece of activism," he tells the campers, who sit at attention on folding chairs outside their tents.

Sadly, it's a classic piece of activism they didn't think of. The manure stunt was the brainchild of an animal rights group, one of the countless organizations in town to protest outside the convention. "They made the front page," White tells the campers, "because their message is clear and there was a high-impact action that could be photographed!"

Over the course of the camp's seven days, White will teach the eager young pro-lifers—most of whom are homeschooled and were born into families with pro-life activist parents—debating skills, abortion history, specifics on the legality of protests, and activist tactics (including the importance of being "chummy" with the police). As for dealing with the press, White tells the young campers that journalists can't be trusted.

Pointing dramatically toward me, he says, "We're fairly certain that your magazine wants you to write that the campers are brainwashed pawns of radical, right-wing, male-led, religious loonies." A few minutes later, as the campers pose for a magazine photographer, Jeff chimes in again. "Be sure to look stiff and close-minded! That's probably what they want you to look like!" (During my day with them, most of the campers look neither stiff nor particularly close-minded. They do, however, seem resigned to the fact that most of the world sees them that way.)

After a brown-bag lunch, we get in a van and drive to Barbra Streisand's house, where word is that some celebrities and politicians have gathered for brunch. Sadly, the Secret Service seems intent on ruining a perfectly good activist opportunity: access to her house is blocked by agents and about forty police vehicles. Still, Reverend Pat Mahoney, a proud Democrat pro-lifer who often works with White, is all smiles as he chats up the bored Secret Service agents and offers instructions to the campers. "If you can engage in conversation, do that," Mahoney tells them. "Don't be afraid to say what's on your mind!"

Mostly, though, Mahoney can't stop thinking about Cher. "What Cher said really speaks to a disingenuous argument," he tells me. "People say, 'Oh, you're led only by *white men,*' which is not true, but if we were led by African-American women, would that make our argument any more valid? And are only women allowed to have an opinion about abortion? If you're pro-life and a man, you're automatically narrow-minded and bigoted. I don't know a single man in this movement who is pro-life because he wants to control women."

I meander over to fourteen-year-old Arianna Grumbine, one of the fifteen girls at the camp. Before I can ask her anything, she blurts out, "People always assume that I'm brainwashed! They want to think that I was made to think this way by my parents, that I can't think for myself. But when I invite people to talk to me, they don't, because I think they're afraid to find out whether I'm brainwashed or not!" Arianna won't have a chance to prove anyone wrong today. The celebrities leave the brunch surreptitiously, speeding past us in their limos and tinted-window vans.

THERE'S MORE WAITING around that night as we stand outside a party sponsored by the Democratic National Committee. Jeff White's fifteen-year-old son, Nick, passes the time by balancing a poster of an aborted fetus on his skater shoes and then pouring a bottle of water on the head of a fellow camper, Kenny Read. Read, who is fourteen, walks away shaking his head. "Nick can be such a dork sometimes," he tells me later.

Nick is one of eight brothers and sisters, and I ask him what would happen if any of them decided to be prochoice. He thinks about it for a few seconds. "Wow, that's a good question," he says. "I don't know . . . I mean, that just wouldn't happen!"

I walk over to Mahoney, who's in the midst of telling some campers that being a pro-life activist in today's world takes strength, courage, and remarkably thick skin. "We are the Rodney Dangerfield of social movements," he says. "We get virtually no respect. We're demonized in the press. We're made fun of." A father of one of the campers eyes me warily as I write down what Mahoney's saying. "If this story turns out negative," the father warns me, "I will find out where you live and burn down your house."

With that cleared up, we all pile back into the van. "Let's stop at Starbucks!" shrieks seventeen-year-old Sarah Dawson as the campers cruise down Santa Monica Boulevard toward another protest opportunity.

"We are *not* stopping at Starbucks," Mahoney tells them. "We're *protesting*."

"But God put Starbucks there for us to go to!" says Dawson, whose persistence is rewarded ten minutes later when we do, in fact, stop at Starbucks. While the kids get caffeinated, Cheryl Conrad, the mother of camper Jason Conrad, stands outside the van and tells me that she's invisible to most pro-choice people. "It bothers me that women will attack our men and say, 'Why are all your leaders men?'" Cheryl says. "And I'll be standing right in front of them, and I'm a *woman,* and I'm a *leader,* but it's like they don't even see me."

Mahoney, who's standing within earshot, smiles and shakes his head. "Um, Cheryl, were you sure to check with the men first to make sure you could speak?"

WE FINALLY ARRIVE at the Mondrian Hotel, the site of an exclusive DNC party. And we hit activist pay dirt: as the politicians and celebrities arrive, they have no choice but to walk by the campers and their posters. "Your party is killing babies! Where is your compassion?" the campers and their leaders belt out to the arriving guests.

Annoyed party organizers huddle together at the doorway and finally decide to create makeshift curtains to block the signs from the arriving guests. "That's just about the dumbest thing they can do," Mahoney tells me. "Any time you try to squelch free speech, it just brings more attention to the message."

The campers also try to engage passersby who stop to see what all the commotion is about. Jason, the eighteen-year-old camper, argues with a loud guy in a leather jacket who insists that Jason's too young to know anything about anything. "I believe that abortion is wrong," Jason says, although not particularly enthusiastically. "It's a belief of mine. These are my own conclusions."

The guy doesn't buy it. "You're brainwashed," he says. "You're fucking brainwashed."

"Can you debate this without resorting to those kinds of words?" another camper asks the man.

"Which words?" the man wants to know. "Brainwashed or fucking?"

"Try both," White tells him.

"Go fuck yourself!" the man says.

White laughs. "I'll be sure to take that under advisement."

The man finally moves along, and the campers get back to ruining the party. "They're seriously pissed off," Mahoney says of the party organizers. "The beautiful thing is, there's nothing they can do. Today, we win."

Trouble in Paradise

The battle for the soul of San Francisco's gay neighborhood: Gay homeless youth versus the residents who want them out.

JADE, A SEVENTEEN-YEAR-OLD HOMELESS teenager, skateboards around the corner onto Collingwood Street in San Francisco's predominantly gay Castro District, whizzing past the middle-aged men smoking cigarettes outside the Edge, a bar with a twenty-four-foot erect penis suspended from the ceiling. It's 11 p.m. on Valentine's Day, and Jade is coming from the nearby two-story building where homeless youths—mostly teenage lesbians—sit on couches, watch TV, eat, sleep, do drugs (pot, cocaine, crystal meth), and fend off the come-ons of the house's owner, a man they call "The Reverend."

Jade skates across the street and stops at the cigarette-littered front steps of the Eureka Valley Recreation Center (EVRC). "I'm so bored," she tells me, tucking her skateboard under her right arm and surveying the small group of homeless young people gathered on the center's steps. Jade wears baggy jeans, a blue jacket over a black hooded sweatshirt, and her signature green New York newsboy hat with beer bottle caps glued to the brim.

She's been on her own since her mother died five years ago while the two were homeless. Left to fend for herself, Jade has led what she calls a "hippie life," traveling from city to city with young people she meets along the way. She arrived in San Francisco four months ago.

"I came to the Castro with a friend," she tells me, "and when we walked down the hill and all I saw was that big gay flag, I was, like, 'Wow, lesbian *heaven*!' We were also on acid, which made it even trippier. It was weird to walk down Castro and see the guys kissing and the girls kissing and everyone so open. It was beautiful."

About thirty feet away, hidden from the street by bushes, a twenty-three-year-old named Paul—he's clad in green pants, a green army jacket, and a black beanie—sits propped up against a rain-damaged mural of children playing. Paul waves me over as he prepares to inject heroin. He needs little time to find a vein in his muscular left arm, sliding the needle carefully in, then back out, smiling as he does.

Suddenly energized ("Heroin has the opposite effect for me than it has for most people!" he says), Paul gathers his paraphernalia and wraps it neatly in his green duffel bag. He stands up, slings the bag over his right shoulder, turns his back, and blows the contents of his runny nose into a small puddle on the concrete. He takes off his beanie, revealing a shaved head. He is attractive and looks several years younger than he is, which he says is an advantage when panhandling. On an average day, about ten men in the Castro ask him to have sex with them for money.

"I have this innocent and boyish face, but I'm also seen as this little dirty, grubby street kid," Paul tells me, adding that he identifies as bisexual. "Some guys can't get enough of that combination."

Paul joins Jade and the other kids on the front steps of EVRC. Normally vibrant and flirtatious, Jade is depressed tonight. She says she likes San Francisco, but she doesn't much care for her options when the sun goes down: the street or the Reverend's house. The mostly gay residents of this neighborhood have lobbied against a shelter for these teens, claiming that it will attract crime to the neighborhood.

"[The Reverend] is always trying to get in my pants," Jade says, shaking her head. "Now that he realizes he's not getting any, I'm not a priority of his anymore. But why does he think he's going to get sex? He's so stupid. He's got like seventeen lesbian homeless kids in his house, and he thinks he's going to get sex!"

"Straight guys aren't known for their intellect," Paul quips.

"What I need is some fierce sugar momma with a leather jacket and a Harley-Davidson to roll up here and save me," Jade tells me, laughing and standing on her skateboard. "That's *exactly* what I need. Except that in the Castro, there are plenty of sugar daddies. Where are all the sugar mommies?"

"They're all at home taking care of their cats!" Paul says, his eyes now the size of golf balls. Jade looks toward the sky, as if expecting a fierce sugar mommie to fall from the heavens. "Damn lesbians! Don't they know they need to come save me?"

A MONTH LATER, a white van rolls to a stop in front of the small, two-story Golden Gate Metropolitan Church in San Francisco's quaintly upscale Noe Valley neighborhood (about a five-minute drive from the Castro). It's 10 p.m. on a weeknight, and it's only the third night that this church will provide temporary shelter for ten homeless gay and lesbian youths from the Castro. The rag-tag, sleepy-eyed group piles out of the van and into the pouring rain, walking quickly inside the church while San Francisco Patrol Special Police Officer Jane Warner stands at the door. "I'm just here so the neighbors can see me, so the neighbors know there is supervision," she says.

A tall, gangly, twenty-three-year-old named Glitter (so named, he says, because of his "charmingly hyperactive personality") takes me by the hand and leads me on a tour of the church. "This, as you can hear, is the *noisy* part," he says as we walk under a light well, where rain crashes loudly against the roof. We pass a small bathroom, then take a right into a spacious kitchen, where several teens sit eating pasta and salad at a large dining room table. Standing at one end, a handsome and well-built boy named J.D. takes off his gray T-shirt to show off his Florida tan (he arrived in San Francisco only a few days ago).

"Ooooh, baby!" Glitter says, playfully grabbing J.D.'s butt before leading me into the church's carpeted, wood-paneled sanctuary. As we walk past two rows of five mattresses on the floor, Glitter warns me that "J.D. is my boyfriend, so keep your hands off him." I tell him I had no intention of doing otherwise. "Good," Glitter says, "because I'm not a big fan of competition. I can get *mean*." Glitter takes me to the room's far corner, next to the street-side stained-glass window, where a small bookcase is overflowing with Bibles. "If we want to get *saved,*" he says, "there are plenty of copies for everyone."

By 10:30 p.m., most of the youths have put sheets and blankets on their single mattresses, and some are already asleep. Glitter sits on his bed, his shirt off, changing into his pajamas. J.D. stands near the kitchen, politely requesting that I mention that he wants to be a fashion model. "Everyone tells me that I should get into that, you know?" he says.

Mark Leno, a member of San Francisco's Board of Supervisors, has arrived, still wearing a suit from his workday. Leno circles the room, stopping to talk to anyone who is still awake. He plans to drop by the church most nights on his way home, as he did at another temporary shelter last year. "Two nights ago here, I remember this moment when everyone was sitting quietly and eating dinner," Leno says. "No one was making a sound, and I sat there wondering, 'This is what all the community fuss in the Castro was about?' This is what the neighbors were so afraid of?'"

THE TEMPORARY NOE Valley shelter is the latest imperfect, short-term solution to the increasing numbers of homeless young people in the Castro. While some Noe Valley residents opposed the shelter at the Golden Gate Metropolitan Church, they asked at least one question that's been dogging the denizens of America's most famous gay neighborhood for several years: Why can't the Castro take care of its own?

According to some, the answer is simple: the historically civic-minded residents of the Castro have grown up, made some money, and misplaced their collective gay soul. The latest symbol of this sell-out, they say, is the vocal neighborhood resistance to a twenty-bed shelter for gay and lesbian youths at a former athletic club in the heart of the neighborhood. A three-team, twenty-one-person panel of Castro residents called the Community Advisory Committee, which was formed to advise the city but does not have legal power, voted 14–7 against the facility. (The CAC is divided into three teams: proshelter, neutral, and opposing.)

Tommie Avicolli Mecca, a short, fiery, outspoken forty-eight-year-old member of the CAC's "pro" team, angrily stormed out of the meeting when the CAC voted down the shelter. "Some of the people in that room make me sick," he said at the time. "Their philosophy is 'I've made it, I've got my little castle here, and I'm going to protect it, I'm going to put a moat up and an electric fence and put the guards out and keep *those people* out.'"

"Those people" are the growing numbers of homeless youths and adults, and they're radically changing the landscape of a neighborhood long lauded for feeling like a gay version of small-town America. According to San Francisco's Coalition on Homelessness, there are approximately 1,500 shelter beds in San Francisco for the city's twelve thousand to fourteen thousand homeless. Of those, an estimated 5 to

10 percent are under the age of eighteen. Although exact numbers are not known, experts believe that many of the city's homeless teens and young adults are lesbian, gay, bisexual, or transgender.

In the Castro, there are usually thirty to forty homeless youths (most social service organizations define a youth as being under twenty-five) at any one time. Most self-identify as "queer," although a handful are straight. Some were thrown out of their homes for being gay, but a majority came from abusive homes, homeless families, or a foster care system ill equipped to protect them. (Several Castro youths say they were raped by older boys in foster homes.)

Many runaways and throwaways stay in San Francisco for a few months, then move on, only to return months or years later, often still homeless. Gay homeless youth can also be found in the Polk Street and Haight-Ashbury areas, but most choose the Castro, because it's where they can find other homeless young people like themselves. Some also hope it's where they'll find compassion and support from the neighborhood's gay residents. "But that doesn't really happen here," Paul tells me. "People say 'No, no drop-in centers in our neighborhood, no this, no that.' Even in this diverse neighborhood, the compassion stops when it comes to us."

To its credit, the Castro does offer an array of services for homeless youth during daylight hours. For the past five years, Mitch Thompson has run the Eureka Valley Teen Program out of EVRC's second-floor recreation room (the program is funded by the city and various local gay groups). Across the street, the Lavender Youth Recreation

& Information Center (LYRIC), organizes daytime and evening activities—including tutoring, computer training, and movie nights—for youth, homeless or not. Outreach workers from several youth social service organizations are also regulars in the Castro, offering condoms, tampons, toothbrushes, snacks, clean needles, clean socks, vitamins, bottled water—and, perhaps most important, referrals to social service organizations.

But because there is no shelter or transitional housing facility in the neighborhood, many of the Castro's homeless sleep in doorways, behind bushes, and in parks. Though there are several shelter options in other neighborhoods, many young people say they don't feel comfortable there. "I know a lot of people would rather sleep on the street with their friends than go to a shelter where they might have to deal with real homophobic assholes," one young homeless Castro resident told me.

MICHAEL (NOT HIS real name) pulls down his jeans, revealing white boxer shorts. He sits on a swing in the sandy portion of the children's play area of EVRC, about twenty feet from the sign that says, NO LOITERING IN THE CHILDREN'S PLAY AREA BY ADULTS and about ten feet from an empty 40-ounce bottle of King Kobra on its side in the sand.

Michael pulls out his penis. He stands up and takes off his shirt. His body is thin, white, and undefined. He paces in a circle on the sand, holding the back of his pants with his left hand so they don't fall to his ankles. He walks over to the slide, then back to the swing, trying to get aroused. Finally hard, he sits back down on the swing.

Seated next to him, a middle-aged man with a shaved head (except for the top, which is a Mohawk) pulls a small video camera from his backpack. Michael leans back in his seat, holding the swing's chain with his left hand to keep his balance. With his right hand, he masturbates.

Several of the Castro's male homeless youths say they have posed for the man, who works for a pornography company based in Australia. Most of the Castro's gay and straight homeless young people say they do what's necessary to make money, from pornography to prostitution. "There is one thing you have to understand about the Castro," says Jaiya, twenty-two, who has been homeless (on and off) in the Castro for several years. "*Everyone* is for sale."

ANDREW BERTAGNOLLI'S LARGE living room window looks directly out onto the front steps of EVRC. In recent years, he says the view has changed for the worse. More homeless have come to the area, and with them has come an increase of things that Bertagnolli does not like: used syringes in the small alleyway next to his apartment, loud noise at all hours of the night, and what he calls a "harsher and meaner" kind of homeless youth.

They are the kind of kids that Trevor Hailey—a long-time neighborhood resident who has been giving her historical "Cruisin' the Castro" tour for ten years—has little empathy for. "I have had to change my tour because of them," says Hailey. "I used to go to Collingwood Park and now I don't, and it's because my groups are consistently met with rudeness, vulgarity, and total disrespect. I think it's unfortunate that [in this whole homeless debate], everyone is so concerned with the rights of the homeless, but who is concerned with the rights of those of us who have to work in the neighborhood?"

Hailey's concern for her livelihood recalls the Castro's first significant battle over the neighborhood's homeless population. In the winter of 1997–1998, local merchants placed "Create Change, Don't Hand It Out" signs in their street windows as a reaction to the growing number of panhandlers in the area. The merchants thought the homeless were using the money for drugs, and they were mostly right.

Still, the campaign created an outcry, mostly because merchants were offering little in the way of "creating change." Tension came to a head for the second time a year later, when the city—ignoring a healthy dose of neighborhood opposition—opened a thirty-bed temporary drop-in shelter for queer youths at EVRC. People were livid. "There have been some great things that went on inside, but what went on outside overshadowed that for many neighbors," says Bertagnolli. "The neighbors thought they had no say, no stake in the shelter. People were frustrated and angry."

Tommie Avicolli Mecca, the proshelter CAC member, was surprised at the extent of the anger. He and others say that the increasingly gentrified neighborhood's gay organizations and upper-middle-class residents routinely rally together to tackle issues that directly affect them, such as AIDS or gay marriage, but ignore problems—including young gay homeless people—that they can't relate to.

Pastor Jim Mitulski of the local Metropolitan Community Church agrees. "This is very much a class issue," says the respected forty-two-year-old activist. "We have a gay movement and a gay neighborhood like the Castro that has never incorporated a serious economic analysis, and the result is the spectacle of a gay neighborhood saying, 'Oh, we don't want to shelter homeless gay youth.' It's appalling, and a huge source of embarrassment. There was a time when this neighborhood came together in the name of compassion. Now there is tremendous tension in the neighborhood. Marx would say it's class warfare, and I think there is a certain truth in that."

IT IS TWILIGHT on an evening in late February, and six homeless youth sit amid a clutter of shopping carts, sleeping bags, duffel bags, pillows, teddy bears, empty Doritos bags, and small cartons of Häagen-Dazs vanilla ice cream next to the mural on the front patio of EVRC.

Hunched over in the corner, holding his stomach, twenty-three-year-old Israel can hardly keep his eyes open. His face is broken out. His brown hair, which he has not washed in nearly a week, stands straight up, revealing a tattoo on the left side of his head. He has two sores on his bottom lip. His thin hands are black from dirt and sweat. His white Nike sweatshirt is brown, and the stained collar of his blue inside-out undershirt protrudes from the top. Nearly twenty hours ago, Israel injected heroin, overdosing in the EVRC bathroom. He was rushed to a hospital by ambulance.

About 80 percent of the Castro's homeless youth say they use crystal meth or speed regularly (often daily), and another 30 percent say they use heroin daily. Neither is hard to get in the Castro, a neighborhood that Jennifer Friedenbach—project coordinator for the substance abuse mental health work group of the city's Coalition of Homelessness—says has "a huge drug trade, and a huge amount of hypocrisy when it comes to criticizing the homeless for their drug problems."

When homeless youths are ready to get drug treatment (and many eventually are), they find an unfortunate loophole in city services. For those under eighteen, there are no treatment programs or detox centers. Those over eighteen can access methadone treatment for heroin, but they're greeted with a waiting list of, on average, three hundred people.

"The city sets these kids up for failure," says John Wood, a political activist and party promoter who has lived on and off in the Castro since 1989. "And it's sad, because [Castro residents] see these kids as junkies. If they saw them as human beings, you would see this neighborhood coming to their aid."

For her part, Jade, the lesbian skateboarder, says she's done waiting for aid. She sits on the front steps of LYRIC, talking about why she's planning to leave the neighborhood. "San Francisco is a great city and the Castro is cool in a lot of ways, but I never stay in one place longer than, like, six months," she says. "And I need a change. I need to get away from the scene here. This [neighborhood] is all about drugs, and no one seems to want us here. I need something a little more real."

In a few hours, Jade plans to leave for the East Coast with a friend who has a car. Word has gotten out that she's taking off, and for the next few hours, dozens of homeless youths come to wish her well. Glitter, who has already said his good-bye, watches Jade from a distance, picking at some dirt in the nail of his left-hand pinkie finger. He asks me if I can spare change for a soda. I say yes, although I doubt he will use it for soda. He thanks me, then looks toward the group of homeless teens standing around Jade.

"It's always sad when people leave," he tells me. "But you get used to it. That's what homeless kids do. They show up, they stay, they leave. Sometimes they come back, sometimes you never see them again. And sometimes you hear they're dead."

The War on Frat Culture

And why maybe that's not so totally great, dude.

BY MODERN FRATERNITY STANDARDS, Phi Delta Theta's tailgate party was a real rager. For one thing, there were kegs. I couldn't see them just then, but proof of their existence was everywhere. Packed into a backyard near the campus of Northwestern University in Evanston, Illinois, were some one hundred drunken college students, beer spilling from plastic cups, industrial-size ketchup bottles overturned on the grass near the grill, and gaggles of hard-drinking sorority girls (including one self-described "Phi Delt groupie") keeping pace with the boys.

Amid the revelry I spotted a lanky, easygoing Phi Delt sophomore from Texas who goes by the nickname Two-Shot, because two shots is about all it takes to get him acting silly. "Two-Shot!" I yelled as he meandered through the crowd in a hooded sweatshirt and jeans, gripping a beer in one hand and a cheap plastic bottle of vodka in the other. "Where's the keg?"

"Hey, homey," he said, pointing toward a far corner. "The beer's over there."

"You going to the game?" I asked.

"Man, that's a good question," he said. "I got great intentions, you know. But stuff happens. Sometimes I don't make it."

I wished him luck ("Keep it real!" he replied) and made my way toward the keg, where I bumped into Theo Michels, Phi Delt's likable chapter president, and Greg Bok, a big, sarcastic, deceptively smart sophomore. (Bok looks like a meathead but scored 1,550 out of 1,600 on the SAT.) Both Michels and Bok were marveling at the success of the day's tailgate.

"Six kegs and no cops!" Michels said. "This has to be some sort of record. Last year, we had an off-campus party that started at 10:30, and by 11 the police came with a paddy wagon. A *paddy wagon*! We're college students trying to have a party off campus, because we can't have one in our own fraternity house, because we're not allowed to drink there. So we try to have one off campus, and it gets broken up. Basically, we can't have a party anywhere."

Peter Micali, a square-jawed Phi Delt sophomore who had wandered within earshot, chimed in, "Yeah, it was easier to party in high school."

Bok shook his head sadly. "The good old-fashioned fraternity experience is dead," he said, pausing for dramatic effect. "So long, *Animal House*."

• • •

IT'S DOOM-AND-GLOOM TIME for many fraternity boys at Northwestern and at colleges across the country. Alarmed by the extent of binge drinking on their campuses, university administrators are cracking down on the excesses of Greek life, saying it's high time for fraternity boys to shape up and sober up. While all kinds of college students binge drink, the 2001 College Alcohol Study by the Harvard School of Public Health found that fraternity house residents are twice as likely to do so as other students.

Eleven national and international fraternities, including Phi Delta Theta, now require most of their chapter houses to be alcohol-free, no matter what their university's policy is. (Sororities have long banned drinking in their chapter houses.) Take away the booze, the new alcohol-free theory goes, and fraternities will be safer, on more solid economic footing (fewer lawsuits, cheaper liability insurance), and more conducive to the creation of real bonds of brotherhood: friendships will be forged out of genuine respect, not the shared misery of hazing or the shared fog of drink.

"We just didn't see a way to dramatically change the fraternity culture without removing alcohol," said Bob Biggs, executive vice president of Phi Delta Theta, when we met last fall in his office at the fraternity's spotless, museumlike international headquarters in Oxford, Ohio.

But what, exactly, would a dry fraternity look like? And would anyone want to join? As I listened to the brothers in that backyard go on about life at one of Northwestern's "alcohol-free" fraternities, I couldn't help feeling a little sorry for them. I was a Phi Delt at Northwestern in the mid-1990s—not that long ago, to be sure, but seemingly a different time entirely. Though we considered ourselves tamer than fraternities at many state schools (where Greek affiliation can often take precedence over just about everything else), my brothers and I still saw drunken debauchery in the chapter house as our fraternal mandate.

We threw rowdy keg parties. We got drunk in our rooms and then broke into other fraternities, stealing their sacred robes and toaster ovens. Some of us smoked marijuana, which we grew and harvested in an off-campus apartment. And many of us eagerly participated in drunken hazing, which most of the hazers and hazed saw as a kind of comic relief integral to fraternal bonding. To my brothers and me, a dry fraternity would have been inconceivable.

In less than a decade, though, the inconceivable has happened. When I told a friend from college that his fraternity, Theta Chi, was now dry, he was baffled. "What's the point?" he wanted to know. Indeed, what is the point of a fraternity if you can't throw a party—or drink a beer in your room with a brother and watch *Cops* at 3 a.m.? Wasn't alcohol what enabled fraternity boys to be, well, fraternity boys?

When I first heard of the move to ban alcohol from fraternity houses, I was reminded of a scene in the film *Roger Dodger* when a sixteen-year-old boy sneaks into a bar with his uncle, who promises to teach him the fine and complicated art of picking up women. When the boy declines an alcoholic beverage, the uncle becomes apoplectic. "You drink that drink!" he demands. "Alcohol has been a social lubricant for thousands of years. What do you think, you're going to sit here tonight and reinvent the wheel?"

A number of fraternities are brazenly trying to do just that, arguing that the fraternity wheel is broken—and badly in need of a redesign. But what does this new, redesigned American fraternity look like? I was back at Northwestern to find out, and to try to make sense of my own fraternity experience. Had I joined for the drunken keg parties, or was brotherhood about more than that? And was I really a "frat guy" or an anomaly—a guy who played sports and wore baseball caps but who really should have been hanging out with fraternity-mocking English majors?

Nearly a decade removed from college, I still view my fraternity experience with a mixture of pride and embarrassment. And I'm not alone. Two fraternity brothers told me that while they loved being Phi Delts, I was not, under any circumstance, to mention their names in this article. I understood. Never mind that Frank Lloyd Wright, Paul Newman, Walter Cronkite, and Ted Koppel—not to mention nearly half of all U.S. presidents and 40 percent of Supreme Court justices—belonged to a fraternity in college. The stereotype of the fraternity guy as party-loving imbecile is alive and well.

In that backyard in Evanston, though, surrounded by beer-guzzling fraternity boys and the girls who love them, I didn't feel ashamed. I felt *old*. "Dude, you're the reporter dude, right?" one brother said, grinning wildly. "Let me introduce you to some freshman girls! You want to meet some freshman girls? You're with Phi Delts, man. You remember how it is! It's all about the girls!"

Word spread among the brothers that I was a Phi Delt from way back in the 1990s, and before long several cornered me. They wanted answers: "How often did you have keg parties in the house? Was the house packed with girls? Were the girls hotter? How much cooler was it?"

They listened intently as I held court in the backyard, recounting salacious stories of riotous fraternal living—a little exaggerated in the retelling, of course. But the more I went on about our "huge keg parties," the more pathetic I felt. Was I really trying to impress college students? And were all of my favorite fraternity stories really about getting loaded?

SINCE 1997, THE year I graduated, Northwestern has expelled five fraternities—in cooperation with their national organizations—for alcohol and hazing violations. One casualty was Kappa Sigma, banished after its 2003 formal dance party at the Shedd Aquarium in Chicago. In a gaffe almost too dopey to be believed, a Kappa Sigma brother dropped a flask into the aquarium's beluga whale tank. Already on probation for an alcohol-related incident that sent a pledge to the hospital, the fraternity was booted off campus by Northwestern administrators, but not before the brothers could make going-away T-shirts. They read, *KAPPA SIGMA—A WHALE OF A GOOD TIME.*

Of the seventeen fraternities now at Northwestern, thirteen are alcohol-free, and any new chapter starting at the school also must be dry. (In 1997, not a single Northwestern fraternity was dry.) Across the country, some thirty colleges—including the University of Iowa, the University of Oklahoma, and the University of Oregon—have gone even further, banning alcohol in all their fraternity houses. (Some have also made their residence halls alcohol-free.)

And many schools are increasingly placing fraternities on probation, requiring that they meet specific academic and behavioral standards. Others are moving fraternity rush from fall to winter, heeding the words of the Arizona Supreme Court, which in 1994 opined that "we are hardpressed to find a setting where the risk of an alcohol-related injury is more likely than from under-age drinking at a university fraternity party the first week of the new college year." To try to combat the tendency of fraternity members to simply move their parties to off-campus apartments and houses, university officials are also cooperating more than ever with local police.

And then there's Alfred University in western New York and Santa Clara University in California, which have taken the most drastic step of all: they did away with fraternities altogether. "The Greek system is beyond repair," Robert McComsey, the chairman of Alfred's board, told *The New York Times* in 2002.

Fraternities have done little to improve their image in recent years, making headlines across the country in hazing and alcohol-related deaths. At Colorado State University, Samantha Spady, a sophomore, was found dead in a lounge at the Sigma Pi chapter house by a member giving his mother a tour of the fraternity. At the University of Oklahoma, Blake Adam Hammontree, a freshman, died at the Sigma Chi house from alcohol poisoning. And at the University of Colorado, Lynn Gordon Bailey, Jr., a Chi Psi pledge, was found dead after drinking during an initiation ritual.

Some fraternity leaders point out that drinking-related deaths at fraternity houses make up fewer than a dozen of the 1,400 alcohol-related deaths at colleges each year (car accidents are involved in approximately 1,100 of those). Whatever the numbers, none of those deaths occurred at dry chapters, which would seem to bolster the argument that alcohol-free fraternities can and do make a difference.

In 1997, Phi Delt was among the first fraternities to announce its plan to go dry, arguing that it would save lives, lift grade point averages, improve the condition of chapter houses, boost slumping recruitment numbers by attracting a new kind of college student (fraternity membership nationwide is down 25 percent from its peak in 1990), and help its members return to the core principles on which the fraternity was founded: friendship, sound learning, and moral rectitude. The policy called for all chapter houses to be dry by 2000.

In July 2005, Phi Delta Theta celebrated its fifth anniversary of being alcohol-free. And though some fraternity leaders still question how effective the policy is in stopping binge drinking ("We're not sure that focusing on where a person drinks will have any impact on how much that person drinks," Mark Anderson, the president of the Sigma Chi Corporation, said), Phi Delt's executive vice president, Bob Biggs, insists the policy is improving the daily lives of members—and keeping them safe.

For the first time since he can remember, Biggs said, the fraternity isn't facing any lawsuits. "It was common before we instituted this to have four, five, six claims at any one time," Biggs told me. To go with its newfound sobriety, Phi Delt even has a new motto: "Brotherhood—Our Substance of Choice."

But sobering up chapter houses isn't easy, and the backlash has been fierce. Some chapters have refused to go dry, choosing instead to break away from their national organizations. And many theoretically dry chapters are anything but—there's plenty of alcohol, pot, and harder drugs behind closed doors.

"I don't think anyone is naive enough to think that there's no alcohol in many dry houses," one fraternity chapter president at Northwestern told me. "If it's done in a somewhat covert way, you're fine." It's often not, and both Biggs and Dave Westol, executive director of Theta Chi, whose chapters started going dry in 1998, have recently closed chapters that brazenly ignored the no-alcohol policy.

But the greatest opposition to dry fraternities often comes from alumni. Westol has received hundreds of e-mail messages from angry alums who, he said, "can't imagine that a fraternity can be fun without alcohol." He went on to say that among the biggest challenges in persuading current fraternity members to take the dry policy seriously are alums who return to the chapter armed with countless stories about the fraternity's drunken past—or, worse yet, with six-packs. When I sheepishly admitted to having done just that (minus the six-packs), Westol went easy on me. "Don't beat yourself up," he said, "but you see what I'm talking about."

• • •

MANY FRATERNITY MEMBERS can't help thinking that alcohol-free fraternity houses came about not out of genuine concern for their well-being but because the fraternities were worried about their pocketbooks. Though Biggs denies that fear of costly lawsuits was the primary factor in going dry, he concedes that increases in litigation and liability premiums played a part in Phi Delta Theta's decision.

In the 1980s, the number of lawsuits and insurance claims resulting from fraternity binge drinking and hazing skyrocketed, causing the National Association of Insurance Commissioners to rank fraternities and sororities as the sixth worst risk for insurance companies—right behind hazardous waste disposal companies and asbestos contractors. Some insurance companies began refusing to cover fraternities, forcing fraternities to take measures to minimize their risk.

In the mid-'90s, Phi Delt's executive board considered going even further. "We wondered, Can we conceive of a fraternity that doesn't allow alcohol in its chapter houses?" Biggs said when I met with him. "But we knew it wouldn't be easy. When we decided to do it, someone made the analogy to when John Kennedy said, 'Let's go to the moon and back by the end of the decade.' So that's what we did."

At its annual convention in 1998, the fraternity broke out fireworks to celebrate its 150-year anniversary and its alcohol-free future. But back at Northwestern that fall, "we thought the world was ending," said Nick Logan, the chapter president at the time. "Northwestern had actually told us that we needed to go dry that year, so unlike other Phi Delt chapters that had two years to prepare, we didn't. It was absolute pandemonium. I mean, we're like nineteen, twenty, twenty-one, many of us have been drinking regularly since high school, we join a fraternity partially for the social scene, and now we're supposed to just not drink? It was like telling a monk that he can't pray."

Many dry chapters still have members who try to skirt the dry rule. Chapter presidents, who are sometimes underage, are put into the difficult position of policing the drinking of members who are twenty-one. But even fraternities that do follow the rules insist that administrators, in their efforts to crack down on drinking, have failed to do just that—and managed to take much of the fun out of fraternity life in the process.

At the Sigma Phi Epsilon fraternity house at Northwestern, members told me of their fruitless attempt this fall to show the classic 1978 fraternity movie *Animal House* at one of their philanthropic events, cosponsored by a campus sorority. The Sig Eps were all set to make a special T-shirt for the event—*FAT, DRUNK, AND STUPID IS NO WAY TO GO THROUGH LIFE, SON*, a famous line from the film—when they say the university "very strongly suggested" they not show the film.

"It was really a very ironic event, of course, because most fraternities now are pretty far from the *Animal House* model," one Sig Ep brother told me. "But the administration and the Panhellenic Association, which oversees the sororities, didn't see the humor in it. They acted very disappointed in us, because we'd been a frat that had worked hard to dispel the *Animal House* stereotype."

Then there was the controversy surrounding Sig Ep's annual prep school party, at which female undergraduates traditionally arrive in their best Catholic schoolgirl attire. As one of the school's four "wet" fraternities, Sig Ep can have parties with alcohol in their house, as long as the beer is sold by an outside vendor and no one under twenty-one drinks. But this year the party was going to be dry. "The university brought our attention to some clause in the student handbook," said Jordan Cerf, the chapter's vice president of recruitment, "that says that any event that freshmen attend during the fall quarter in a house has to be dry."

The Sig Eps were still expecting a huge crowd when I talked to them in October. "Here's what the school has done by making this party dry," Nick Johnson, the chapter president, explained. "Before coming to the party, everyone is going to get loaded at their dorm, or off campus, or in their car. They're going to drink more, and they'll drink faster, so that their buzz lasts them through the party. That's really the disingenuous thing about this policy. I don't see how this is keeping anyone safer. It's just moving the binge drinking somewhere else."

I NEVER EXPECTED to be a hard-drinking fraternity boy when I arrived at Northwestern in the fall of 1993. I considered myself far too much of a "freethinker" to join a fraternity, and I certainly wasn't going to be "paying for friends," which is what I considered the monthly dues to be.

There was also my father's fruitless fraternity experience to consider. In 1958, he joined Lambda Chi Alpha at the University of Wisconsin–Madison, a fraternity, he says, "for guys other fraternities wouldn't take." Still, it was a welcome social outlet for my shy dad, and he happily went along with the heavy drinking and the endless talk of sorority house panty raids if it meant having friends. But things went awry when my father wanted to attend a racial equality march, which didn't gel with the fraternity's conservative views. The chapter president told him not to go, and when my father said he was going anyway, the president insisted that he not wear his fraternity pin. Outraged, my father moved out of the chapter house and started writing antifraternity letters to the school newspaper. He was expelled from the fraternity soon after.

My dad's experience played right into my stereotype of fraternities: they were for close-minded people. But as the fall quarter of my freshman year progressed, my antifraternity stance softened. I realized that a third of Northwestern's undergraduates (including plenty of people who seemed perfectly decent) belonged to fraternities or sororities. I also loved fraternity parties—my friends and I spent many weekend nights stumbling from one fraternity kegger to the next.

And as much as I liked to mock fraternity guys, I desperately wanted to belong to *something*. I was a mostly clueless drifter in high school, and I didn't want to be one in college, too. As an only child, I was intrigued by the idea of brotherhood—by the concept of guys contractually obligated to have my back. Maybe paying for friends wasn't such a bad idea, after all.

So I didn't object when my classmate and new friend Dave, who struck me as even less of a fraternity guy than I was (he was a film major prone to outbursts of hypersensitivity), suggested we head up to Phi Delta Theta and enjoy the free food at its Rush Week event. I didn't know much about the chapter, but Dave apparently knew a brother there. That evening I was introduced to many of the members, and everyone seemed cool enough to me. Dave and I went back the next night, and I was summoned to a room and offered a "bid"—an invitation to "pledge" membership to the fraternity. I had a Groucho Marx moment—did I really want to join a fraternity that would have me?—but I got over it and accepted on the spot.

They threw a pledge T-shirt on me, and we ran downstairs, out the front door, and onto the porch, where there was a lot of congratulatory hollering and a few "Who's that skinny dude?" whispers from pledges who didn't know me. Before I knew it, I was being hurled high into the cold night air, and everyone started singing a ditty you won't find listed among the official songs of Phi Delta Theta:

> I'm a Phi from NU, and I don't give a damn,
> I came to school to fuck the girls and flunk the damn
> exams.
> To hell, to hell with Fiji, to hell with Sigma Nu,
> And if you're not a Phi Delt, to hell, to hell with you,
>
> So listen to me lassie, so listen to my plea,
> Don't ever let a Phi Delt an inch above your knee.
>
> He'll take you to the back shed and fill you full of rye,
> And soon you'll be the mother of a bouncin' baby Phi.

Be a Phi, be a Phi, Phi Delt do or die,
So fuck you SAE, and piss on Sigma Chi!

Soon after pledging, I learned that I wasn't joining a chapter with the most sterling reputation. We were told that in the 1980s, our house had been known for spawning "obnoxious jerks." One night some brothers apparently got drunk, shouted obscenities, and "threw things" at marchers during a Take Back the Night rally. University officials booted the fraternity off campus, but not before the brothers got drunk and trashed the place.

I was horrified by this news, but soon I was too busy being hazed to think about it. We had weekly "lineups" in the main room of the chapter house, where active members, drinking and wielding flashlights, would belittle our physiques and quiz us on arcane fraternity history. We were made to do push-ups until we couldn't anymore, and we were told to lie on our stomachs and cover our behinds, because the Betas, who lived in the chapter house next door, were apparently coming after us. The Betas didn't seem particularly gay to me (we mostly knew them as bigger potheads than we were), but we were made to believe that they wanted nothing more than to have their way with us.

There was also a lot of forced drinking. We were told to down copious amounts of liquor, and most any effort to avoid it (an earnest explanation that alcoholism ran in the family, for example) was usually laughed off. To haze effectively, many of the active brothers had to get drunk, too. After all, hazing isn't much fun when you're sober—a fact that isn't lost on fraternity leaders who hope that going alcohol-free will reduce hazing.

And maybe it has. The current Phi Delts at Northwestern seem to value the humiliation of freshmen a lot less than we did. "When I was a pledge last year," Peter Micali told me, "we would be at some off-campus apartment and the actives"—full members—"would be, like, 'Here, drink this.' But if you didn't want to, they were like, 'Okay, no problem, that's cool.' So we don't do much hazing." One night at a bar, Micali admitted that he actually would have liked to have been hazed a little harder. "I wanted them to be like, 'Okay, *you worthless dirtbag*, walk through that wall!' That would have been funny."

As much as the actives tried to humiliate us a decade ago, we stayed cocky throughout, and we did the minimum required during our months as pledges: we fetched food, cleaned the house, took our morning Wheaties with beer instead of milk. Soon enough we were initiated and taught the secret handshake and the secret sign, both of which I promptly forgot.

We told ourselves that we were clearly the best fraternity at Northwestern, and we could drink you under the table to prove it. My senior year, though, was to be the beginning of the end. Just after I graduated and stepped awkwardly into the real world, the brothers were faced with the daunting, incomprehensible, surreal prospect of fraternal sobriety. They didn't react well. Brothers disagreed about following the alcohol-free mandate. In May 1999, the university informed the fraternity that its members needed to find a new place to live the following fall. According to the

Chicago Sun-Times, the school's list of the chapter's infractions included "a sink that was pulled from the wall and used as a urinal; a member who set off a fire alarm by smoking marijuana; throwing garbage, urine, paint and other debris."

David Sykes, the chapter president at the time, told a skeptical reporter that Phi Delt was "no Animal House" and that many of the charges were overblown. The brothers sued Northwestern, but a Cook County Circuit Court judge dismissed the case as "an unnecessary drain" on the courts. Remarkably, the university let the brothers return to the fraternity house the following year. Everyone was on his best behavior. But over the last three years, the brothers haven't always agreed on how seriously to take their alcohol-free mandate. In that way, they're not much different from the Phi Delts who came before them.

THE PHI DELTA Theta international fraternity—now home to nearly two hundred chapters in forty-four states and six Canadian provinces—was founded by six serious and determined students at Miami University in Ohio on a December night in 1848. Conceived as a secret literary and social society for men of intellectual vigor and upstanding character, the Miami University chapter enjoyed a brief period of fraternal harmony before all hell broke loose.

By 1850, the fraternity was "chaotic with dissension between fraternal idealists and hedonists," writes Hank Nuwer in his book *Wrongs of Passage: Fraternities, Sororities, Haz-*

ing and Binge Drinking. Phi Delt's members—including a transfer student named Benjamin Harrison, who would later become the twenty-third president of the United States—disagreed about what a fraternity should be.

Was Phi Delta Theta, as its six founding fathers envisioned, about friendship, sound learning, and moral rectitude? Or was it a place for boys to be boys, no matter how juvenile and tasteless that might appear to the outside world? Or could it be some ingenious combination of the two, making space for both righteousness *and* debauchery?

A hard-liner, Harrison quickly got himself elected fraternity president: Phi Delt was to be a place of honor and respectability. He was more than a little displeased, then, when two fraternity members became obscenely drunk at a reception for Pierson Sayre, the last living Revolutionary War soldier. He gave the offending men a second chance after they promised to shape up, but soon enough they were back to their old ways. Harrison threw them out, upon which several other members, who backed the banished brothers, resigned.

The growth of Phi Delta Theta (in 1859, it became the first Greek organization at Northwestern) and other fraternities stalled during the Civil War. But Phi Delt rebounded between 1870 and 1900, as fraternities expanded west. The first reported alcohol- and hazing-related fraternity deaths also occurred during this time, Nuwer recounts. In 1873, a Kappa Alpha Society pledge at Cornell University died when he fell into a gorge after fraternity brothers left him alone in the woods. Nine years later, a blindfolded Delta Kappa Epsilon pledge at Yale pierced himself with a sharp object on a carriage while following orders from fraternity brothers to run down the street. He subsequently died from the injury.

In 1897, the South Carolina State Legislature voted to ban fraternities at the state school; in 1901, Arkansas followed suit. The president of the University of Michigan, James Angell, neatly summed up the feelings of many college presidents who disliked the lack of discipline in fraternity houses when he said, "The great dangers to the residents of these houses are waste of time . . . a substitution of social life for hard study. If the upperclassmen are not of high moral strain, the lowering of the character of the members is inevitable."

During the 1920s, fraternity members proved adept at procuring liquor despite Prohibition. In 1930, a commentary in *The New York Times* warned that colleges needed to be wary of the "gay-dog alumnus" who visited his old fraternity house, alcohol in tow. Hazing incidents increased in the 1930s, leading officials at fourteen colleges to join together to crack down on the practice.

Fraternity enrollment dropped off during World War II, but it bounced back soon after. While alcohol wasn't technically allowed on many college campuses and in fraternities until the mid-1960s, fraternity members were known to ignore the rule. In 1957, Northwestern's Interfraternity Council began conducting "liquor checks" in chapter houses to catch offenders.

Throughout the Vietnam War era, fraternity enrollment dropped off significantly as the Greek system came to be seen by many as an outdated symbol of establishment culture. But by the mid-1970s, fraternities were again soaring in popularity, openly celebrating mischief and mayhem, while universities did very little to stop them. At Northwestern, Sigma Chi held beer-chugging contests on its front lawn, which it advertised prominently around campus: "Chug for Charity," read one Sigma Chi poster in 1976, just two years before *Animal House* hit movie theaters.

"Back then," Patrick M. Quinn, an archivist at Northwestern, said, "they had kegs inside their frats so they could drink beer all day long. You could smell the weed all the way down to Tech"—referring to the technology building midway between north and south campus. "It was a crazy time. These days, you walk by the fraternities and everything is so quiet. It's eerily quiet."

APPEARANCES CAN BE deceiving. From the outside, the brick, four-story, ivy-covered Phi Delta Theta house at Northwestern looks like a nice place to live—it certainly has more charm than the dorm the school recently built across the way. But walk inside the chapter house, and you discover an unmitigated disaster, a job that even the team from *Queer Eye for the Straight Guy* would surely dismiss as hopeless. As one freshman put it, "It's shockingly nasty."

During most of my two weeks at Northwestern this fall, the chapter's third-floor hallway was strewn with garbage, and the toilets were indescribably foul. ("I won't even go to the bathroom here," one brother said.) In the main room, tossed carelessly underneath a pool table littered with cups, flyers, magazines, and Papa John's Pizza menus, I found the fraternity's '95–'96 framed group photo. It should have been hanging prominently on the wall with the others, but the brothers had apparently run out of space and found the floor a suitable alternative.

Kyle Pendleton, Northwestern's director of fraternity and sorority life, told me that one "effective" way to get fraternity members to take care of their chapter house is to ask them these questions: "What would your fraternity's founders think if they came back to life and walked into your house? Would they *approve*? Would they want to join?" Either those questions hadn't been asked at Phi Delt or, more likely, the Phi Delts laughed them off.

"Most of us don't take any of this fraternity stuff too seriously," Will Johnson said, strumming a guitar in his room. He acknowledged that he and his brothers are most likely not what the fraternity's leadership had in mind when they went dry. "Yeah, they were probably thinking that if we weren't drunk all the time in the house, that we would get really into being the best fraternity we could be or something. But this is just a place to live and hang out with your friends. I don't think it should be taken as much more than that. All that fraternity ritual and stuff, it's a little silly."

The current brothers are a study in cocky, amused detachment. Their laid-back attitude extends to rush, which at Northwestern happens in the winter instead of the fall. The extra months give Northwestern freshmen ample time to be courted, although the current Phi Delts are too lazy to do much of that. "The whole rush thing is really pretty gay," said Matthew Rosenthal, a goofy, curly-haired Phi Delt junior who was nursing a hangover one weekday afternoon in his large room, which is decorated with Frank Zappa and

Grateful Dead posters. "Sometimes it feels like we're trying to get them to sleep with us, you know?"

Phi Delts acknowledge that their dry policy initially gives the recruiting advantage to Chi Psi (better known as the Lodge) and Delta Tau Delta, their two biggest competitors, both of which are wet. "There really is no way to positively spin not being able to drink in your chapter house, even when you're twenty-one," said Michels, the chapter president.

When I visited in October, though, both Delta Tau Delta and the Lodge were on probation and were temporarily dry. The former home of David Schwimmer, one of the stars of *Friends,* Delt had been in trouble since last spring, following an incident in its chapter room. A freshman girl and a Delt pledge were apparently cavorting privately when other fraternity members—some underage and drunk—burst in and started taking pictures. The girl told her story to *The Daily Northwestern,* claiming that she heard the stunt was a Delt "tradition," and before long local television crews were parked outside the fraternity, eagerly reporting on this salacious fraternity sex scandal.

The Lodge has had no similar public relations disasters, but the Phi Delts find plenty of reasons to make fun of it, too. Like an aggressive politician going right at an opponent's strength, Phi Delts like to mock the Lodge's notorious—and in some freshmen circles, deeply revered—"floor parties," which are usually packed with sweaty freshmen drunkenly hitting on each other. At mostly dry Northwestern, the floor parties are about as close to *Animal House* as anyone is going to get (and it's still pretty far). "The parties are fun when you're a freshman," admitted Matthew Rosenthal, "but freshmen are happy with whatever as long as they're drunk."

Still, many Phi Delts confessed that as freshmen they considered pledging the Lodge. "Joining a wet house is definitely tempting for most guys," Rosenthal said. But Rosenthal eventually chose Phi Delt, mostly, he said, because of the colorful personalities of the guys in the house. I heard the same from other brothers. "A lot of fraternities have guys who look, talk, and act the same," said Alex Wu, an engaging Phi Delt junior known for his rapping skills. "We have such a cast of characters, and that meant more to me than being able to drink in the house."

The same was true of the fraternity a decade ago. We had football players, swimmers, nerds, preppies, writers, artists, liberals, and right-wingers. We were an eclectic bunch, unpredictable in our perspectives on life. The chapter became a little more unpredictable when I came out as gay my junior year. After a plethora of drunken attempts to convince myself that I liked girls "in that way," I finally accepted what part of me had known since I was twelve: I was gay. Once I accepted it, I really wasn't interested in lying about it, and I told my family and some of my friends.

But I was living in the fraternity house that year—was I going to tell my brothers, too? If I did, would they disown me—or, worse yet, keep me around as a courtesy but mock me behind my back? My fraternity was diverse, all right, but it wasn't that diverse. There wasn't anyone in the chapter who was openly gay, and some brothers were clearly homophobic. My freshman year, one brother told me, "Thank God we don't have any fags in this house."

The current Phi Delts at Northwestern don't have an openly gay member and also like to throw the words "gay" and "fag" around a lot (they assumed I was straight), but I'm not convinced the words actually mean much to them. I watched in surprise as two brothers who only hours earlier had jokingly labeled Lodge members "a bunch of pretty-boy fags from Long Island" ridiculed a freshman who walked out of a room when he saw two guys kissing on television. "Dude, what are you, homophobic or something?" one brother asked him. "Grow up, man."

I would have loved to have heard something like that a decade ago. Instead, I drank and drank and became very good at changing pronouns (my boyfriend became a girlfriend, although she was always too busy to come by the house). I didn't like lying, and I tried desperately to build up the courage to tell my brothers. I suspected that my closest friends in the house would be fine with it. As for the others, I was really hoping that brotherhood actually meant something. Would they have my back?

When I finally told my close friends in the house, they promptly told their girlfriends, who then told the whole school. Most important, though, most of my brothers surprised me by accepting me completely. For many of them, I was the first gay guy they'd really known—and some of them claimed to be heartbroken when I told them that, no, I didn't find them attractive. "If I can't even get gay guys into me," one drunken brother asked me, "how am I supposed to get *girls*?"

• • •

KYLE PENDLETON, NORTHWESTERN'S director of fraternity and sorority life, kept urging me to visit Sigma Chi. It is, he told me, "the model fraternity in many ways."

I could see immediately why Pendleton liked the place so much. The house is spotless and majestic. (Frankly, it looks and feels a lot like a sorority.) But more than that, Sigma Chi takes its mission as a new and redesigned fraternity very seriously, and it is, according to most fraternity guys on campus, the driest of the dry fraternities.

"We don't want to be a house that thinks the only way to have fun is to be drunk, stupid, and belligerent," Diego Berdakin, a sophomore and Sigma Chi's president, told me one afternoon as he gave me a tour of the house, with its beautiful woodwork and king-size beds (both thanks to big-spending alumni). "We're looking to live up to the ideals that the fraternity was founded on. At the same time, we're trying to build our own legacy, a whole new model of what a fraternity can be. We're not interested in being anything like *Animal House*.

"If you look at this chapter five or six years ago," Berdakin continued, "we were considered one of the top fraternities on campus, but I don't think the brothers back then really respected the fraternity. You could spend two straight days just trying to think up everything a fraternity could do wrong, and I'm sure they did it all."

In 2000, this chapter of Sigma Chi was shut down by its national headquarters for being too unruly, a far cry from what it is today. Last spring, as part of its New Chapter Initiative, the fraternity's leadership recruited about forty-five Northwestern students to start the chapter again. Some had never expected to join a fraternity but were intrigued by the idea of starting one from scratch. Others, like Berdakin, are popular and likable students who wanted to join a chapter that wasn't about partying and hazing. And some joined because, as members of several other fraternities told me, "no other chapter would take them."

Though it's difficult to take issue with Sigma Chi's focus on things that actually matter (Berdakin spoke often about wanting to have a house "with integrity"), something about the place spooked me. It struck me as too clean, too perfect. At one point, I had to use the bathroom and found myself staring at a sign above the sink that read: WASH YOUR HANDS. DIRTY HANDS SPREAD DISEASE. Was this the redesigned American fraternity?

Pendleton also spoke highly of Sigma Phi Epsilon, saying that although the chapter is wet, its focus isn't on drinking. The house was hard to miss, with a moose head and strobe light protruding from its top window. Most Sig Ep chapters, including Northwestern's, have adopted the Balanced Man Program, which Sig Ep's national leadership developed in the early 1990s to combat what the fraternity's national spokesman, Scott Thompson, called "a fraternity culture of boozing, drugging, and hazing."

The program doesn't restrict drinking in the chapter house, but it does something nearly as radical and arguably more meaningful: it has done away with the "pledge system," meaning that new members who join the fraternity have nearly all the rights and responsibilities of active members.

"New members don't pledge for a certain period of time, get hazed, get initiated, and then show up for parties until they graduate," Thompson said. "In the Balanced Man Program, men join, and they are developed from the time they join until the time they graduate. Part of that development focuses on building a sound mind and sound body, a simple philosophy that we took from the ancient Greeks."

Thompson supports Sig Ep chapters that choose to go dry on their own (a dozen have), but he says the fraternity doesn't force the issue. "We believe that if we recruit smart men and put them in an environment where they respect each other, they're going to make smart decisions," he said. I heard similar reasoning from Nick Johnson and Jordan Cerf, Sig Ep seniors who spoke fondly of the Balanced Man philosophy and clearly valued their fraternity experience. They pride themselves on being a well-liked chapter where girls "feel safe" and know "the door will be held open for them."

But Johnson and Cerf also talked a lot about having a good time. They were visibly giddy at the news that Kappa Alpha Theta, considered one of Northwestern's top sororities, had chosen to do Homecoming with them. "That would have *never* happened ten years ago," Cerf said.

When I asked them why, they struggled to put it delicately. "I wouldn't want to use the word 'cooler,' exactly, to describe us versus the guys from back then," Cerf said. "But, you know, those guys were just starting out and weren't really known on campus."

Johnson assured me, "They were all-around nice guys, but maybe, in terms of social presence, they weren't quite *there*." Before spending time with the Sig Eps, I was skeptical of the Balanced Man Program. Fraternities often coin new initiatives that mean very little in practice. But I left feeling thoroughly impressed. More than any fraternity boys I visited at Northwestern, the Sig Eps seem to be, well, balanced men. And they're proof that a wet fraternity doesn't necessarily mean an unruly one.

They're also proof that there are other ways, besides outlawing liquor, to redesign the American fraternity. Going dry may be a necessary step for some chapters, but the more I hung around Northwestern's fraternity boys, the less I saw regulating alcohol as particularly relevant to the health and personality of fraternities. For me, the ideal fraternity would somehow combine the strengths of Northwestern's Sigma Chi, Sig Ep, and Phi Delt chapters. It would stress integrity, character, and leadership. But it would also be a place where fraternity boys are allowed to be fraternity boys, however unseemly and absurd their choices may appear to the rest of us. Without that, the redesigned American fraternity may be no more balanced than the one that was scrapped in the first place.

SEX

Boy Crazy

The Untold Story of the North American Man/Boy Love Association, a group of unapologetic radicals who badly overestimated the breadth of the sexual revolution.

BOYS FLOCKED TO THE three-story, wood-shingled house on Mountain Avenue in Revere, Massachusetts, for the teenage version of the Holy Grail: an endless supply of beer and weed. Being drunk and stoned made everything—from the air hockey to the movie watching—significantly more enjoyable. There was also money to be had. The pocket cash came from the local men (teachers, construction workers, businessmen), who especially liked it when the local boys (hustlers, gay teens, straight teens) lounged around the house with their shirts off. Then there were smiles all around.

There was also sex. The boys had sex with each other. The boys had sex with the men. All of this was done quietly, because neighbors would later say that they didn't see or hear anything unusual coming from the house. There were no naked boys loitering in the doorway, no drunken men stumbling in the backyard, no obvious signs of depravity. It was a normal house, the neighbors thought, until they learned that it wasn't.

In June 1977, police arrested the house's owner and announced that it was the national headquarters of a sordid, pornographic sex ring. It was a stretch to call it a "ring," but Suffolk County District Attorney Garrett Byrne declared that the arrests were just "the tip of the iceberg." There had to be other perverted people in other wood-shingled houses. And Byrne had a way to catch them: a hotline people could call with anonymous tips about molesters.

In fact, man-boy relationships had been flourishing—not particularly secretly—for years in Revere. Revere Beach, on the eastern fringes of this working-class city, was a notorious cruising ground for men and boys. "It's surprising that no one has stumbled onto a 'sex ring' in Revere before this," Frank Rose wrote in a 1978 *Village Voice* piece about the scandal.

Everybody was talking about the case, which led to the indictments of twenty-four men. During an interview on a Boston television station, the poet and outspoken boy-lover Allen Ginsberg joked about the scandal. "I had sex when I was eight with a man in the back of my grandfather's candy store in Revere, and I turned out okay!" Ginsberg declared before being hurried offstage as the station cut to a commercial.

That moment aside, there was little to chuckle about that year for gays in general and men who liked boys in particular. In Florida, the beauty queen Anita Bryant was pushing her "Save Our Children" campaign, spearheading the repeal of budding gay rights ordinances. In Toronto, police raided the city's gay newspaper after it published an article entitled "Men Loving Boys Loving Men." From coast to coast, states began enacting tougher laws against child pornography, alluding to the need to protect children from the clutches of homosexual adults.

Staffers at *Fag Rag,* a now-defunct Boston-based radical gay paper, decided to fight back. They formed a committee to defend the suspects in Revere and rally against police harassment. Two groups emerged from that committee. One, the Gay & Lesbian Advocates & Defenders, is still a respected legal organization. The other, the North American Man/Boy Love Association, would become one of the most despised and ridiculed groups in America.

TWO "BOY-LOVERS," AS they call themselves, sit at a small table in a Boston coffee shop. "Everyone's telling me not to talk to you," says one, a gray-haired, sixty-two-year-old NAMBLA founder who goes by the pseudonym Socrates. "I mean, really, what's the point? It may be naive to think that an article that is really honest about NAMBLA can be published in any major magazine in America. We are the poison group. This is the poison story."

It's a story that began unremarkably enough. In 1978, NAMBLA was just another oddball sexual group proposing another oddball, radical philosophy: that kids should have more rights, particularly the right to have sex with whomever they please. Age should not be a consideration in anything, especially sex and love, and age-of-consent laws should be repealed. It was a more permissive time, a time before AIDS, and during NAMBLA's infancy in Boston (it would later move its headquarters to New York), the group enjoyed the support of a vocal minority in the gay community, who believed that attacks on boy-lovers were veiled attacks on all homosexuals. To NAMBLA's greater surprise, it found that even many straight people were willing to discuss adult-youth relationships without resorting to name-calling and finger wagging.

"The seventies were an incredible time," says Socrates. "We were at a time when things were changing, when our voices could be heard. We began to believe the rhetoric that the revolution was coming, that we were going to create a free society."

They could not have been more wrong. More than a quarter century after forming in the Community Church of Boston, NAMBLA finds itself close to extinction. It has achieved nothing except brand recognition. Its members live in fear, victims in their own minds, captives of their political blunders, their misreading of popular sentiment, and a sustained, multipronged attack from right-wingers, feminists, homophobes, gays, abuse survivors, police, politicians, and the media.

"Today, we are seen as worse than murderers," says a longtime NAMBLA member, Bill Andriette, who sits, unshaven and shoulders hunched, across the table from Socrates. Andriette joined NAMBLA in 1981, when he was fifteen. "But if I was fifteen today, I don't think I would join

NAMBLA. NAMBLA itself has become pretty irrelevant, except as a symbol invoked by its enemies."

And there are plenty of those. The 1997 murder of a ten-year-old Cambridge boy, Jeffrey Curley, by two men, one allegedly a NAMBLA member, and the Curley family's subsequent wrongful death lawsuit against the organization have stoked popular outrage. While many legal experts describe the Curley lawsuit's prospects as slim, it is another offensive against a group that has spent most of its time defending itself. "That case is probably going to break our back, even if we win, which we will," says Socrates. "Out of the closet since 1979, today we must hide again in America."

Could NAMBLA's founders have had any idea that they would become America's symbol of organized depravity? That a group founded mostly by eccentric, boy-loving leftists would come to be considered public enemy number one in the nation's battle against child sexual abuse?

"Never mind the fact that NAMBLA has never been a very large or influential organization," says Philip Jenkins, a professor of history and religious studies at Pennsylvania State University and the author of *Moral Panic: Changing Concepts of the Child Molester in Modern America*. "But it fit our need then, and still does today, to think of child molesters as being part of an immense, vast, powerful conspiracy that moves in elite circles. NAMBLA has become the acceptable symbol to blame for a lot of what has gone wrong morally in America over the last twenty years."

For its part, the organization has tried to point out the hypocrisy of its critics. NAMBLA argues that Americans go to remarkable lengths to pretend that kids aren't sexual, even as we promote youth sexuality in music, films, beauty pageants, and advertising. Still, if NAMBLA had any chance at even counterculture legitimacy, it wasn't going to achieve it by convincing Americans of their supposed hypocrisy.

It would succeed only as a passenger on the bandwagon of gay liberation, which long tolerated (and in fact celebrated) the inclusion of outcasts and deviants. Though NAMBLA's founders never expected the mainstream gay movement to be as radical as they were, they also never expected gay culture to shed its pre-AIDS sexual radicalism and ditch boy-lovers in the name of mainstream legitimacy.

Meanwhile, NAMBLA and its members made a series of perplexing, misguided, irrational political choices. Theirs is the story of a small group of unapologetic radicals who badly overestimated both the inclusiveness of gay liberation and the breadth of the sexual revolution.

DAVID (NOT HIS real name) is a sixty-two-year-old cab driver who likes, among other demographic groups, teenage boys. More than anything, though, he likes to be left alone to sit on the couch in the cozy, carpeted living room of his San Francisco apartment, where he can watch *Monday Night Football* on mute while listening to classical music on high.

Today, he's also talking about how it feels to receive telephone calls like this one: "Hey, fuck you and all your NAMBLA friends! You fuck little boys up the ass! I'm going to find out where you live, and I'm going to kill you. I'm going to bash your skull in with a baseball bat!"

That call, which he reported to police, is one of several he has received since the antipedophile crusader Mike Echols posted David's name, address, and phone number, and those of about eighty other suspected NAMBLA members, on Echols' anti-NAMBLA Web site. (David insists he's not a member and doesn't act on his attraction to teenagers.)

In small towns and big cities, suspected NAMBLA members are being warned to stay the hell away from kids. In New Mexico, a suspected member's tires were slashed and the word "pedophile" was graffitied on his truck. In San Francisco, an eighty-two-year-old former NAMBLA member received a death threat at his nursing home. In European countries, angry mobs have staked out the homes of men convicted of sex crimes with minors, calling for nothing less than public lynchings.

"It's a bad time to be a pedophile and an even worse time to be a NAMBLA member," says Tim Painter, an inspector on the district attorney's child sex abuse unit in Alameda County, California. He has worked on several cases involving NAMBLA members. "NAMBLA has done more good for those who want to stop them than they have for themselves. What NAMBLA has done is put a face to the enemy."

These days, NAMBLA's face fronts for little more than a publishing collective and several hundred scared, paranoid members. There are no more annual conventions, no more public appearances, no more city chapters, no more NAMBLA contingents in gay pride marches, no more eager new recruits. Times are so bad, in fact, that most members would just as soon not talk about them. Of the fifty members (or suspected members) I contacted by phone, mail, or e-mail, only a handful agreed to talk. Others wrote responses like these:

> I'm under court order not to have anything to do with NAMBLA, so I would appreciate it if you didn't send me anything else, or I could get in a whole heap of trouble.

> I got your letter today. . . . I would imagine we will want to use encryption to e-mail each other as it is easy for someone to read our e-mail. I do not know how to use encryption. You will have to instruct me.

Encryption? The need for silence and pseudonyms is particularly agonizing to NAMBLA's founders, who have historically been open about their attraction to boys. Only seconds after sitting down at an Upper West Side restaurant in New York, "Steve," a NAMBLA founder who asks that his real name not be used, says, "I absolutely hate having to be not up front. I find this very painful. But I think the climate has really gotten bad, and I have no doubt that I would be fired from my job if it came out that I was a NAMBLA member. What's so sad is that it didn't used to be this way. We used to celebrate our lives."

That was before NAMBLA began its baffling pattern of self-destruction. The group, somehow unaware—or unconcerned—that police might want to infiltrate its meetings, unwittingly voted undercover law enforcement officials to its steering committee. "Working against NAMBLA members is like stealing candy from a baby, only easier," says Echols, seated at a seafood restaurant in Dallas and never failing to plug his two true-crime books about child sex abuse (*Brother Tony's Boys* and *I Know My First Name Is Steven*). He says he personally infiltrated several NAMBLA meetings and also got his hands on the group's "top secret" membership list.

Perhaps hoping to improve their image, several NAMBLA members cooperated with the making of a 1994 documentary about them, *Chicken Hawk: Men Who Love Boys*. It was a rare chance to show the world that maybe they weren't nearly as despicable as people made them out to be. Typically, NAMBLA blew that chance. Several members came off as unhappy, childlike, nerdy, predatory, even delusional. The film's undisputed star is longtime NAMBLA member Leland Stevenson, a fifty-five-year-old former Mormon missionary who is seen chatting up boys at shopping mall pay phones, interpreting their aloofness and resistance as flirtation, and saying things like "Okay, that will be our little secret."

If NAMBLA members were bad at security and public relations, they were even worse at staying out of jail. Members (and those "with NAMBLA ties," as prosecutors and the media described them) were arrested for possession of and distribution of child pornography, statutory rape, and molestation. In 1989, at least one NAMBLA member was arrested in Thailand after police said he was running an orphanage that served as a front for child prostitution. (NAMBLA member Bill Andriette insists the organization had no knowledge of the purported orphanage, a claim police reject.)

Arguably most damaging to NAMBLA, though, was its

refusal to change its position calling for the repeal of all age-of-consent laws, despite the argument made by a vocal minority of members that such a stance—with its implication, sometimes stated and sometimes not, that a prepubescent child can consent to sex—was political suicide.

"I have been trying to convince the NAMBLA people for years that they should argue for an age of fourteen or fifteen, something that people could see as a little more *reasonable,*" says William A. Percy, a professor of history at UMass/Boston and the author of *Pederasty and Pedagogy in Archaic Greece*. "But they're a small group of inbred and fanatical ideologues. They only talk to each other. They won't listen to ideas of compromise."

They also failed, for the most part, to attract boys to their cause. While an occasional voice seconds NAMBLA's outrage over age-of-consent laws ("They are just one of the countless ways we discriminate against gay people and treat teenagers like second-class citizens," says Mike Glatze, an editor at *Young Gay America*, an Internet magazine for young gay men and women), the question is clear: just where is the army of boys backing NAMBLA and fighting for the rights of teens to have sex with whomever they wish? The short answer is that there is no army. The North American Man/Boy Love Association is, and always has been, remarkably short on boys.

"I AM AN ethical man," says Socrates, sitting in the kitchen of his modest Boston home next to several framed pictures of former teenage lovers. "I never hurt or manipulated the boys who have been my lovers. And they were my friends, not just my lovers. They are all part of what I consider my family."

The first was James Dubro, now a Canadian crime writer and documentary filmmaker. In 1961, Dubro was an openly gay, sexually active fourteen-year-old living on Beacon Hill in Boston and Socrates was a college student just coming to terms with his attraction to boys. The pair met in a Charles Street coffee shop, where Dubro stopped every day after school to sell copies of the *Boston Record-American*.

"[He] chatted me up and offered to buy the five or so papers I had left," Dubro recalls. Socrates took the teen back to his college dorm room, where the pair had the first of many sexual encounters and began a friendship that continues to this day. "[Socrates] is extremely loyal to the boys he has had relationships with," says Dubro. "And a lot of the boys could not have survived without his assistance. To my personal knowledge, he has never abused anyone—and is, if anything, too trusting and self-denying to a fault."

Socrates is attracted primarily to teenagers fourteen and older and men in their early twenties. He is the legal adoptive father of one of his former lovers, considers himself a surrogate father to another eight, and says that about thirty young men have lived with him at one point or another. Socrates travels often to meet with his three current teenage lovers in a foreign country. "Today, it's too dangerous in America," he says.

That danger has sent some NAMBLA members, and many boy-lovers, running to Internet boy-love communities, where men of all ages post tortured poetry about their ten-year-old neighbors, debate the best place to take a thirteen-year-old on a date (WWE wrestling matches, toy stores), and share advice about how to charm unsuspecting mothers. Many of NAMBLA's founders and key members insist that they now avoid sexual relationships with underage boys. Chris Farrell, a longtime NAMBLA member, made that decision after serving four years in prison in the early 1990s for sodomy with three teenage boys.

"For me, contact with young people was not only a means of sexual satisfaction but an enormous and important part of my broader social relationships," Farrell says, standing in the cluttered Manhattan office of his mail-order book and video company. "But to have those relationships so severely truncated is a difficult thing. And it's so hard to stomach. For years, in many societies, my love for boys was valued."

That hasn't been the case since the early 1980s, when America discovered, with much media sensation, that its day care centers seemed to be run by perverted Satanists. There were convoluted tales of children being flown to cultlike churches, where they were raped and videotaped by chanting, mask-wearing preschool teachers. Though abuse did occur in some cases, these stories were often as wrong as they were unbelievable.

A decade later, the discovery of the Internet as a powerful and very real tool for the sexual abuse of children only served to heighten national anxiety over child sexual abuse, making it nearly impossible for anyone—least of all NAMBLA—to engage the country in a discussion about youth sexuality.

"We live in a culture that's hysterical about children and assumes they have no sexual agency or desire," argues Dan

Savage, an author and nationally syndicated sex columnist. "But anyone who can remember what they were like when they were eleven knows that kids are sexual, and whether it was messing around with their cousin, playing doctor with their neighbor, or making passes at people ten years older, they were horny. So NAMBLA steps out to articulate all this, albeit in its usual highly dysfunctional and creepy way, and because we know what they say to be true on this issue, we've got to label them as insane perverts. Any attempt at rational discussion about youth sexuality and intergenerational sex is simply shouted down."

Which may explain what happened in 1998, when a journal of the American Psychological Association published the results of a study of college students who, as youths, had been involved in sexual relationships with adults. The study found that the harm done was less than generally believed and that some people—particularly males who had been involved in the relationships as teenagers—didn't view those relationships as abusive. In fact, many valued them. Finally, the study suggested that not all such instances should be automatically labeled as "abusive" and the youths involved as "victims."

Predictably, Dr. Laura Schlessinger was aghast. So was the U.S. House of Representatives, which took the unusual step of condemning (by a 355–0 vote) a scientific study. The resolution's sponsor, Representative Matt Salmon of Arizona, called the study "the Emancipation Proclamation of pedophiles." The APA, under intense pressure, distanced itself from the findings, saying it should have considered the "social policy implications" before publishing it.

"The reaction surprised us tremendously," says Bruce Rind, one of the study's coauthors and an assistant professor of psychology at Temple University. "But I think it goes to the heart of the extent of America's current insane moral panic."

That panic, argues James Kincaid, the author of *Erotic Innocence: The Culture of Child Molesting,* is a result of America's love-hate relationship with stories about gothic sexual demons. "If we didn't have NAMBLA, we would undoubtedly find a new national monster," says Kincaid, an English professor at the University of Southern California. "We need an enemy, because the endless talk of child sex abuse allows us the vicarious, titillating thrill of talking about children and sex, while at the same time allowing us to shake our heads at someone else's depravity. And while we find a threat to loathe and deplore, we will continue to promote child sexuality [in entertainment] and we will continue to position at the center of our national desirability women—and sometimes men—who look fourteen years old."

AS MUCH AS a ten-year-old can, Jeffrey Curley owned his East Cambridge neighborhood. Charming and mischievous, Jeffrey liked playing hockey and baseball, speeding around town on his bike, and bragging about his two older brothers and the many girls who invariably wanted him.

Still, on October 1, 1997, it was two young men—Charles Jaynes, twenty-two, and Salvatore Sicari, twenty-one—who wanted Jeffrey Curley most. Jaynes was an auto detailer and lifelong outcast who was deeply disturbed by his obesity. He made occasional appearances at Boston-area gay youth group meetings and became a NAMBLA member in 1996, receiving copies of the NAMBLA *Bulletin,* the group's quarterly magazine. In his diary, Jaynes wrote poetry about his love for boys.

Sicari was a pale, dark-haired housepainter who lived near Jeffrey with his mother, two sisters, younger brother, and a stepfather he did not like. Nicknamed "Salvi," he strutted through the blue-collar East Cambridge neighborhood wearing hooded sweatshirts and trying to act tough. Sicari could be violent, and in 1997 he confessed in court to beating his girlfriend. A year later, Sicari's seventeen-year-old brother, Robert, was found guilty of raping a ten-year-old boy he had lured to a parking garage with the promise of a bike.

At about 3:15 p.m. on October 1, Jeffrey left his grandmother's house wearing a maroon and gold football jersey with the number 32 on it. Also reportedly lured by the promise of a new bike, he joined Jaynes and Sicari in Jaynes's 1983 gray Cadillac, where several copies of the NAMBLA *Bulletin* were in an envelope behind the driver's seat.

The three drove to a grocery store in Newton. There, Sicari later told police, Jaynes dragged the eighty-pound boy into the back seat and tried to sexually assault him. Jeffrey struggled to get away, police said, but the nearly three-hundred-pound Jaynes sat on him, then suffocated Jeffrey with a gasoline-soaked rag. "Don't fight it, kid, don't fight it," Jaynes told the boy, according to Sicari.

The pair drove to Jaynes's apartment in Manchester, New Hampshire, where Sicari claims Jaynes sodomized the boy's dead body. They then stuffed the body into a container, drove to Maine, and dumped it from a bridge into the Great Works River. Two days later, Sicari, correctly sensing that the Curley family suspected him, confessed his role to police but pinned the murder on Jaynes. Police charged both of them with kidnapping and murder.

The alleged act of necrophilia was quickly reported as fact, even though Maine's chief medical examiner found no evidence that the body had been sexually abused. "It went from 'Sicari said' to 'police said' to simply being fact, and there wasn't a shred of evidence that it happened," says Jaynes's attorney, Robert Jubinville. "The way the sexual aspect of this case played out in the press was absolutely ludicrous."

The reports outraged the public. Declaring that Sicari and Jaynes "should not see the light again," Governor Paul Cellucci joined a campaign to reinstate the death penalty, falling one vote shy when a Democratic legislator changed his mind at the last minute. Sicari was eventually convicted of first-degree murder, while Jaynes got second degree. Because Jaynes had copies of the NAMBLA *Bulletin* in his car, NAMBLA quickly became a focus of the story. Sensing yet another PR disaster, the group issued this statement: "The alleged actions of these two individuals run absolutely contrary to everything we believe in and stand for. NAMBLA condemns the use of threat or violence against anyone."

That did not appease the Curley family, which filed a $200 million civil suit against NAMBLA—specifically, its purported members Roy Radow, Joe Power, David Thorstad, David Miller, Peter Herman, Max Hunter, Bill Andriette, Denny Mintun, and Arnold Schoen, most of whom were singled out because they were listed in the NAMBLA *Bulletin* as part of its publishing collective. The suit claims that "As a direct and proximate result of the urging, advocacy, conspiring, and promoting of pedophile activity by . . . NAMBLA . . . Charles Jaynes became obsessed with having sex with and raping young children."

The Curley family attorney, Larry Frisoli, flatly compares NAMBLA to the Mafia. "NAMBLA is a criminal organization that teaches its members how to rape kids," he says during a conversation in his Cambridge office. "To say that age-of-consent laws should be changed is fine; it's legal. But to actually encourage and assist in the abuse of children is illegal. If you look at *The Godfather*, in the forties and fifties the Corleones always got up there and said, 'We don't exist.' Yet they did exist. And NAMBLA does exist. And it has tiers of membership. And like the Mafia, the question becomes how much can you blame the Godfather for what the foot soldier on the street is doing?"

Many question the extent to which NAMBLA can be called a criminal organization, let alone one that resembles the Mafia. The FBI and local law enforcement agencies have been trying for years to find NAMBLA in violation of laws against the sexual exploitation of children. The most organized attempt, which included a year of police infiltration in the mid-1980s, produced nothing, and the U.S. Senate Permanent Subcommittee on Investigations found that NAMBLA did not engage in criminal activity.

The Massachusetts chapter of the American Civil Liberties Union, which is defending NAMBLA, agrees. "This lawsuit is akin to someone getting killed by the permissive attitude of sex, drugs, and rock 'n' roll and then suing *Rolling Stone* for creating a climate when the murder was possible," says John Reinstein, the lead ACLU attorney on the case. "NAMBLA is *not* the Mafia."

ON A HOT and sunny Sunday afternoon in San Francisco, NAMBLA the Clown sits on the stage at the Folsom Street Fair, a popular and eclectic yearly gathering of leather daddies, bondage lovers, drag queens, and curious gay suburbanites. NAMBLA the Clown looks exactly as he said he would: hell raiser after a messy shopping spree at the Home Depot. He wears a heavy black robe, eight-inch mirrored platform boots, pushpins in his head (complete with fake blood), and black makeup to accentuate harsh black eyebrows.

The self-described "postmodern joke that dare not speak its name," NAMBLA the Clown is actually a real person. His name is Ggreg Taylor (he spells it with three Gs), and he is a celebrity of sorts in San Francisco's artistic gay circles. "There are two things that really scare people in this world: NAMBLA and clowns," he says, sweating as he leans over the side of the stage. "So, being the twisted guy I am, I thought I would combine them and create some real mental havoc. Unfortunately, I am a joke that a lot of people don't get. Some people think I am in bad taste."

Many of those people are gay people. Standing next to a booth selling X-rated videos, vibrators, and glow-in-the-dark dildos, a young man wearing only tight leather shorts says, "NAMBLA has no place in gay culture. Gay culture celebrates everything, as long as it is consensual. Fucking kids is *not* consensual."

The Folsom Street Fair is a collection of gay culture's fringiest elements, and there was a time when NAMBLA shared a place at the table. That table is the freaks' table, where everyone not quite ready for prime-time television has taken a backseat to a mainstream gay movement concerned with looking respectable, all-American, and decidedly not after the little boy next door.

In the early 1990s, the gay community watched in horror as the Christian right used NAMBLA's presence in gay pride marches to attack gay rights legislation and tell Americans that homosexuals were after their kids. The tactic worked. "Starting in 1994, it would have been easier for Jerry Falwell to march in a gay pride parade than for NAMBLA," says Echols, the antipedophile crusader.

Today, as gay organizations fight for the rights of gays to marry and adopt, they officially condemn NAMBLA. Even *XY,* the national magazine for young men that champions teen sexuality and argues for a lowering of the age of consent, published an opinion piece by writer Karen Ocamb that dripped with anti-NAMBLA anger: "I watched the NAMBLA creeps [at the 25th anniversary of the Stonewall Riots] rub their hands in glee. . . . My skin crawled as these pasty-white, nerdy, hunched-over men scurried away from my tape recorder like cockroaches afraid of the light. . . . These men aren't gay, and we mustn't let them co-opt our movement. . . . They are simply perverts who like to fuck children, using the gay community as a Trojan horse to storm the barricades of legitimacy."

Gay bookstores are putting up barricades of their own, choosing not to carry the NAMBLA *Bulletin* for the first time in the organization's history. At Giovanni's Room in Philadelphia, the store's owner, Ed Hermance, says he pulled the NAMBLA *Bulletin* off the shelves after his staff threatened to strike if he didn't.

"I think it's a strange day for gay culture when we start banning something because it makes us uncomfortable," Hermance says. "Especially when that thing is a foundation of gay literature. If we pulled all the books that had adult-youth sexual themes, we wouldn't have many novels, memoirs, or biographies left."

THE SHIRTLESS KID has a huge smile on his face. After all, he's years away from puberty, about seven or eight years old, but he's already shaving. He has a razor in one hand and a glob of shaving cream in the other. He looks happy.

Two shirtless boys stand on a beach. The older boy, about twelve or thirteen, has spiky brown hair and a surfboard tucked under his right arm. He's talking to the younger boy, who looks about eight and is holding a toy shovel in his right hand.

Those are two of the images from an issue of the NAM-

BLA *Bulletin*. The *Bulletin* publishes news pieces, opinions, semierotic short stories, and pictures of boys, most of whom have not reached puberty.

"I never felt very comfortable with how the *Bulletin* had pictures of so many young kids," says Steve, the NAMBLA founder from an eastern city. "I felt that it was politically stupid."

NAMBLA members have long disagreed over what they are and what kind of unified front they should show the public. Socrates insists that the group is made up of a majority of pederasts (people attracted to boys in or after puberty) and a minority of pedophiles (people attracted to prepubescent children). Yet the *Bulletin* has rarely reflected that, angering many of NAMBLA's members.

"The *Bulletin* is turning into a semipornographic jerk-off mag for pedophiles," NAMBLA cofounder David Thorstad wrote in a December 1996 letter to the magazine. "Has the *Bulletin* forgotten that NAMBLA has always consisted not only of pedophiles, but also of pederasts? In fact, were it not for the pederasts, there would never have been a NAMBLA. . . . What has happened to the political goals of NAMBLA, which are to struggle for sexual freedom and liberation, not merely for the right of dirty old men to get their vicarious jollies?"

The *Bulletin*'s then editor, Mike Merisi, replied angrily in print: "I well remember visiting Mr. Thorstad's NYC apartment in the early '70s, and viewing in his library books and magazines . . . [that] featured nude boys apparently between six and sixteen, and I can assume Mr.

Thorstad has since shredded these artifacts of our culture, at which time he became a good pederast, only interested in age-appropriate teens, leaving the rest of us bad 'pedophiles' behind, in much the same way as the larger gay movement left him."

Nearly every year at NAMBLA's annual convention, a small faction requested that the organization decide on an age at which the group believed a boy could give consent. Every year, NAMBLA chose not to do so. "Politically, we made a disastrous choice," says Socrates. "We were going to lose with that choice, and we did, big time. And while we could have said, 'Okay, we favor an age of consent at twelve or fourteen,' that goes against our philosophy that the important issues to consider are coercion, manipulation, and ultimately violence, not age. We hoped we could strike a blow to the core of the problems in society. Philosophically, we know we made the right choice."

The right choice? To everybody except NAMBLA, that choice was dumbfounding both politically and philosophically. "They lost everybody who might have supported them by arguing that [prepubescent kids] can consent to sex with adults," says Savage, the sex columnist. "The problem with NAMBLA is that it packages reasonable arguments about teen sexuality and age-of-consent laws with irrational, insane arguments about seven-year-olds. That's why the group is where it is today."

And that's why some NAMBLA members wonder if any of this was worth it. "I sometimes ask myself whether organizing NAMBLA was a good thing to do," says Steve. "Because I do wonder if things would be as bad today if we hadn't organized, or if we had tried to approach this topic in an entirely different way. Did we create the backlash? [Socrates] says that we didn't, that the forces of repression didn't need us to bring us where we are today. I don't know. I hope he's right."

Cosmetically Correct

Lipstick lesbians unite! A Boston social group for girly girls who (gasp!) like other girls.

VERONICA LAROUCHE IS A petite forty-seven-year-old with shoulder-length auburn hair, a small head, and the serious, taut look of a proper Bostonian. She wears dresses, lipstick, and makeup, and she is the kind of woman who takes her sweet time in front of a mirror before leaving the house.

When she does, it's likely to be with her current love interest, a talkative and opinionated blonde named Kim, whom Larouche met two years ago at a monthly social gathering for "lipstick lesbians" called Cosmetically Correct. Larouche founded the Boston group three years ago for "feminine women who love and prefer the same," and although she never expected to meet the love of her life there, there was no resisting Kim, who combines a natural femininity with a strong earthiness. These days, Larouche spends most of her time at Kim's and, in a true sign of lesbian devotion, has up and moved her two cats into Kim's place.

For now, though, Kim and Larouche are socializing with about forty other Cosmetically Correct members in a back room at Laurel's Restaurant in Boston's South End neighborhood. I'm the only guy present (not counting the waiter, who dutifully serves cocktails), but I'm not, to my surprise, the only person sans lipstick. "You didn't think that *all* lipstick lesbians actually wear lipstick, did you?" says a tall blond group member who isn't wearing lipstick. "How cute that you would think that!"

I lose the patronizing blonde and walk over to Larouche and Kim, who are chatting with a beautiful twenty-eight-year-old named Jenny (not her real name). Jenny looks about twenty and is affectionately called "Baby Dyke." She also looks like Marisa Tomei, a fact that she denies even though most everyone she meets says, "Wow, you look like Marisa Tomei!" Tall, radiant, and always smiling, Jenny is the most attractive woman in the room, which might explain why she always has someone to talk to.

"So it's like *this,*" she says as we sit at a table, her right hand grabbing my knee for effect. "I would give you my name, but I'm *undercover*. I'm, like, a secret agent, man. A secret agent! No one knows I'm here. No one knows I'm a *lesbian*."

Jenny isn't alone. Cosmetically Correct is home to all kinds of women—some are openly gay, some are bisexual, and some are cheating on their husbands. Jenny, who is in the early stages of coming out, says she doesn't have a husband and wouldn't want one, anyway. "I'm definitely a lesbian," she says, squeezing my knee again. "And I'm a feminine lesbian. I don't relate to butch, masculine lesbians at all. I just came here to meet other lesbians like myself."

MISUNDERSTOOD BY MAINSTREAM society and discounted as apolitical window dressing by some lesbians, lipstick and femme lesbians are joining social groups and Internet communities, proudly rejecting the idea that femininity is somehow reserved for straight women. While still heavily outnumbered by social groups for, say, lesbian bikers, femme and lipstick lesbians are organizing in ways not seen before: In Boston, feminine lesbians who prefer the same can choose between two social groups, Cosmetically Correct and Femme4Femme. Atlanta boasts the Atlanta Lipstick Lesbians. And on the Internet, there are many new Web sites devoted to femmes (not counting the thousands of pornographic sites promising steamy pictures of "hot lipstick lesbian lust").

"Femmes are uniting in a new kind of way—a femme sisterhood almost," says Joan Nestle, a lesbian historian and author. "I think this is what happens when a community grows in valuing itself."

It's also what happens when femme and lipstick lesbians loudly reject the gender stereotypes that still permeate much of this country's simplistic thinking about sexuality: namely, that feminine women can't possibly be lesbians (maybe bisexual, but definitely not dykes). And by discounting men completely, feminine lesbians are a subversive force, leading socially and sexually fulfilling lives without men—and debunking the theory that femininity is nothing without masculine appreciation.

(Meanwhile, a similarly seditious movement is evident in gay male culture. More and more sports leagues and social groups for "masculine" gay men are rejecting the idea that heterosexuality and masculinity are inextricably linked, arguing that not all gay men prefer show tunes to college football.)

So what's wrong with breaking a few stereotypes? Nothing, really, except that groups like Cosmetically Correct can't seem to do it without upsetting people—namely, the politicized lesbians who fought for decades to make it possible to have lesbian social groups at all. Larouche and her lipstick lesbian sisters happily bite the hand that used to feed them.

"Really butch lesbians kind of scare me," says Larouche. "Lesbian culture around Boston is essentially run by them, and they require that you look, act, and talk a certain way, and that way is definitely not feminine, because they see femininity as buying into the patriarchy. So we create one group that they don't feel includes them, and they're calling for our heads!"

UNDERSTAND THIS: IT'S not easy being a lipstick lesbian. Sure, she can pass for straight—but what's the use in that when she has to deal with *men*? Hoping to deflect their attention, she informs her male admirers that she doesn't play on their team. This usually backfires: now guys are even more interested (and in a creepy, can-I-watch? kind of way).

Then there's the problem of scoring a date, because feminine lesbians aren't easy to find if you don't know where to look. What with their lipstick, eyeliner, dresses, and high heels, they're often mistaken for heterosexual bombshells. Some lipstick lesbians venture out to traditional lesbian bars and social groups, only to find that the lesbian social scene is home to thousands of women who wouldn't dream of wearing makeup.

Christine Drinkwater, the editor of the online magazine *Femme,* is used to the strange looks she gets at lesbian bars. "I show up and am often told at the door, 'You don't belong here. This is a *dyke* bar,'" she says. "People still assume that because you don't look butch or boyish, that you must be straight."

Disheartened and dateless, the lipstick lesbian's luck turns when she learns of Cosmetically Correct. She shows up, meets other feminine lesbians, and can hardly contain her enthusiasm. No longer must she hang out in lesbian coffee shops or join a lesbian softball team for companionship (the sporty lesbians always stick her out in right field, anyway).

"Cosmetically Correct is for women who don't relate to mainstream lesbian culture and who feel they don't fit in with the butches who are afraid to put on a dress," says Larouche, who lives and works in Boston as a translator. "When I started it, I hoped this group would really fill a need."

Larouche also hoped to come up with a name that would get the group noticed. And she came up with a zinger, courtesy of a conversation many years ago. "I was seeing a woman when the term 'politically correct' came into usage," recalls Larouche. "She would always watch me in amazement as I got ready in front of the mirror before we went out, and finally she looked at me and said, 'You're not politically correct. You're cosmetically correct!' I always remembered that, and it seemed like a perfect name for the group."

It was, to be sure, perfectly controversial. By choosing Cosmetically Correct, was Larouche insinuating that butch lesbians are somehow cosmetically incorrect? "People were upset by the name, but I can't really worry about people's insecurities," she says. "What I wanted to do with the name is poke fun at the political correctness that runs rampant in the gay and lesbian community."

Larouche hosted the group's first social event in January 2000. She wasn't sure anyone would come, but nearly thirty people did, including a writer for the gay weekly *Bay Windows*. And that's when the trouble began. "It's really unfortunate that the lesbian community has embraced this whole concept of androgyny," Larouche told *Bay Windows* that night. "It's fine for some people, but some of us are not comfortable with that, and there are some of us that would like to see a little style and class returned to the gay community among lesbians."

Style? Class? In scathing letters to the editor (one entitled "Snobs in Makeup," another "Cosmetically Incorrect"), *Bay Windows* readers called Cosmetically Correct members classist, delusional, self-hating, and "self-involved princesses." Larouche defended her group, reiterating that she has no "litmus test" for femininity and that all kinds of lesbians are welcome as long as they understand that the group celebrates feminine women.

Cosmetically Correct survived the initial negative buzz and is going strong—nearly three hundred women are on the listserv, and an average of forty lesbians attend the monthly gatherings. (The group also sponsors newcomer brunches and informal get-togethers and card nights.)

IN THE LATE 1800s and early 1900s, psychologists and sex researchers were faced with a head-scratcher: pretty, feminine women were happily coupling with butch, masculine "boy-girls."

Bewildered, the researchers discounted the femmes as the passive prey of aggressive, militant lesbians who probably wouldn't take no for an answer. But femmes were, in fact, equal and eager participants in butch-femme relationships, which were the first "publicly visible lesbian community," according to Joan Nestle. These couplings were popular in urban working-class neighborhoods in the 1920s, '30s, and '40s, although the terminology differed from community to community. Among African-Americans, for example, butches were called "studs" or "bulldaggers," while a femme was called "my lady."

Butch-femme relationships were also popular in gay male culture in the 1950s. The late Harry Hay, a radical activist and founder of the Mattachine Society (the country's first major gay rights group), told a biographer that butch-femme couples were the norm in southern California. At parties, the butch man would wear a suit, while his femme boyfriend usually donned a flowered Hawaiian shirt.

Though gay men mostly dropped the butch-femme categories, lesbian butch-femme couplings flourished until the 1970s, when lesbian feminists angrily labeled them re-creations of oppressive, heterosexual gender roles. "Femmes were seen as traitors to the lesbian-feminist cause, and old-time butch-femme couples were basically ostracized from the movement," says Nestle. "The story of the seventies is the story of women's movement history—when in the heat of ideological battle, overly simplistic lines are drawn, when desire, so at the heart of being a femme for me at least, is given little attention. It is too seemingly fragile, too nuanced, for such doctrinaire times."

There was a noticeable resurgence of butch-femme relationships in the 1980s and '90s as butch-femme became an acceptable erotic choice, a lesbian-specific challenge to the norms of gender, and a popular subject of drag and performance art. But today, many femme and lipstick lesbians insist there is a new backlash against lesbian femininity.

"It isn't nearly as focused as in the seventies, but it's definitely there," says Amie Evans, the femme founder of the Boston-based lesbian burlesque drag troupe The Princesses of Porn with the Dukes of Dykedom. "But unlike in the seventies, we aren't simply taking off our femme trappings and trying to fit an acceptable mold. We're embracing our femininity. I think there is a large portion of the community that is appreciative of diversity and what femme is really about, but there are many lesbians who read us as either unlesbian or somehow slipping by and not really being part of the struggle for equality."

That animosity toward femmes is ironic, because "many of the same [lesbians] who are critical of femmes are also trying to sleep with them," points out Cathy Cohen, a lesbian professor of political science and director of the Center for the Study of Race, Politics, and Culture at the University of Chicago. "But seriously, we have to be careful not to separate lesbians into only two groups, butches and femmes. It's a bit more fluid than that, and many lesbians don't fit neatly into a category. There are also many variations within butch and femme—some women start out as strong butches and soften over time."

To complicate things further, many lesbians argue that there is even a distinction between lipstick lesbians and femme lesbians. "While femmes can pass as straight, most are really adamant about being known to be queer, while lipstick lesbians are often in the closet," says *Femme* magazine's Drinkwater. "While lipstick lesbian is a description of what someone *looks* like, femme is a deep and meaningful identity that someone claims. Being a femme is really about sexual and feminine power, and we just radiate femininity. I can spot a femme wearing no makeup and Birkenstocks. For femmes, femininity isn't something you play with or apply with makeup. It's at your core."

So what's at the core of most Cosmetically Correct members? Certainly not a need to be open or outspoken about their sexuality—with about half its members in the closet, lesbian and/or femme pride isn't at the top of the group's laid-back social agenda. Cosmetically Correct members don't pretend to be part of any larger lesbian social or political struggle, nor do they mind poking fun at the butch lesbians who Larouche says, "often act more like boys than girls."

That kind of talk even upsets some femme lesbians. "The group is certainly allowed to favor whatever kind of women they want, but I do take issue with how they present themselves," says Dawn Dougherty, a femme lesbian writer and performer who usually dates butches. "It's hard enough to be a butch dyke in America as it is, because butches are already a pariah in the eyes of many straight people. I really tense up when any group, especially a lesbian group, says they want women who look like real women."

THE LIPSTICK LESBIANS are getting drunk. It's nearing the end of their monthly gathering, and everyone has loosened up—maybe a bit too much. Jenny, the Marisa Tomei lookalike, is grabbing my leg harder now and reiterating that she's "undercover." Kim, Larouche's girlfriend, won't stop talking about the transgender lesbian (a biological man who lives as a woman and identifies as a lesbian) who attended one of the group's events.

In one corner, a blond lipstick lesbian is straddling her friend and pretending to lick her neck. Seated at a table, another blonde recounts a hilarious nugget from her romantic past, after which she smiles and says, "Of course, you can't use that for your article." She also won't give me her name, even though she insists she is comfortably and openly gay. "Actually, I'm *bisexual,*" she says. "I've dated a lot of guys.

One of them was totally obsessed with lesbian porn. He would bring it home and try to get me to watch it with him, but I would just go to bed and let him do his thing. I mean, I didn't even realize I liked women in that way at the time. Sometimes you're just clueless!"

At a nearby table, Kim finally stops talking long enough for Larouche to get a word in. The happy couple then spend several minutes making fun of butches before insisting that they don't have any real animosity toward them. The couple says they would, in fact, like to participate in more mainstream gay and lesbian events. "We were thinking of having a float in the gay pride parade, but we really would like to avoid getting booed," Kim says. "I mean, I could see some butches throwing rocks at us. Could you imagine the scene? Angry butches throwing rocks the size of softballs and lipstick lesbians in dresses and high heels running for their lives!"

Such a scene isn't likely to play out in reality, but it underscores one of the most important developments in gay and lesbian culture: That the monolithic "gay community," if such a thing ever did exist, certainly doesn't anymore. With greater acceptance and increased visibility comes a new freedom for gays and lesbians to openly be what they want and find others to be that with, even if it means irking old-school activists and national gay organizers who sometimes prefer everyone on the same page.

For Cosmetically Correct, that means invading the South End (the epicenter of Boston gay life) for its social events but leaving the politics of gay liberation to others. The key, I suppose, is not to take any of this too seriously. While Larouche talks a mean game to butches, she actually doesn't mind them. Poking fun at them is her shtick.

And, true to her word, Larouche doesn't reject butches at the door to her events. As the tipsy lipstick lesbians wrap things up at Laurel's Restaurant, Cheryl, a group member who is very feminine and very pregnant, sits next to her butch girlfriend, Kerry, who has short blond hair, strong arms, and a tattoo. The couple is expecting their first child soon (through artificial insemination).

"I came tonight because Cheryl wanted me to, but I never would have come by myself," Kerry says. "This isn't my scene. But it isn't so bad. Everyone is friendly, and a lot of people are talking to me. And what do you expect? I'm really popular, now that everyone knows I can get women *pregnant*."

Abercrombie Nation

Mike Jeffries turned a moribund company into a multibillion-dollar brand by selling youth, sex, and casual superiority.

MIKE JEFFRIES, THE SIXTY-ONE-YEAR-OLD CEO of Abercrombie & Fitch, says "dude" a lot. He'll say, "What a cool idea, dude" or, when the jeans on a store's mannequin are too thin in the calves, "Let's make this dude look more like a dude" or, when I ask him why he dyes his hair blond, "Dude, I'm not an old fart who wears his jeans up at his shoulders."

On my second day at Abercrombie & Fitch's three-hundred-acre headquarters in the Ohio woods, Jeffries—sporting torn Abercrombie jeans, a blue Abercrombie muscle polo, and Abercrombie flip-flops—stood behind me in the cafeteria line and said, "You're looking really A&F today, dude." (An enormous steel-clad barn with laminated wood accents, the cafeteria feels like an Olympic Village dining hall in the Swiss Alps.)

I didn't have the heart to tell Jeffries that I was actually wearing American Eagle jeans. To Jeffries, the "A&F guy" is the best of what America has to offer: he's cool, he's beautiful, he's funny, he's masculine, he's optimistic, and he's certainly not "cynical" or "moody," two traits Jeffries finds wholly unattractive.

Jeffries's endorsement of my look was a step up from the previous day, when I had arrived in a dress shirt, khakis, and dress shoes, prompting A&F spokesman Tom Lennox—at thirty-nine, he's a virtual senior citizen among Jeffries's youthful workforce—to look concerned and offer me a pair of flip-flops. Just about everyone at A&F headquarters wears flip-flops, torn Abercrombie jeans, and either a polo shirt or a sweater from Abercrombie or Hollister, Jeffries's brand aimed at high school students.

When I first arrived on "campus," as many A&F employees refer to it, I felt as if I had stepped into a pleasantly parallel universe. The idyllic compound took two years and $131 million to complete, and it was designed so nothing of the outside world can be seen or heard. Jeffries has banished the "cynicism" of the real world in favor of a cultlike immersion in his brand identity.

The complex does feel like a kind of college campus, albeit one with a sound track you can't turn off. Dance music plays constantly in each of the airy, tin-roofed buildings, and when I entered the spacious front lobby, where a wooden canoe hangs from the ceiling, two attractive young men in

Abercrombie polo shirts and torn Abercrombie jeans sat at the welcome desk, one checking his Friendster.com messages while the other swayed subtly to the Pet Shop Boys song "If Looks Could Kill."

It's a fitting song. If looks could kill, everyone here would be dead. Jeffries's employees are young, painfully attractive, and exceedingly eager, and they travel around the campus on playground scooters, stopping occasionally to chill out by the bonfire that burns most days in a pit at the center of campus. The outdoorsy, summer camp feel of the place is accentuated by a tree house conference room, barnlike buildings and sheds with gridded windows, and a plethora of wooden decks and porches. But the campus also feels oddly urban—and, at times, stark and unwelcoming. The pallid neoindustrial two-story buildings are built around a winding cement road, reminding employees that this is a workplace, after all.

Inside, the airy, modern work spaces are designed to encourage communication and teamwork, and everywhere you look, smiley employees are brainstorming or eagerly recounting their weekends. "I'm not drinking again for a *year,*" one young employee said to another as they passed me in the hall. There are few "offices" and even fewer doors at A&F central. Jeffries, for example, uses an airy conference room as his office, and he spends much of his days huddling with designers who come armed with their newest ideas and designs.

The press-shy Jeffries rarely grants interviews, but he invited me to his Ohio headquarters to promote the opening of his first flagship store, a four-story, 23,000-square-foot behemoth across the street from Trump Tower in Manhattan. To celebrate the opening, Jeffries threw a packed, ritzy, invitation-only party at the store, at which slightly soused women paid $10 apiece to have Polaroids of themselves taken with shirtless A&F model Matt Ratliff.

And why not throw a party? Life is good for Jeffries, who in fourteen years has transformed Abercrombie & Fitch from a struggling retailer of "fuddy-duddy clothes" into the most dominant and imitated lifestyle-based brand for young men in America. Valued at $5 billion in 2005, the company has revenues approaching $2 billion a year rolling in from more than eight hundred stores and four successful brands. For the kids there's abercrombie, aimed at middle schoolers who want to look like their cool older siblings. For high schoolers there's Hollister, a wildly popular surf-inspired look for "energetic and outgoing guys and girls" that has quickly become the brand of choice for midwestern teens who wish they lived in Laguna Beach.

When the Hollister kids head off to college, Jeffries has a brand—the preppy and collegiate Abercrombie & Fitch—waiting for them there. And for the postcollege professional who is still young at heart, Jeffries recently launched Ruehl, a casual sportswear line that targets twenty-two to thirty-five-year-olds.

Though Wall Street analysts and the companies' many critics gleefully predict A&F's impending demise every year or so, they have yet to be right. And as his A&F brand has reached iconic status, Jeffries has raised prices, only to find that the brand's loyal fans will gladly pay whatever he asks. Next, Jeffries plans to open his first store overseas, in London, and continue the transformation of A&F from American frat-bro wear to sexy, luxury lifestyle brand. I wouldn't bet against him. If history is any indication, Jeffries won't let anyone—"girlcotting" high school feminists, humorless Asians, angry shareholders, thong-hating parents, lawsuit-happy minorities, copycat competitors, uptight moralists, or nosy journalists—get in his way.

MIKE JEFFRIES IS the Willy Wonka of the fashion industry. A quirky perfectionist and control freak, he guards his aspirational brands and his utopian chocolate factory with a highly effective zeal. Those who have worked with him tend to use the same words to describe him: driven, demanding, smart, intense, obsessive-compulsive, eccentric, flamboyant, and, depending on whom you talk to, either slightly or very odd.

"He's weird and probably insane, but he's also unbelievably driven and brilliant," says a former employee at Paul Harris, a midwestern women's chain for which Jeffries worked before becoming CEO of Abercrombie & Fitch in 1992.

Examples of his strange behavior abound. According to *Business Week,* at A&F headquarters Jeffries always goes through revolving doors twice, never passes employees on stairwells, parks his Porsche every day at the same angle in the parking lot (keys between the seats, doors unlocked), and has a pair of "lucky shoes" he wears when reading financial reports.

His biggest obsession, though, is realizing his singular vision of sexy, idealized all-American youth. He wants desperately to look like his target customer (the casually flawless college kid), and in that pursuit he has aggressively transformed himself from a classically handsome man into a cartoonish physical specimen: dyed hair, perfectly white teeth, golden tan, bulging biceps, wrinkle-free face, and big Angelina Jolie lips.

But though he can't turn back the clock, he can—and has—done the next best thing, creating a parallel universe of beauty and exclusivity in which his attractions and obsessions have made him millions, shaped modern culture's concepts of gender, masculinity and physical beauty, and made over himself and the world in his image, leaving them both just a little more bizarre than he found them.

Much more than just a brand, Abercrombie & Fitch successfully resuscitated a 1990s version of a 1950s ideal—the white, masculine "beefcake"—during a time of political correctness and rejection of '50s orthodoxy. But it did so with profound and significant differences. A&F aged the masculine ideal downward, celebrating young men in their teens and early twenties with smooth, gym-toned bodies and perfectly coiffed hair.

While feigning casualness (many of its clothes look as if they've spent years in a washing machine, then a hamper), Abercrombie actually celebrates the vain, highly constructed male. After all, there is nothing *casual* about an A&F sweatshirt worn over two A&F polos worn over an A&F T-shirt. (A&F has had less of a cultural impact on women's fashion. Its girls' line is preppy, sexy, and popular, but the company has remained focused mostly on pleasing the all-American college boy.)

For many young men, to wear Abercrombie is to broadcast masculinity, athleticism, and inclusion in the "cool boys' club" without even having to open their mouths, which may be why the brand is so popular among some gay men who want desperately to announce their noneffeminacy. But because A&F's vision is so constructed and commodified (and because what A&F sells is not so much manhood but perennial *boyhood*), there is also something oddly emasculating about it. Compared to the 1950s ideal, A&F's version of maleness feels restrictive and claustrophobic. If becoming a man is about independence and growing up, Abercrombie doesn't feel very masculine at all.

In that way, the brand is a lot like its creator. Although Jeffries wears A&F clothes, the uniform doesn't succeed in making him seem boyish or particularly masculine. And for a man obsessed with creating a "sexy and emotional experience" for his customers, Jeffries comes off as oddly asexual. He is touchy-feely with some of his employees, both male and female, but the touch seems decidedly paternal.

REMARKABLY LITTLE IS known about Jeffries's personal life. There are few people who claim to know him well, and those who do wouldn't comment. What is known is that Jeffries has a grown son, lives separately from his wife, and, according to *BusinessWeek*, has a Herb Ritts photo of a toned male torso hanging over the fireplace in his bedroom.

Jeffries wouldn't discuss any of that with me, and he fidgeted nervously and grew visibly agitated when I asked about several of the many controversies and lawsuits he has weathered at the helm of A&F. Our first bump came when I mentioned the 2002 uproar over the company's thongs for middle school girls, which had EYE CANDY and WINK WINK printed on their fronts.

"That was a bunch of bullshit," he told me, sweating profusely. "People said we were cynical, that we were sexualizing little girls. But you know what? I still think those are cute underwear for little girls. And I think anybody who gets on a bandwagon about thongs for little girls is crazy. Just crazy! There's so much craziness about sex in this country. It's nuts! I can see getting upset about letting your girl hang out with a bunch of old pervs, but why would you let your girl hang out with a bunch of old pervs?"

Later I brought up the brouhaha surrounding the *A&F Quarterly,* which, until it was discontinued in 2003, boasted articles about the history of orgies and pictures of chiseled, mostly white, all-American boys and girls (but mostly boys) cavorting naked on horses, beaches, pianos, surfboards, statues, and phallically suggestive tree trunks. The magalog so outraged the American Decency Association that it called for a boycott and started selling anti-Abercrombie T-shirts: DITCH FITCH: ABERCROMBIE PEDDLES PORN AND EXPLOITS CHILDREN. Meanwhile, gay men across America were eagerly collecting the magazines, lured by photographer Bruce Weber's taste for beautiful, masculine college-aged boys playfully pulling off each other's boxers.

Jeffries nearly fell over in exasperation when I mentioned the magalog, although I'm not sure which charge—that he sells sex to kids or that his advertising is homoerotic—

bothered him more. "That's just so wrong!" he said. "I think that what we represent sexually is healthy. It's playful. It's not dark. It's not degrading! And it's not gay, and it's not straight, and it's not black, and it's not white. It's not about any labels. That would be cynical, and we're not cynical! It's all depicting this wonderful camaraderie, friendship, and playfulness that exist in this generation and, candidly, does not exist in the older generation."

Jeffries alternates his grumpy defensiveness with moments of surprising candor, making him at times oddly endearing. He admitted things out loud that some youth-focused retailers wouldn't (which may be why he panicked and pulled his cooperation from this story two days after I left A&F headquarters, offering no explanation). For example, when I ask him how important sex and sexual attraction are in what he calls the "emotional experience" he creates for his customers, he says, "It's almost everything. That's why we hire good-looking people in our stores. Because good-looking people attract other good-looking people, and we want to market to cool, good-looking people. We don't market to anyone other than that."

As far as Jeffries is concerned, America's unattractive, overweight, or otherwise undesirable teens can shop elsewhere. "In every school there are the cool and popular kids, and then there are the not-so-cool kids," he says. "Candidly, we go after the cool kids. We go after the attractive all-American kid with a great attitude and a lot of friends. A lot of people don't belong [in our clothes], and they can't belong. Are we exclusionary? Absolutely. Those companies that are in trouble are trying to target everybody: young, old, fat, skinny. But then you become totally vanilla. You don't alienate anybody, but you don't excite anybody, either."

JEFFRIES'S OBSESSION WITH building brands began when he was five. He grew up in Los Angeles, where his father owned a chain of party supply stores for which a young Jeffries liked to organize and design the windows and counters. "I would always say to my parents, 'We need another store. We need another!'" Jeffries recalls. "I always wanted to expand and get bigger, and I would get off on saying 'Why do we do the fixtures like this? Why don't we do it another way?' That totally turned me on."

Jeffries says he had a "very classic American youth," although he was not good at sports. "I broke my dad's heart because I wasn't good at basketball," he says. In high school in the late 1950s, Jeffries always wore Levi's jeans. "Actually, don't write that," he tells me, laughing. "But Levi's was definitely the uniform back then, kind of like what A&F has become. If you didn't wear 501s you were considered weird."

No one cool wore Abercrombie & Fitch when Jeffries went off to Claremont McKenna College and then to Columbia University, where he earned a master's degree in business administration. In fact, the company's best years were long behind it. Founded in 1892, in its heyday it served Presidents Hoover and Eisenhower (they bought their fishing equipment there), Ernest Hemingway (guns), and Cole Porter (evening clothes). During Prohibition A&F was where the in crowd went for its hip flasks. But by the 1970s it had become a fashion backwater, holding on for dear life.

Leslee O'Neill, A&F's executive vice president of planning and allocation, remembers what the company was like before Jeffries got there. "We had old clothes that no one liked," she says. "It was a mess, a total disaster. We had this old library at our headquarters with all these really old books. There were croquet sets lying around. It was very English."

The company, which since 1988 had been owned by The Limited, was losing $25 million a year when Jeffries arrived and announced that A&F could survive and prosper as a "young, hip, spirited company." "We're all there thinking, Oh yeah, right. Abercrombie & Fitch?" recalls O'Neill. "But in the end we were, like, Well, why not? It can't get any worse." Jeffries, then in his late forties, dressed in Oxford shirts and corduroy pants. "He was a lot more normal then," O'Neill says. "Today he's much more eccentric, obviously."

Maybe, although former coworkers at Paul Harris recall that Jeffries had an odd personal style even back then. "He wore the same outfit to work every day," recalls Thomas Yeo, a Paul Harris colleague. "Nearly worn-out suede loafers, a pair of gray flannel pants, and a double-breasted navy blazer. I don't think he ever changed his clothes. All that seemed to matter to him was the success of the brand."

Jan Woodruff, who also worked with Jeffries at Paul Harris, remembers him as a workaholic. "If he had a life outside work, it wasn't something people knew about," she says. But Woodruff and others say he has a superlative fashion mind. "It's so rare to find someone who is brilliant at both the creative and the business sides. But Jeffries is both. He's good at thinking in broad terms, but he's also obsessed with details. And I've never seen anyone as driven as Mike. I had no doubt he would be incredibly successful if he found the right venue. And he found it."

Soon after taking over A&F, Jeffries went looking for the right man to help him make A&F a sexy, aspirational brand. He settled on Bruce Weber, already a renowned photographer known for his male nudes. "But back then we couldn't afford him for an actual shoot," Jeffries told me, "so we bought one picture from him and hung it in a store window."

Fourteen years later, Jeffries's success is the envy of the fashion world. In a feature called "The Abercrombie Effect" in *DNR*, a newsmagazine about men's fashion and retail, the magazine noted that "not since Ralph Lauren's ascent in the 1980s has a single brand perfected a lifestyle-based look so often alluded to and imitated." Now Ralph Lauren's doing the imitating, opening a chain of collegiate, WASPy Polo knockoff stores called Rugby for young customers, featuring in-store grunge bands and beautiful salespeople.

"Imitation is the sincerest form of flattery," says Margaret Doerrer, national sales manager for young men at Union Bay, another youth-oriented label. "In the young men's market, for the longest time no one was creating a 'lifestyle.' Particularly in the department stores, everyone was focused on hip-hop and urban brands, and no one was creating that average, American Joe look. Jeffries never lost sight of who his customer is, and he created a quality brand that caters to the cool clique and has a sense of exclusivity, yet it still has a mass appeal, because people want to be a part of it. It's genius."

MAYBE IT'S JUST the price of success, but it's not a normal day in America if someone isn't suing (or boycotting, or "girlcotting") Abercrombie & Fitch, which has become a lightning rod for both the Left and the Right. In 2004, A&F paid $40 million to settle a class action suit brought by minority employees who said they were either denied employment or forced to work in back rooms, where they wouldn't be seen by customers.

Though A&F denied any wrongdoing, Jeffries said the suit taught him a lesson: "I don't think we were in any sense guilty of racism, but I think we just didn't work hard enough as a company to create more balance and diversity. And we have, and I think that's made us a better company. We have minority recruiters. And if you go into our stores you see great-looking kids of all races."

In the latest episode, a group of high school girls from Allegheny County, Pennsylvania, made the rounds of television talk shows to protest the company's "offensive" T-shirts. Of particular concern were shirts that read: WHO NEEDS A BRAIN WHEN YOU HAVE THESE?, GENTLEMEN PREFER TIG OL' BITTIES, and DO I MAKE YOU LOOK FAT?

"Abercrombie has a history of insensitivity," the group's well-spoken Emma Blackman-Mathis, sixteen, told me, "and there is no company with as big an impact on the standards of beauty. There are kids starving themselves so they can be the 'Abercrombie girl,' and there are guys who think they aren't worthy if they don't look exactly like the guys on the wall."

The protest (which resulted in A&F pulling WHO NEEDS A BRAIN WHEN YOU HAVE THESE? and GENTLEMEN PREFER TIG OL' BITTIES but retaining DO I MAKE YOU LOOK FAT? and others) began after my visit, so I couldn't ask Jeffries about it. But I did ask him about other T-shirt dustups, including IT'S ALL RELATIVE IN WEST VIRGINIA (which West Virginia's governor didn't find funny), BAD GIRLS CHUG. GOOD GIRLS DRINK QUICKLY (which angered antiaddiction groups), and WONG BROTHERS LAUNDRY SERVICE—TWO WONGS CAN MAKE IT WHITE (which triggered protests from Asian groups).

Remarkably, Jeffries says he has a "morals committee for T-shirts" whose job it is to make sure this sort of thing doesn't happen. "Sometimes they're on vacation," he admits with a smile. "Listen, do we go too far sometimes? Absolutely. But we push the envelope, and we try to be funny, and we try to stay authentic and relevant to our target customer. I really don't care what anyone other than our target customer thinks."

What about shareholders? In 2005, Abercrombie shareholders filed a suit against the company alleging that Jeffries's compensation was excessive. (The suit was settled; his $12 million "stay bonus" was reduced to $6 million, and he gave up some stock options. In 2004, he had made approximately $25 million.) Other suits accuse Jeffries of misleading stockholders about the company's profits.

"You settle because it's a distraction," Jeffries told me. "I can't let anybody be distracted here. Me included. We are passionate about what we do here on a daily basis, and if any of us is tied up with this nonsense, it's counterproductive. We're a very popular company. We have a lot of money. And we're targets."

Jeffries dismisses the idea that he deliberately courts controversy to sell clothes, although the endless complaints about Abercrombie perverting the minds of America's youths undoubtedly make the brand even more appealing to them. Meanwhile, the slogan-free items, which are for the most part as unthreatening as those of any other, less controversial label, fly under the parental radar. "Abercrombie remains a very acceptable look for Mom," says Union Bay's Doerrer. "I don't think many mothers of sixteen-year-old boys dressed in Abercrombie will make them go upstairs and change."

JEFFRIES SAYS THAT A&F is a collaborative environment ("a diva-free zone," is how he put it to me), but in the end he makes every decision—from the hiring of the models to the placement of every item of clothing in every store. There are model stores for each of the four brands at A&F headquarters, and he spends much of his time making sure they're perfect. When they are, everything is photographed and sent to individual outlets to be replicated to the last detail. If there's an A&F diva, it's Jeffries.

I got a firsthand look at his perfectionism when he invited me along for the final walk-through for the Christmas setup of his stores. "How does a store look? How does it feel? How does it smell? That's what I'm obsessed with," Jeffries said as we walked quickly toward the Hollister model store surrounded by a handful of his top deputies, including Tom Mendenhall, a senior vice president whom Jeffries recently lured away from Gucci.

Inside the dimly lit Hollister store, which is designed to look like a cozy California beach house (there are surfboards, canoes, comfy chairs to lounge in, magazines to read, and two screens with live shots of Huntington Beach, courtesy of cameras permanently affixed to a pier), Jeffries paused in front of two mannequins and shook his head. "No, no, we're still not there, guys," he shouted over the No Doubt song "Spiderwebs," which blasted throughout the store. He stared at the jeans on the female mannequin. "The jeans are too high. I think she has to be lower."

A guy named Josh got down on his knees and started fidgeting with the jeans, trying to pull them down so they hung to the ground. "And we need to make the leg as skinny as we can," Jeffries said. "Should we clip the back of the leg in the knee?" Two employees scurried off to get clips. "We want it bigger at the top and skinnier at the legs. Yes, that's sexier. Much better. That's *less butch*." (Jeffries isn't a fan of the "butch" look, though when they were all the rage he grudgingly incorporated camouflage army pants into his Hollister line for girls.)

Jeffries then turned his attention to the male mannequin. "Okay, how rugged and masculine can we make this guy?" he asked, prompting a couple of his assistants to fidget with the jeans, making them bigger in the leg. "Good, he looks cooler now. He's got more attitude. We love attitude."

There was more mannequin fixing at the A&F store,

where a male one decked out in jeans wasn't looking very manly. "We have to fix this guy's package," Jeffries said. "We could stuff him," a girl suggested while a guy fiddled with the crotch, trying to make it poofier. With that fixed, Jeffries turned to a male mannequin in cargo pants. To make sure it looked realistic, he had a very attractive male employee put on a pair of the pants and stand next to the mannequin. "That looks great," he said as the young man did a 360, the pants sagging off his ass. Jeffries looked at the mannequin again. "Are the pants low enough? This guy's got it lower."

"They're right at the edge of falling off," said an assistant.

"Okay, that's good," Jeffries said. "Let's get them as low as we can without them falling off. We don't want him looking like an *old guy*."

What's in a Street Name?

Meet the residents of a small Ohio town who changed the name of their street from Gay Road to Green Apple Road.

BACK WHEN GAYS WERE queers, life wasn't this complicated for the folks on Gay Road. They figured—when they thought about it at all—that they lived on a *happy* road. It was named, they say, after Mr. Gay, who lived there in the early 1900s but died at the hands of his two-timing wife's boyfriend.

It's a sordid tale, and Gay Road residents love to tell it. Apparently, Mr. Gay came home one afternoon to find his unclad wife in bed with another man. A heated discussion ensued, after which Mr. Gay figured he would settle the matter with his shotgun. But Mr. Gay's wife was a step ahead of him (alas, she always was), and she had removed the shell from its casing. On cue, her boyfriend shot Mr. Gay.

A century later, Mr. Gay was in for another surprise. Nineteen residents of Gay Road in Miami Township, Ohio, signed a petition to rename it Green Apple Road. "The repercussions of living on a road called 'GAY' are not pleasant," one resident, Sharon McKinney, wrote in the official petition. "The snide remarks and thoughtless comments about one's address being 'GAY' are intolerable."

Not only that, but the single road sign was a magnet for persistent, mysterious thieves. They stole it once or twice a month until township officials tired of the routine, elevating the street sign four years ago to an unheard-of fifteen feet. Undaunted, the thieves climbed. But officials insist that the fifteen feet served as a deterrent, because thefts decreased to once or twice a year.

So what kind of people steal gay road signs? And are there, as these residents claim, serious "repercussions" to living on a road called Gay? Could these be the same repercussions as actually *being* gay? I traveled to Miami Township, a mostly rural community of 25,000 near Dayton in southwestern Ohio, to find out. Miami Township is Republican country, and Gay Road and its surrounding area is a white, middle- and working-class community with dense forests, rich farmland, meandering creeks, spacious parks, and small country roads. Homes with American flags outnumber those without them, and BEWARE OF DOG signs are everywhere.

I arrived on Gay Road at noon on an overcast Monday. The street sign had already been changed—this was officially

Green Apple Road now. I parked my car near the sign, on the corner of Green Apple and Cranes Run Road, right next to a creek that dumps into the Miami River. I made my way up the winding country road, stopping at a one-story brick house with a basketball hoop in the driveway, where a scruffy, mean-looking man told me that he wasn't interested in talking to any magazine (especially, he said, "a magazine for *the gays*").

My first successful Gay Road contact came courtesy of a tall, radiant blond woman who welcomed me into her spacious home and promptly introduced me to her husband, Wade Gates, who was apparently going to do the family's talking. A friendly, boyishly handsome businessman and Baptist youth pastor, Gates led me to his downstairs study, where I tried to get him to talk about Gay Road, while he tried to convert me to Christianity.

"I hope you will study the Bible," he said, smiling and handing me a pamphlet called "How to Study the Bible."

"Don't just read the Bible," he insisted. "*Study* it. That's the neat thing about the Word of God. It's established soundly in one book. But we live in a world today where we've taken the truth, set it aside, and said, 'Let's take an opinion poll!'"

By the time I reached the small, country-style house of seventy-four-year-old Richard Johnson and his seventy-one-year-old wife, Arlene, who have lived on the road since 1952, word had apparently spread of my presence in the neighborhood. "Are you the guy from New York?" Richard asked, all smiles as he walked into his kitchen from his cluttered front porch, where two hanging signs read CHILDREN

LEFT UNATTENDED WILL BE SOLD AS SLAVES and NO RIDERS EXCEPT BRUNETTES, BLONDES, AND REDHEADS.

A former papermaker, Richard is an upbeat man with piercing blue eyes, a gold tooth, and gray hair that juts out from under his baseball cap. Richard likes to tell long-winded tales, and he has the spastic storytelling style of a man on crystal meth.

"Don't let him get started," Arlene warned me.

But it was too late. "So one day I went to see my friend and get a tractor tire fixed," Richard said. "This fellow that worked for him asked me my address, and I told him Gay Road, and my friend, the boss, started laughing. He looked over at me and said, 'I see you have the same problem I have.' I didn't know what he was talking about. Then he said, 'I live on *Fairy Lane*!'"

So, I ask him, are there really unpleasant repercussions of living on a road called Gay?

"Oh, people sometimes make a comment, but it wasn't a big deal to me," Richard said. "We aren't prejudiced against anybody. There are probably even some gay people in our family if you search back far enough. Sure, sometimes we might be puzzled by the lifestyle people choose, but—"

"Yeah, I don't really agree with the gay life," Arlene interrupted.

"Now, now, don't say you don't *agree* with it," Richard said. "Just say you don't *understand* it. The gays can maybe accept that better."

Right then, the couple's adult grandson dropped by and told me that he had endured some good-natured ribbing in the late 1980s when the school bus dropped him off at the corner of Gay Road and Cranes Run. "Yeah, kids would make fun of me because I lived on Gay Road," he said with a smile. "It was a big joke."

"So who was stealing the sign?" I asked them.

"That's a big mystery," Richard said, shaking his head.

Further up Green Apple, Dale and Boots Vaughn think they know who stole the sign. "I think it was the queers," said Dale, a stocky thirty-six-year-old in a T-shirt, jeans shorts, and a baseball cap. He stood next to his father, Boots, in front of their small house near the end of Gay Road. (The Vaughns, who were friendly and outgoing, assumed that I was straight.)

"Do you think it was one queer or queers working as a *team*?" I asked. "I don't know," Dale said. "But if you weren't gay, why would you want to steal a gay sign?"

The next day, Jon Zimmerman—a gay man who grew up a block from Gay Road in the 1950s and '60s, and who now lives in a nearby town—took me on "the tour that the neighbors don't want you to see." As we drove, he pointed out a yellow house where he says there were once extravagant drag shows, a park where he says men are often arrested for public sex, and a former general store that he insists used to double as a whorehouse.

"But no, God forbid the neighborhood has a *Gay Road*," said Zimmerman. "The truth around here is that people would rather see a gay kid dead than see a gay kid come out, and they'll do anything to avoid having to face the word 'gay,' including changing a street name."

Later that afternoon, I drove across the county to the city of Kettering, where there is a small, unspectacular stretch of road called Gay Drive. My reason for coming here was simple: I needed to know if the folks on Gay Road in Miami Township are, as I suspect, an aberration, or if there are, unbeknown to us all, thousands of Americans who live tortured lives because of their gay-themed postal addresses. Do the folks on Gay Drive want to change their street name, too?

"Nah man, 'gay' is just a word," said Justin Collinsworth, a college student who lives on the street. "And you know, it's great when you're giving directions, because people don't forget that. They're, like, 'Yeah, I should be able to find *that*.'"

After speaking with several other residents (all of whom insisted that living on Gay Drive wasn't a big deal), I headed back to Gay Road, suspecting, as I often do, that I had missed something. And I had. About a hundred yards past the small home of Dale and Boots Vaughn, after Gay Road turns into Staley Road, I came upon a street that had to be some kind of joke. But I went with it, taking a right on Queen Avenue. And that's when it hit me: I might just be in the gayest neighborhood in America.

Double Lives on the Down Low

Secret Lives, AIDS, and the Black Homosexual Underground.

IN ITS UPPER STORIES, the Flex bathhouse in Cleveland feels like a squash club for backslapping businessmen. There's a large gym with free weights and exercise machines, and men in towels lounge on couches and watch CNN on big-screen TVs.

In the basement, the mood is different: the TVs are tuned to pornography, and the dimly lighted hallways buzz with sexual energy. A naked black man reclines on a sling in a room called "the dungeon play area." Along a hallway lined with lockers, black men eye each other as they walk by in towels. In small rooms nearby, some men are having sex. Others are napping.

There are two bathhouses in Cleveland. On the city's predominantly white West Side, Club Cleveland—which opened in 1965 and recently settled into a modern 15,000-square-foot space—attracts many white and openly gay men. Flex is on the East Side, and it serves a mostly black and Hispanic clientele, many of whom don't consider themselves gay.

I go to Flex one night to meet Ricardo Wallace, an African-American outreach worker for the AIDS Task Force of Cleveland who comes here twice a month to test men for HIV. I eventually find him sitting alone on a twin-size bed in a small room on the main floor; next to him on the bed are a dozen unopened condoms and several oral HIV-testing kits.

Twenty years ago, Wallace came here for fun. He was twenty-two, and AIDS seemed to kill only gay white men in San Francisco and New York. If Wallace and the other black men who frequented Flex in the early 1980s worried about anything, it was being spotted walking in the front door.

Today, while an increasing number of black men are openly gay, many black men who have sex with men still lead secret lives, products of a black culture that deems masculinity and fatherhood as a black man's primary responsibility—and homosexuality as a white man's perversion. And although Flex now offers baskets of condoms and lubricant, Wallace says that many of the club's patrons still don't use them.

Wallace ticks off the grim statistics: blacks make up only 12 percent of the population in America, but they account for half of all new HIV infections. Though intravenous drug use is a large part of the problem, experts say that the leading cause of HIV in black men is homosexual sex (some of which takes place in prison, where blacks disproportionately outnumber whites). According to the Centers for Disease

Control, one third of young urban black men who have sex with men in this country are HIV-positive, and 90 percent of those are unaware of their infection.

We don't hear much about this aspect of the epidemic, mostly because the two communities most directly affected by it—the black and gay communities—have spent the better part of two decades eyeing each other through a haze of denial or studied disinterest. For African-Americans, facing and addressing the black AIDS crisis would require talking honestly and compassionately about homosexuality—and that has proved remarkably difficult, whether it be in black churches, in black organizations, or on inner-city playgrounds. The mainstream gay world, for its part, has spent twenty years largely fighting the epidemic among white, openly gay men, showing little sustained interest in reaching minorities who have sex with men but refuse to call themselves gay.

Rejecting a gay culture they perceive as white and effeminate, many black men have settled on a new identity, with its own vocabulary and customs and its own name: Down Low. Though there have always been men—black and white—who have had secret sexual lives with men, the creation of an organized, underground subculture largely made up of black men who otherwise live straight lives is a phenomenon of the last decade.

Many of the men at Flex tonight—and many of the black men I have met these past months in Cleveland, Atlanta, Florida, New York, and Boston—are on the Down Low, or on the DL, as they more often call it. Most date or marry women and engage sexually with men they meet only in anonymous settings such as bathhouses and parks or through the Internet. Many of these men are young and from the inner city, where they live in a hypermasculine "thug" culture. Other DL men form romantic relationships with men and may even be peripheral participants in mainstream gay culture, all unknown to their colleagues and families. Most DL men identify themselves not as gay or bisexual but first and foremost as black. To them, that equates to being inherently masculine.

DL culture has grown, in recent years, out of the shadows and developed its own contemporary institutions, for those who know where to look: Web sites, Internet chat rooms, private parties, and special nights at clubs. Over the same period, Down Low culture has come to the attention of alarmed public health officials, some of whom regard men on the DL as an infectious bridge spreading HIV to unsuspecting wives and girlfriends. In 2001, almost two thirds of women in the United States who learned they had AIDS were black.

With no wives or girlfriends around, Flex is a safe place for men on the DL to let down their guards. There aren't many white men here (I'm one of them), and that's often the norm for DL parties and clubs. Some private DL events won't even let whites in the door. Others will let you in if you look "black enough," which is code for looking masculine, tough, and "straight." That's not to say that DL guys are attracted only to men of color. "Some of the black boys here love white boys," Wallace tells me.

While Wallace tests one man for HIV, I walk back downstairs to change into a towel (I've been warned twice by Flex employees that clothes aren't allowed in the club). By the lockers, I notice a tall black man in his late teens or early twenties staring at me from a dozen lockers down. Abruptly, he walks over to me and puts his right hand on my left shoulder.

"You wanna hook up?" he asks, smiling broadly.

His frankness takes me by surprise. Bathhouse courtship rituals usually involve a period of aggressive flirtation, often heavy and deliberate staring. "Are you gay?" I ask him. "Nah, man," he says. "I got a girl. You look like you would have a girl, too."

I tell him that I don't have a girl. "Doesn't matter," he says, stepping closer. I decline his advances, at which he seems genuinely perplexed. Before I go back upstairs, I ask him if he normally uses condoms here. As a recurring announcement comes over the club's loudspeaker—"HIV testing is available in Room 207. . . . HIV testing in Room 207"—he shakes his head. "Nah, man," he says. "I like it raw."

IF CLEVELAND IS the kind of city many gay people flee, Atlanta is a city they escape to. For young black men, Atlanta is the hub of the South, a city with unlimited possibilities, including a place in its vibrant DL scene.

I travel to Atlanta to meet William, an attractive black man in his thirties on the DL who asked to be identified by his middle name. I met him in the America Online chat room DLThugs, where he spends some time most days searching for what he calls "real" DL guys, as opposed to the "flaming queens who like to pretend they're thugs and on the DL." William says he likes his guys "to look like real guys," and his Internet profile makes it clear what he isn't looking for: "No stupid questions, fats, whites, stalkers or queens."

I told him I was a writer, and he eventually agreed to meet me in Atlanta and take me around to a few clubs. With one condition: "You better dress cool," he warned me. "Don't dress, you know, *white*."

William smiles as I climb into his silver Jeep Grand Cherokee, which I take as a good sign. Two of William's best friends are in the car with him: Christopher, a thin, boyish thirty-two-year-old with a shaved head, and Rakeem, an outgoing thirty-one-year-old with dreadlocks who asked to be identified by his Muslim name. We drive toward the Palace, a downtown club popular with young guys on the DL.

William doesn't date women anymore and likes guys younger than he is, although they've been known to get more attached than he would prefer. "Yeah, he's always getting *stalked*," Rakeem says enthusiastically. "The boys just won't leave him alone. He's got this weird power to make boys act really stupid."

It's easy to see why. William radiates confidence and control, which serve him well in his daytime role as an executive at a local corporation. He says his coworkers don't know he likes men ("It's none of their business," he tells me several times) or that after work he changes persona completely, becoming a major player in the city's DL scene, organizing parties and events.

Christopher, who sits in the backseat with me, is the only

one of the three who is openly gay and not on the DL (although he won't tell me his last name, for fear of embarrassing his parents). Christopher moved to Atlanta when he was twenty-four and was surprised when black men in the city couldn't get enough of him. "They would hit on me at the grocery store, on the street, on the train, always in this sly, DL kind of way where you never actually talk about what you're really doing," he says. "That's actually how I met my current boyfriend. He followed me off the train."

Rakeem, a roommate of William's, moved to Atlanta five years ago from Brooklyn. He says he's "an urban black gay man on the DL," which he says reflects his comfort with his sexuality but his unwillingness to "broadcast it." People at work don't know he's gay. His family wouldn't know, either, if a vindictive friend hadn't told them. "I'm a guy's guy, a totally masculine black gay man, and that's just beyond my family's comprehension," he says.

While Rakeem and William proudly proclaim themselves on the Down Low, they wouldn't have been considered on the DL when men first started claiming the label in the mid-1990s. Back then the culture was completely under the radar, and DL men lived ostensibly heterosexual lives (complete with wives and girlfriends) but also engaged in secret sexual relationships with men. Today, though, an increasing number of black men who have sex only with men identify themselves as DL, further muddying an already complicated group identity. And as DL culture expands, it has become an open secret.

For many men on the Down Low, including William and Rakeem, the DL label is both an announcement of masculinity and a separation from white gay culture. To them, it is the safest identity available—they don't risk losing their ties to family, friends, or black culture.

William parks the car in a secluded lot about a block from the Palace. As he breaks out some pot, I ask them if they heard about what happened recently at Morehouse College, where one black student beat another with a bat supposedly for looking at him the wrong way in a dormitory shower. "I'm surprised that kind of stuff doesn't happen more often," William says. "The only reason it doesn't is because most black guys are sly enough about it that they aren't gonna get themselves beaten up. If you're masculine and a guy thinks you're checking him out, you can always say: 'Whoa, chill, I ain't checking you out. Look at me. Do I look *gay* to you?'"

Masculinity is a surprisingly effective defense, because until recently the only popular representations of black gay men were what William calls "drag queens or sissies." Rakeem takes a hit from the bowl. "We know there are black gay rappers, black gay athletes, but they're all on the DL," Rakeem says. "If you're white, you can come out as an openly gay skier or actor or whatever. It might hurt you some, but it's not like if you're black and gay, because then it's like you've let down the whole black community, black women, black history, black pride. You don't hear black people say, 'Oh yeah, he's gay, but he's still a real man, and he still takes care of all his responsibilities.' What you hear is 'Look at that sissy faggot.'"

I ask them what the difference is between being on the DL and being in the closet. "Being on the DL is about having fun," William tells me. "Being who you are but keeping your business to yourself. The closet isn't fun. In the closet, you're lonely."

"I don't know," Christopher says. "In some ways I think DL is just a new, sexier way to say you're in the closet."

Both have a point. As William says, DL culture does place a premium on pleasure. It is, DL guys insist, one big party. And there is a certain freedom in not playing by modern society's rules of self-identification, in not having to explain yourself—or your sexuality—to anyone. Like the black athletes and rappers they idolize, DL men convey a strong sense of masculine independence and power: *I do what I want when I want with whom I want*. Even the term Down Low—which was popularized in the 1990s by the singers TLC and R. Kelly, meaning "secret"—has a sexy ring to it, a hint that you're doing something wrong that feels right.

But for all their supposed freedom, many men on the DL are as trapped—or more trapped—than their white counterparts in the closet. While DL guys regard the closet as something alien (a sad, stifling place where fearful people hide), the closet can be temporary (many closeted men plan to "come out" someday). But black men on the DL typically say they're on the DL for life. Since they generally don't see themselves as gay, there is nothing to "come out" to—there is no next step.

When sufficiently stoned, the guys decide to make an appearance at the Palace. More than anything, the place feels like a rundown loft into which somebody stuck a bar and a dance floor and called it a club. Still, it's one of the most popular hangouts for young black men on the DL in Atlanta.

William surveys the crowd, which is made up mostly of DL "homo thugs," black guys dressed like gangsters and rappers (baggy jeans, do-rags, and FUBU jackets).

"So many people in here try so hard to look like they're badasses," he says. "Everyone wants to look like they're on the DL. You have no idea how many of the boys here tonight would let me fuck them without a condom. These young guys swear they know it all. They all want a black thug. They just want the black thug to do his thing."

While William and many other DL men insist that they're strictly "tops"—meaning they do the penetrating during sexual intercourse—other DL guys proudly advertise themselves as "masculine bottom brothas" on their Internet profiles. They may play the stereotypically passive role during sex, they say, but they're just as much men, and just as aggressive, as DL tops. As one DL guy writes on his America Online profile, "Just 'cause I am a bottom, don't take me for a bitch."

Still, William says that many DL guys are in a never-ending search for the roughest, most masculine, "straightest-looking" DL top. Both William and Chris, who lost friends to AIDS, say they always use condoms. But as William explains, "Part of the attraction to thugs is that they're careless and carefree. Putting on a condom doesn't fit in with that. A lot of DL guys aren't going to put on a condom, because that ruins the fantasy." It also shatters the denial—stopping to put on a condom forces guys on the DL to acknowledge, on some level, that they're having sex with a man.

• • •

IN 1992, E. Lynn Harris—then an unknown black writer—self-published *Invisible Life,* the fictional coming-of-age story of Raymond Tyler, a masculine young black man devoted to his girlfriend but consumed by his attraction to men. For Tyler, being black is hard enough; being black and gay seems a cruel and impossible proposition. Eventually picked up by a publisher, the book went on to sell nearly 500,000 copies, many purchased by black women shocked at the idea that black men who weren't effeminate could be having sex with men.

"I was surprised by the reaction to my book," Harris said. "People were in such denial that black men could be doing this. Well, they were doing it then, and they're doing it now."

That behavior has public health implications. A few years ago, the epidemiological data started rolling in, showing increasing numbers of black women who weren't IV drug users getting infected with HIV. Though some were no doubt infected by men who were using drugs, experts believe that many were infected by men on the Down Low.

Suddenly, says Chris Bell, a twenty-nine-year-old HIV-positive black man from Chicago who often speaks at colleges about sexuality and AIDS, DL guys were being demonized. They became the "modern version of the highly sexually dangerous, irresponsible black man who doesn't care about anyone and just wants to get off." Bell and others say that while black men had been dying of AIDS for years, it wasn't until "innocent" black women became infected that the black community bothered to notice.

For white people, Bell said, "DL life fit in perfectly with

our society's simultaneous obsession [with] and aversion to black male sexuality." But if the old stereotypes of black sexual aggression were resurrected, there was a significant shift: this time, white women were not cast as the innocent victims. Now it was black women and children. The resulting permutations confounded just about everyone—black and white, straight and gay.

How should guys on the DL be regarded? Whose responsibility are they? Are they gay, straight, or bisexual? If they're gay, why don't they just tough it up, come out, and move to a big-city gay neighborhood like so many other gay men and lesbians? If they're straight, what are they doing having sex with guys in parks and bathhouses? If they're bisexual, why not just say *that*? Why, as the CDC reported, are black men who have sex with men more than twice as likely to keep their sexual practices a secret than whites? Most important to many, why can't these black men at least get tested for HIV?

The knee-jerk answer to most of these questions is that the black community is simply too homophobic: from womanizing rappers to moralizing preachers, much of the black community views homosexuality as a curse against a race with too many strikes against it. The white community, the conventional wisdom goes, is more accepting of its sexual minorities, leading to fewer double lives, less shame, and less unsafe sex. (AIDS researchers point to shame and stigma as two of the driving forces spreading AIDS in America.)

But some scholars have come to doubt the reading of black culture as intrinsically more homophobic than white culture. "I think it's unfair to categorize it that way today, and it is absolutely not the case historically," says George Chauncey, a professor of gay and lesbian history at the University of Chicago. "Especially in the 1940s and '50s, when antigay attitudes were at their peak in white American society, black society was much more accepting. People usually expected their gay friends and relatives to remain discreet, but even so, it was better than in white society."

Glenn Ligon, a black visual artist who is openly gay, recalls that as a child coming of age in the 1970s, he always felt there was a space in black culture for openly gay men. "It was a limited space, but it was there," he says. "After all, where else could we go? The white community wasn't that accepting of us. And the black community had to protect its own."

Ligon, whose artwork often deals with sexuality and race, thinks that the pressure to keep homosexuality on the DL doesn't come exclusively from other black people but also from the social and economic realities particular to black men. "The reason that so many young black men aren't so cavalier about announcing their sexual orientation is because we need our families," he says. "We need our families because of economic reasons, because of racism, because of a million reasons. It's the idea that black people have to stick together, and if there's the slightest possibility that coming out could disrupt that, guys won't do it." (That may help explain why many of the black men who are openly gay tend to be more educated, have more money, and generally have a greater sense of security.)

But to many men on the DL, sociological and financial considerations are beside the point; they say they wouldn't come out even if they felt they could. They see black men who do come out either as having chosen their sexuality over their skin color or as being so effeminate that they wouldn't have fooled anyone anyway. In a black world that puts a premium on hypermasculinity, men who have sex with other men are particularly sensitive to not appearing soft in any way.

Maybe that's why many guys on the DL don't go to gay bars. "Most of the guys I've messed around with, I've actually met at straight clubs," says D., a twenty-one-year-old college student on the DL whom I met on the Internet and then in person in New York City. "Guys will come up to me and ask me some stupid thing like 'Yo, you got a piece of gum?' I'll say, 'Nah, but what's up?' Some guys will look at me and say, 'What do you mean *what's up*?' but the ones on the DL will keep talking to me." Later he added, "It's easier for me to date guys on the DL. Gay guys get too clingy, and they can blow your cover. Real DL guys, they have something to lose, too. It's just safer to be with someone who has something to lose."

D. says he prefers sex with women, but he sometimes has sex with men because he "gets bored." But even the DL guys I spoke with who say they prefer sex with men are adamant that the nomenclature of white gay culture has no relevance for them. "I'm masculine," as one college student from Providence, Rhode Island, who is on the DL, told me over the phone. "There's no way I'm gay." I asked him what his definition of gay is. "Gays are the faggots who dress, talk, and act like girls. That's not me."

That kind of logic infuriates many mainstream gay people. To them, life on the DL is an elaborately rationalized repudiation of everything the gay rights movement fought for—the right to live without shame and without fear of reprisal. It's a step back into the dark days before liberation, before gay bashing was considered a crime, before gay television characters were considered family entertainment, and way, way before the Supreme Court ruled that gay people are "entitled to respect for their private lives."

Emil Wilbekin, the black and openly gay editor in chief of *Vibe* magazine, has little patience for men on the DL. "To me, it's a dangerous cop-out," he says. "I get that it's sexy. I get that it's hot to see some big burly hip-hop kid who looks straight but sleeps with guys, but the bottom line is that it's dishonest. I think you have to love who you are, you have to have respect for yourself and others, and to me most men on the DL have none of those qualities. There's nothing 'sexy' about getting HIV or giving it to your male and female lovers. That's not what being a real black man is about."

Though the issues being debated have life-and-death implications, the tenor of the debate owes much to the overcharged identity politics of the last two decades. As Chauncey points out, the assumption that anyone has to name his sexual behavior at all is relatively recent. "A lot of people look at these DL guys and say they must really be gay, no matter what they say about themselves, but who's to know?" he says. "In the early 1900s, many men in immigrant and African-American working-class communities engaged in sex with other men without being stigmatized as queer. But it's hard for people to accept that something that seems so intimate and inborn to them as being gay or straight isn't universal."

Whatever the case, most guys on the DL are well aware of the contempt with which their choices are viewed by many out gay men. And if there are some DL guys willing to take the risk—to jeopardize their social and family standing by declaring their sexuality—that contempt doesn't do much to convince them that they'd ever really be welcome in Manhattan's Chelsea or on Fire Island.

"Mainstream gay culture has created an alternative to mainstream culture," says John Peterson, a professor of psychology at Georgia State University who specializes in AIDS research among black men, "and many whites take advantage of that. They say, 'I will leave Podunk and I will go to the gay barrios of San Francisco and other cities, and I will go live there, be who I really am, and be part of the mainstream.' Many African-Americans say, 'I can't go and face the racism I will see there, and I can't create a functioning alternative society because I don't have the resources.' They're stuck. The choice becomes, do I want to be discriminated against at home for my sexuality, or do I want to move away and be discriminated against for my skin color?"

So increasing numbers of black men—and other men of color who are increasingly claiming the DL identity—split the difference. They've created a community of their own, a cultural "party" to which whites aren't invited. "Labeling yourself as DL is a way to disassociate from everything white and upper class," says George Ayala, the director of education for AIDS Project Los Angeles. And that, he says, is a way for DL men to assert some power.

Still, for all the defiance that DL culture claims for itself, for all the forcefulness of the "never apologize, never explain" stance, a sense of shame can hover at the margins. It's the inevitable price of living a double life. Consider these last lines of a DL college student's online profile: "Lookin 4 cool ass brothers on tha down low. . . . You aint dl if you have a V.I.P. pass to tha gay spot. . . . You aint dl if you call ur dude 'gurl.' . . . Put some bass in ur voice yo and whats tha deal wit tha attitude? If I wanted a broad I would get one—we both know what we doin is wrong."

THE WORLD HEADQUARTERS of the Web site streetthugz.com is a small, nondescript storefront next to a leather bar on Cleveland's West Side. The site's founder, Rick Dickson, invites me to watch one of its live Webcasts, which he says feature "the most masculine DL brothers in the world doing what they do best."

Rick opens the door holding a cigarette in one hand and a beer in the other. Inside, a group of young black men sit in a thick haze of cigarette smoke as the song "Bitch Better Have My Money" plays from a nearby stereo. By the far wall, two men type frantically on computer keyboards, communicating in some thirty chat room conversations at once. Near the street-front window, which is covered by a red sheet, there are three more muscular black men in their early twenties.

Rick sits down and lights another cigarette. A part-time comic who goes by the stage name Slick Rick, he has a shaved head, piercing green eyes, and a light-skinned face with a default setting on mean. Twice a week, Rick's thugs, as he calls them, perform a sex show for anyone who cares to log on. Although less than a year old, the site has developed a devoted following, thanks mostly to chat room word of mouth. "We're going to be the next Bill Gates of the Internet industry," he assures me. "We got black DL thugs getting it on, and that's what people want to see!"

One of the site's most popular stars is a tall, strikingly handsome twenty-three-year-old former Division 1 basketball player who goes by the name Jigga. When I first meet Jigga about ten minutes before the show, he's naked, stretching and doing push-ups in an adjacent room as he peppers me with questions about journalism and sportswriting. "I want to be a sportswriter," he says. "Either that or a lawyer. I *love* to argue."

Unlike some of the other streetthugz stars who dropped out of school and hustle for money, Jigga says he comes from a close middle-class family and always did well academically. Considering all that, I ask him how he came to find himself here. "It's some extra cash," he says. "But mostly it's 'cause I like the attention. What can I say? I'm vain." Jigga says he has sex with both men and women, but he doesn't label himself bisexual. "I'm just freaky," he says with a smile.

Like many guys on the DL, Jigga first connected to other DL men through phone personals lines, which still have certain advantages over Internet chat rooms. "You can tell a lot right away by a voice," he says later. "There are guys who naturally sound masculine, and then there's guys who are obviously trying to hide the fact that they're big girls."

At 10:07 p.m., seven minutes behind schedule, Rick announces, "It's showtime at the Apollo." He unfolds a burgundy carpet that serves as the stage, and Jigga and two thugs take their places. The phone won't stop ringing as viewers call to make requests ("Can I talk to Jigga when he's done?"), and Rick answers each call with an enthusiastic reference to the caller's location. "Hey, we got Detroit in the house! Say wuzzup to Detroit!"

The show temporarily goes "off air" when Chi, a thirty-two-year-old promoter for the site, trips over the MegaCam's power cord. While someone else plugs it back in, he takes a seat on the sidelines. Thin and deceptively strong, Chi looks younger than his age. He has a tattoo on his left arm, which he tells me is a reminder of his gang days. Back then, before he moved to Cleveland, his life was a disaster: he had three kids with three women and spent most of his twenties in jail for drug trafficking.

Chi says he doesn't deal drugs anymore—not since his mother, a heroin addict, died with a needle in her arm. Today he works at a fast-food joint in a shopping mall food court and is a talent scout for Rick, which means that if he spots a young black man with "the look" (tough, masculine, and preferably with a wild streak), he'll ask him if he'd like to take some pictures for money—or, better yet, act in one of the site's live sex shows. Chi has a fiancée he's been with for four years. She doesn't know that he's also casually dating a man.

When Rick has seen enough foreplay, he throws condoms at the boys. Rick has been making a big deal to me about how his site promotes safe sex, which he insists is a moral obligation at a time when so many young black men in America are dying of AIDS. But previous viewers of the show told me they didn't see condoms being used and that the site boasts of keeping everything "raw." I ask Rick about the discrepancy. "It's just an expression, man," he says, explaining that the sex is simulated.

The actors seem somewhat bored, but the point, I gather, is not what they do on camera, but how they look. And these guys look straight—in fact, they look as if they might rather be having sex with women. That, Rick knows, is the ultimate turn-on in much of the DL world, where the sexual icon is the tough, unemotional gangster thug.

"Do these guys ever kiss?" I ask Rick.

"Thugs don't really kiss," he explains. "Sometimes they stick their tongues in each other's mouths, but it's not really *kissing*. Gay people kiss. DL thugs don't kiss."

IN MAY 1986, Sandra Singleton McDonald showed up at the Centers for Disease Control in Atlanta, eager to begin her research into diseases affecting blacks in the South. "Well," a young research assistant there told her, "then you'll want to look into AIDS."

McDonald laughed. "Baby, you must have misunderstood my question," she said in her loving, motherly voice. "I'm talking about *African-American* diseases."

"Yes, I know," the man said. "Like I said, you'll want to look into AIDS."

McDonald did, and what she learned floored her. "This

wasn't just a gay white man's disease like we had all been told from the beginning," recalls McDonald, the founder of Outreach Inc., an Atlanta-based nonprofit organization providing services to those affected by AIDS and substance abuse in the city's black communities. "I went out and told the leaders in the black community that we needed to start dealing with this now, and they looked at me like I was crazy. People were outraged that I was even bringing this up. They said, 'Oh, be quiet, that's a *white* problem.' But why would we think that a sexually transmitted disease would stay within one racial group or within one geographic area? It made no sense. Looking back, the public health community made a lot of mistakes and gave out a lot of wrong information. Once we became aware of the impact of the disease, we did a lot of blaming and shaming so that we could feel okay and say, 'This isn't about us.'"

Five years later, that fiction ceased to be viable when Magic Johnson told a national television audience that he was HIV-positive. AIDS organizations were flooded with calls from panicked black men and women wanting to know more about the disease. Meanwhile, Magic dismissed the rumors that he'd slept with men during his NBA career, insisting he hadn't gotten infected through homosexual sex but rather through unprotected sex with a woman. Young black men on inner-city basketball courts weren't so sure. They wondered if maybe Magic had men on the side.

That it took Johnson's announcement to introduce the reality of AIDS to the black community goes to the depth of the denial around the disease. By 1991, 35,990 African-American men had been reported with AIDS (roughly half having contracted it through sexual intercourse), accounting for about a quarter of all AIDS cases in America. But although white gay men quickly mobilized around AIDS in the early 1980s, there was no similar movement among black men with AIDS, black leaders, politicians, clergy, or civil rights organizations.

"There was a real sense in black communities that you had to put your best face forward in order to prove that you deserve equal rights and equal status, and that face didn't include gays and IV drug users with AIDS," says Cathy Cohen, author of *The Boundaries of Blackness—AIDS and the Breakdown of Black Politics*. "It's been a very slow process for the black leadership in America to own up to this disease. Not acknowledge it in passing, but own it."

Black churches, which are the heart of many African-American communities, were particularly slow to respond to the crisis, and many still haven't, despite the disease's ravages within their parishes. In 1999, after female congregants of Cleveland's Antioch Baptist Church told their pastor that they were HIV-positive, the church started an AIDS ministry that has been applauded for its courage and effectiveness. Still, the black church—like many in white America—is careful not to condone homosexual behavior.

"Some gays want a flat-out, standing-on-the-tower affirmation from the church that the gay lifestyle, or the lifestyle of whoring around with men, is acceptable," says Kelvin Berry, the director of the Antioch program. "And that's not going to happen."

Combating AIDS in these communities also means confronting popular conspiracy theories that claim that HIV was created by the U.S. government to kill black people. One study by the Southern Christian Leadership Conference found that 54 percent of blacks thought HIV testing was a trick to infect them with AIDS. In the early 1990s, Spike Lee and the rapper Kool Moe Dee expressed concern that HIV was a part of a calculated campaign intended to rid the world of gay men and minorities, and as recently as 1999, Will Smith told *Vanity Fair* that "possibly AIDS was created as a result of biological-warfare testing."

Pernessa Seele, the founder and CEO of the Balm in Gilead, an international AIDS organization that works with black churches, explained, "For the most part, we don't want to get tested, and we don't want to get treatment, because we really believe that the system is designed to kill us." She continued, "And our history allows us to, or helps us, believe that. We have documented history where these kinds of diseases have been perpetuated on us. And that's why it's so important for the church to get involved. Black people trust the church. We don't trust health care. We don't trust doctors and nurses, but we trust the church. So when the church says, 'Get tested,' when the church says, 'Take your medicine,' people will do it."

Other black AIDS organizations are focused on prevention. In some cases, the strategies are straightforward: push condoms, distribute clean needles. But reaching men on the DL is difficult. James L. King, a publishing executive, spoke about his former DL life at a National Conference on African-Americans and AIDS. "I sleep with men, but I am not bisexual, and I am certainly not gay," King said. "I am not going to your clinics, I am not going to read your brochures, I am not going to get tested. I assure you that none of the brothers on the Down Low are paying the least bit of attention to what you say."

Earl Pike, executive director of the AIDS Task Force of Cleveland, agrees that many of the prevention messages aimed at black men have been unsuccessful. "Up to this point, we've failed to make a convincing case to young black men about why they should listen to us when we tell them to put on a condom, mostly because we've had the wrong people delivering the wrong kind of message," he says. "The usual prevention message for all these years can be interpreted as saying 'Gee, we're sorry about racism. We're sorry about homophobia in your homes and churches. We're sorry that urban schools are crappy. We're sorry that you can't find a good job. We're sorry about lack of literacy. We're sorry about all these things, but you really need to start using condoms, because if you don't, you could get infected tomorrow or next year or some point during the next decade, and if you do get infected, at some point you could get sick and die.'"

Many AIDS organizations now say that frank, sexy prevention messages that use the masculine imagery of hip-hop culture are the only way to reach men on the DL. In Saint Louis, for example, a $64,000 federal grant financed a billboard campaign—depicting two muscular, shirtless black men embracing—aimed at raising AIDS awareness. But Mayor Francis Slay called the billboards inappropriate and ordered them taken down.

• • •

"I NEED A beer," Chi says as we drive through downtown Cleveland on a Saturday night, looking for something to do. It's been three months since I last saw him at the streetthugz .com filming. As we stop at a red light, he turns to get a better look at a young Hispanic woman in the car next to us. "That girl is beautiful," he says. "But she needs to lose the car. What a shame—a beautiful woman driving a Neon!"

Chi loves women. He also likes men, although, like many guys on the DL, he doesn't verbalize his attraction to them, even when he's with like-minded people. When I ask him about this, he's stumped to explain why. "I don't know," he says. "Maybe it's because being black, you just learn to keep that to yourself." Anyway, he always had a girlfriend. "Guys were there for sex."

Unlike many other DL guys, who never tell anyone about their private lives, Chi opens up with little prompting. He says that he loves his fiancée but that he doesn't consider the sex he has with men to be cheating. "Guys are a totally different thing." Unbeknown to his fiancée, he has been casually dating his male roommate for several months. "I told her that he's gay and makes passes at me," he says, "but she doesn't know we have sex."

On some level, Chi says he feels bad about the deception. Right now, though, he isn't feeling guilty. His fiancée just called to tell him that she's going out tonight—and that he needs to come over to pick up their feisty one-year-old son. "She just wants to go out and shake her groove thing with her friends instead of taking care of him like she said she would," Chi says. "Man, she's selfish sometimes. I love her, but sometimes I hate her. You know what I'm saying?"

We pull up to Chi's apartment, where his fiancée and two of her friends are waiting for him in the driveway. Inside the apartment, they argue about whose turn it is to take care of their son while I sit in the dining room and watch him fearlessly attack the four house cats. In the dark living room, Chi's roommate, who is white, lounges on the couch in blue boxers, chain-smoking as he half watches television.

Chi's fiancée eventually leaves, after which Chi changes out of his work shirt and mixes a drink for the road. "We've been on shaky ground," Chi tells me, referring to his roommate. "He loves me, but I'm committed to someone else. I think he has problems dealing with that. Like I tell him, 'I care about you, but I can't be that guy you want.'" What Chi means, I think, is that he can't be *gay*.

Chi puts his son in the backseat of the car and we drive toward Dominos, a black gay bar where we're supposed to meet Jigga. Chi spends most of the ride complaining about his fiancée. His son finally starts crying and kicks the back of Chi's seat. "Yeah, defend yo mama!" Chi says, laughing.

They wait in the car as I walk into Dominos looking for Jigga. The long, rectangular bar is packed with regulars tonight, mostly middle-aged black men—some openly gay, others on the DL—and a few tough-looking younger guys. Jigga spots me first and waves me over to the bar. He tells me a lot has changed since the first time I met him. He's in law school now and has put aside the sportswriter idea. And though he is still on the DL (his coworkers and most of his straight friends don't know he likes guys), he has a serious boyfriend who is also on the DL.

Four months ago, having a serious boyfriend would have

been inconceivable to him. "I think I love this dude," he tells me as we walk to the car. "He's got a lot of attitude, but I kind of like that. We have fistfights all the time, and we don't stop until somebody has blood. Then we have sex." Jigga laughs as he opens the car door. "But I must really love him, because I never got in fistfights with any of my exes!"

I'm about to question his definition of love when Chi interjects. "I *still* need a beer," he says, pointing the way toward a nearby gas station. We pull into a tight parking spot, careful to avoid the young black man with a sideways baseball cap who leans into the car next to us, blocking Chi's passenger-side door. "Move your ass," Chi says, knocking the kid out of the way with the car door. The boy laughs it off, avoiding a possible confrontation.

"I think I hooked up with him," Jigga says, craning his neck from the backseat to get a better look at the kid. "Actually, nah, that's not him. Looks like him, though."

Recently, Jigga told his parents that he's interested in both guys and girls. "I was drunk when I told them," he says. "But I'm glad I did. They've been really cool about it." It takes me a few seconds to process the words. Really cool about it? In six months of talking to young black gay and DL men, I found that Jigga is one of the few who told his parents and the only one who reported unconditional acceptance. "I'm blessed," he says. "I realize that. Black parents don't accept their gay kids. Black culture doesn't accept gay people. Why do you think so many people are on the DL?"

Jigga is proof that being on the DL isn't necessarily a lifelong identity. He seems considerably more comfortable with his sexuality than he was the first time I met him, and I suspect that soon enough, he may be openly gay in all facets of his life without losing his much-coveted masculinity. I tell him what I'm thinking. "Who knows, man?" he says. "Two years ago, I wouldn't have believed that I'd be having sex with guys."

Chi opens the car door, cradling a six-pack of beer. "I love beer," he says, smiling. As we drive away, he checks out a young woman stepping out of a nearby Honda Civic. "Damn, that girl is *fine*!"

Get Out of My Closet!

Can you be white and on the Down Low?

IN 2003, I WROTE a story for *The New York Times Magazine* about black men who have sex with men but don't identify as gay—or even, in many cases, as bisexual. Instead, they adopted the label Down Low and formed a vibrant but secretive subculture of DL parties, DL Internet chat rooms (Thugs4Thugs, DLBrothas), and DL sex cruising areas (parks, bathhouses). Some of the Down Low guys I met were married but had covert sex with men, while others who claimed the label had sex only with men but considered themselves much too masculine to be *gay*. Most equated gayness with effeminacy—and, to a lesser extent, whiteness. From their perspective, to be an effeminate black man (a "punk," a "faggot") is to not really be a black man at all.

The Down Low was a relatively new response to a very

old behavior. Men of all races have long had secret sexual and romantic male relationships, complete with the usual accessories of a double life: lies, deception, and shame. But the Down Low was a uniquely African-American creation. If the closet is a stifling, lonely place for white guys who realize they're gay but aren't ready to admit it publicly, the Down Low is a V.I.P. party for "masculine" black men who will never admit to being homosexual—because they don't see themselves that way. And though men on the DL certainly have their share of shame, among themselves it masquerades as bravado and sexual freedom: They're the ultimate pimps and players, man enough to do their girlfriend on Thursday and do their best guy friend on Friday. And until recently, most black women didn't have a clue.

But then I wrote my story, J. L. King published his memoir (*On the Down Low*), Oprah turned King's book into a best seller, and *Law & Order* devoted an episode to the subculture. The Down Low quickly ceased to be, well, on the down low. And now, in a sure sign of the DL's cultural currency, white boys—apparently unsatisfied with having co-opted hip-hop—are claiming to be on the "Down Low," too.

I knew nothing of this until two months ago, when I met my first white guy who claimed to be "on the DL." He was twenty-four, tall, masculine, attractive, and said "bro" a lot. I met him at a New York City gay club (he had made the trek from Long Island), and I'm embarrassed to say that we sort of hit it off. On the first of a few dates, I asked him where he worked—and whether people there knew he was gay.

"Bro," he said, "I'm on the Down Low."

"Dude," I said, "you're white. You can't be on the Down Low!"

"Bro," he said, "all kinds of white people are saying they're on the Down Low now."

"That's ridiculous," I protested. "Why don't you just say you're in the closet?"

"Because the closet sounds stupid," he said.

I wasn't sure I believed him, so a few days later I went searching on Craigslist, and, sure enough, I found dozens of ads from white men claiming to be on the DL. In Boston, where I live, I saw an ad for a "slightly stocky, hairy, and kinky bi married white guy on the down low." In New York City, a man looking to "take care of a nice guy" who is "kool and looking for some fun" wrote that he needed someone discreet because he's on the Down Low. In the San Francisco Bay Area, a "white boy on the down low" posted that he was looking to "chill with the same."

(Interestingly, white guys also use the expression as an adjective—as in "I have a down-low place" to hook up, or "I need down-low head." By far the most common usage, though, is some variation of "We need to keep this on the Down Low," meaning that if you happen to bump into your hookup around town, you won't bear hug him and shriek, "Bro, last night was awesome!")

Keith Boykin, the author of *Beyond the Down Low: Sex, Lies, and Denial in Black America,* told me he isn't surprised that white men are co-opting the expression. "It's become trendy to be on the DL," he says. "It has always had an appeal because it refers less to sexuality than it does to masculinity. It's an alluring term for men who identify as butch or masculine. The closet has a certain shame and weakness attached to it. The Down Low sounds more powerful, more empowering. It also sounds like a secret group or club."

Maybe so, but white guys claiming to be on the DL is a little like two straight roommates pretending to be domestic partners so they can save on health insurance. While white guys want the perceived benefits of being on the Down Low (being seen as cool, tough, discreet, and masculine), they certainly don't want the unenviable choices facing many black men attracted to other men. For all their supposed freedom and masculine power and independence, black men on the Down Low are stuck: "come out" as anything other than heterosexual, and suddenly they're a double minority, likely to be ostracized by their friends, family, and church. (Black men still have less economic mobility than whites, making their community connections all the more critical.) Don't come out, and live a secretive, dishonest, compartmentalized—but in some ways, safer—life on the DL.

"We know there are black gay rappers, black gay athletes, but they're all on the DL," Rakeem, a black gay man from Atlanta, told me three years ago when I interviewed him for my Down Low story. "If you're white, you can come out as an openly gay skier or actor or whatever. It might hurt you some, but it's not like if you're black and gay, because then it's like you've let down the whole black community, black women, black history, black pride."

I called Rakeem recently to ask him what he thought about white guys claiming to be on the Down Low. "Are you really asking to me to explain the behavior of white dudes?" he asked, laughing. "I'm not even going to try." Next I called

Jimmy Hester, a white former music executive and an expert on the Down Low. "What haven't white people stolen from black culture?" he said. "But seriously, it's incredibly sad that there are still millions of men of every color living in the closet, or on the Down Low, or whatever they want to call it. I say, let's retire the Down Low. It should be extinct, like a dinosaur. People need to free themselves."

The Newlywed Gays!

Inside the lives of the young, gay, and married in Massachusetts.

LAST NOVEMBER IN BOSTON, Joshua Janson, a slender, boyish twenty-five-year-old, invited me to an impromptu gathering at the apartment he shares with Benjamin McGuire, his considerably more staid husband of the same age. It was a cozy, festive affair, complete with some twenty guests and a large sushi spread where one might have expected the chips and salsa to be.

"I beg of you—please eat a tuna roll!" Joshua barked, circulating around the spacious apartment in a blue blazer, slim-fitting corduroys, and a pair of royal blue house slippers with his initials. "The fish is not going to eat itself!"

Spotting me alone by a window seat decorated with Tibetan pillows, Joshua, who by that point had a few drinks in him, grabbed my arm and led me toward a handful of young men huddled around an antique Asian "lion's head" chair. "Are you single? Have you met *the gays*?" Joshua asked, depositing me among them before embarking on a halfhearted search for the couple's dog, Bernard, who, last I saw him, was eyeing an eel roll left carelessly at dog level. (At the other end of the living room, past a marble fireplace, the straights—in this case, young associates from the Boston law firm Benjamin had recently joined—were debating the best local restaurants.)

As the night went on, the gays and the straights—fueled, I suspect, by a shared appreciation for liquor—began to mingle, and before long the party coalesced into a boisterous celebration. Joshua looked delighted. And in a rare moment of repose, he sidled up to his taller, auburn-haired mate.

"Honey," Joshua said, "we may be married, but we still know how to have a good time, don't we?"

Benjamin, sharply outfitted in green corduroys and an argyle sweater over a striped dress shirt, smiled. "Josh is extremely social, and he keeps us busy all the time," he told me. "I think we may be proof that opposites do attract."

"If it were up to him," Joshua said, "we'd barely leave the house! We're actually a terrific team. He calms me down, and I get him out at night. I'll say, 'Honey, this is what we're doing. Now put this on.'"

"I think a lot of straight married couples start hibernating at home once they get married," Benjamin said.

Joshua kissed Benjamin lovingly on the cheek. "No, honey, that's just your parents."

"No, that's a lot of people," Benjamin insisted. "I think—"

"And I love your parents to death," Joshua interrupted, "but it scared me senseless to think that if anything were to happen, if you ended up in the hospital, *your mother* would get to make the decisions." Joshua looked at me with a devilish grin. "I dare her to try! I'd say, 'Woman, get away from my man!' I'm twenty-four, I've been with Ben for a long time, and we've been married for three years. I think I've earned the right—the responsibility—that comes with that."

Benjamin chuckled. "You're twenty-five."

"Oh, God," Joshua said, looking as if he'd just been sucker-punched. "I keep forgetting that I'm twenty-five. I think I'm probably having some issues around that number. Am I desperately trying to hold on to my youth?" He grabbed Ben's arm. "Honey, am I a gay cliché?"

Benjamin shook his head. "You can't be a gay cliché when you get married to a man at twenty-two."

JOSHUA AND BENJAMIN had each only recently come out of the closet—and certainly didn't have marriage in mind—when they became friends seven years ago during Benjamin's freshman year at Brown University.

Benjamin first realized his attraction to men his senior year of high school, but at Brown he tried to put it out of his mind, flirting with female students and playing beer pong with his straight friends. When that became too tedious to bear, he slowly began coming out to friends. Soon he was dating other male students.

Joshua, who was a freshman at Curry College, about forty miles north of Brown, had also recently acknowledged to himself that he was gay. But unlike Benjamin, he had long experimented sexually with boys. In high school, he was a gregarious presence who was beloved—and protected—by the school's popular girls. While many students had assumed he was gay, Joshua insists he was "the last to know" about his orientation, even though he spent an hour or two each night in AOL gay chat rooms and occasionally had furtive sex with members of his high school's football team.

Joshua broke through his denial before graduation, but he was in no mood to settle down with Benjamin when they fooled around during their freshman year of college. "I was, like, 'Well, that was fun, but I'm going to the gay club to find someone to do that with again!'" Joshua said.

"And I was, like, 'Well, we had sex, so I guess we're dating now,'" Benjamin recalled.

Before long, Benjamin's persistence paid off: Joshua moved into his dorm room. "It was all very lesbianish of us," Joshua told me. "It happened pretty quickly, and we did everything but rent a U-Haul."

(Joshua was referencing a long-standing joke—What does a lesbian bring on a second date? A U-Haul!—that is supposed to satirize the way some lesbians rush into cohabitation. The joke is sometimes paired with a second one about gay men rushing into bed: What does a gay man bring on a second date? *What* second date?)

Joshua and Benjamin were deeply committed to each

other by the time Benjamin graduated from Brown in May 2004, the same month that Massachusetts began issuing marriage licenses to gay and lesbian couples. Marrying "seemed obvious and inevitable," Benjamin told me, because he and Joshua had no doubt that they would spend the rest of their lives together. "It seemed silly," he said, "not to get married when we were fortunate enough to live in the only state where we could."

Both of their families were supportive. "My parents didn't have a problem with me marrying a guy," Benjamin said. "Their only question was 'Aren't you a little too young to be doing this?'"

"Oh, my parents said the same thing," Joshua huffed. "But you know what I told the parental units? I said, 'I don't want to hear it, because at our age you were married and pregnant with us.' That shut everyone right up, and soon enough our parents were fighting over who would get to pay for the wedding!"

IN 2004, WHEN I was twenty-eight, CNN asked me to gather together a group of my Boston friends in their twenties for a short segment about gay marriage. The network wanted to know what young gay men in Massachusetts thought about our newfound right.

For nearly an hour, seven of us—five working professionals in our twenties and two college undergraduates—sat in a coffee shop and talked theoretically about what a young gay marriage might entail. In the end, most of us agreed that we would like to be married—just not yet. We still had a lot of living and growing up to do. Though many of our heterosexual peers undoubtedly did as well, we were immune to the pressure some of them felt to marry. No one—not our friends, not our families, not the gay community—expected us to wed.

For the next few years, I didn't give young gay marriage much thought. While thousands of gay men and lesbians in their thirties, forties, or fifties married in Massachusetts, none of us at the table that night did, even as several of us inched into our thirties. I assumed that marriage—what the gay playwright Terrence McNally recently called "the final civil right; the right to love as anyone else loves"—was a right appreciated only in gay middle age.

But then something strange happened. During a ten-day span last August and September, two friends of mine—Brandon Andrew, who was then twenty-five, and Marc Brent, who was twenty-four—announced their respective engagements. Brandon called from his apartment in Boston to deliver the news. "You're not going to believe this!" he told me, pausing for dramatic effect. "I'm engaged!"

He was right. It was hard to believe. Not only was the prospect of two Brandons marrying each other surreal (his boyfriend, who was then twenty-four, is named Brandon Lehr), but Brandon A. didn't strike me as the marrying type. Not at this point in his life, anyway. An outgoing, freethinking, penny-saving art student in his last year at the School of the Museum of Fine Arts in Boston, he seemed far too busy DJ'ing at eclectic dance parties and breaking into construction sites for his installation art projects to worry about marriage.

Marc, a dental office manager who still lived at home with his parents in a Boston suburb, didn't call to tell me about his engagement. I learned about it instead on Facebook, when, with little fanfare, he changed the relationship status on his profile from "In a Relationship" to "Engaged." He had been dating his fiancé, Vassili Shields, who was then twenty-three, for a year.

"Are you actually engaged," I called to ask Marc, "or is that just your way of saying you *really* like Vassili?" He replied that he was, in fact, engaged. They planned to marry in a few months.

I didn't know what to make of these engagements—or of my subsequent discovery that more than seven hundred gay men age twenty-nine or younger had married in Massachusetts through June 2007. On the one hand, I wondered why these guys were marrying so young. What was the rush? It seemed to me that one of the few advantages of being young gay men—until gay marriage was legalized in Massachusetts, at least—was that we were constitutionally protected from ever appearing on *Divorce Court*.

But I could also relate to young gay men yearning for companionship and emotional security. Had gay marriage been an option when I was twenty-three and recently out of the closet, I might very well have proposed to my first gay love. Like many gay men my age and older, I grew up believing that gay men in a happy long-term relationship was an oxymoron. (I entered high school in 1989, before gay teenagers started taking their boyfriends to the prom.) If I was lucky enough to find love, I thought, I'd better hold on to it. And part of me tried, but a bigger part of me wanted to pitch a tent in my favorite gay bar.

I wasn't alone. Everywhere I looked, gay men in their twenties—or, if they hadn't come out until later, their thirties, forties, and fifties—seemed to be eschewing commitment in favor of the excitement promised by unabashedly sexualized urban gay communities. There was a reason, of course, why so many gay men my age and older seemed intent on living a protracted adolescence: we had been cheated of our *actual* adolescence. While most of our heterosexual peers had experienced socialization in their teens around courtship, dating, and sexuality, many of us had grown up closeted and fearful, "our most precious and tender feelings rarely validated or reflected back to us by our families and communities," says Alan Downs, the author of *The Velvet Rage: Overcoming the Pain of Growing Up Gay in a Straight Man's World.* When we did manage to express our sexuality, the experience often came booby-trapped with secrecy, manipulation, or debilitating shame.

No wonder, then, that in our twenties so many of us moved to big-city gay neighborhoods and aggressively went about trying to make up for lost time. And no wonder that some of us—myself included—sometimes went overboard.

"The expectation for many years was that if you did any dating in your twenties, they were essentially 'practice relationships' where you did what heterosexual kids get to do in junior high, high school, and college," says Jeffrey Chernin, a Los Angeles psychotherapist and the author of *Get Closer: A*

Gay Men's Guide to Intimacy and Relationships. "But for many gay men, your twenties were about meeting a lot of different people, going out to bars with your friends, and having a lot of sex. That has long been considered a rite of passage in the gay community."

But young gay men today are coming of age in a different time from the baby-boom generation of gays and lesbians who fashioned modern gay culture in this country—or even from me, a gay man in his early thirties. While being a gay teenager today can still be difficult and potentially dangerous (particularly for those who live in noncosmopolitan areas or are considered effeminate), gay teenagers are coming out earlier and are increasingly able to experience their gay adolescence. That, in turn, has made them more likely to feel *normal*. Many young gay men don't see themselves as all that different from their heterosexual peers, and many profess to want what they've long seen espoused by mainstream American culture: a long-term relationship and the chance to start a family.

"For many young gay men today, settling down in a relationship in their twenties—or getting married if they live in Massachusetts—will feel like a very natural thing to do," says Joe Kort, a psychotherapist and the author of *10 Smart Things Gay Men Can Do to Improve Their Lives*.

But with no model for how to build a young gay marriage, I was curious about how gay men in their twenties would choose to construct and maintain their unions. What would their marriages look like? And would the expectation of monogamy, a long-standing cornerstone of heterosexual marriage, be a requirement for their marriages, too?

To find out, I spent time over the next few months with a handful of young married and engaged gay couples—including Joshua and Benjamin. All were college-educated and white. (A 2008 study of gay and lesbian couples in Vermont, California, and Massachusetts—three states that offer some form of legal recognition for gay couples—found that "couples who choose to legalize their same-sex relationships . . . are overwhelmingly European American." They also tend to be college-educated.)

Although more than twice as many lesbians age twenty-nine and younger have married in Massachusetts than have gay men of that age, I chose to focus on the latter. "Women—straight or gay—tend to want to settle down years before men do," says Dan Savage, a sex advice columnist and the author of *The Commitment*, about the same-sex marriage debate and his decision to marry his long-term boyfriend. Gary Gates, a demographer who studies gay and lesbian population trends, adds that "lesbians are more likely to be partnered than gay men, tend to cohabitate quicker, and are more likely to have children—which is a motivator to get married."

But what, I wondered, was motivating the first generation of young gay married men?

ON A WEEKNIGHT in October, I sat down with Marc and Vassili at the restaurant where Vassili used to work as a waiter. He recently told his former coworkers about the engagement, and two waitresses kept coming over to our table to congratulate the couple. Tall and boyish, with big lips and soft features, Vassili beamed with joy and scooted his chair closer to his preppy, dark-haired fiancé.

They'd met a year before in this restaurant. "I thought he was cute the first night he came in with his friends," Vassili recalled, "but he had one of them climb through the window of the restaurant, instead of walking around and in the front door. So I yelled at him."

"And I'm ridiculously stubborn," Marc said, "so I wasn't about to apologize. For the next month, it was basically a series of dirty looks the times I went in there."

Vassili eventually broke down and asked Marc on a date to the aquarium. Other dates followed, and nearly a year later, while hanging out at Fritz, a gay sports bar, they decided to become engaged. As Vassili explained it, they considered themselves best friends and planned to be together forever. "So why not get married?" he said. "I always knew I wanted to spend my life with one person. And I know I've found him." Besides, they both want to be young dads. They plan to adopt before they turn thirty. (Most of the couples I spent time with for this story said they eventually want children.)

There was no formal exchange of rings to commemorate the engagement, no romantic dinner followed by either of them on bended knee. They also didn't plan on having a wedding ceremony. When I asked them why, they insisted that such formalities were unnecessary. "We don't think there is any set way we have to do this," Vassili told me. "We're not following anyone's model for how an engagement or marriage should go."

They said that philosophy also applied to when they would break the news of their engagement to their families. Vassili said he wasn't sure how his parents would react. "They know that Marc is my boyfriend, but my gayness is not something we ever really talk about," he told me. "My guess is my parents would want to be at any ceremony we have, but I don't know."

Marc said he had no doubt that his own parents would be supportive. "My mom knows and loves Vassili, and one time she asked, 'Why don't you guys just get married?'" he said. "And I was, like, 'Well, maybe we will!' But sometimes I wonder if they would be as excited, or as supportive, about me marrying a guy as they would be if I was marrying a girl. But I'm going to tell my parents soon. I just want to have everything planned out first."

By that, Marc meant that he wanted to know the specifics of when he and Vassili would move in together before announcing to his family that they were going to marry. Both men were living at home with their parents (Vassili had recently moved back to save money).

I asked Marc and Vassili if it was wise for any couple to become engaged before testing their domestic compatibility. Why not live together for a year? The couple deflected the question with the *you-must-not-really-understand-the-power-of-our-love* look common to so many lovesick young couples. "We just know we'll be fine," Vassili told me, rubbing Marc's back. "We love each other, and that's all that matters."

"We know we're compatible," Marc said. "We've thought a lot about household roles. I'm going to clean, and Vassili is going to cook."

"I like doing laundry and ironing," Vassili told me. "He likes yardwork."

"I don't think either one of us is really going to be the *wife,* per se," Marc said.

Still, they insisted they would be "traditional" in one important way: they vowed to be monogamous. "I know that some gay couples who've been together awhile open up their relationships," Marc said, "but we're not going to do that. I mean, we wouldn't be getting married if we didn't plan on being monogamous. To me, that's a fundamental and important part of marriage."

It is for many young gay couples. Frederick Hertz, an attorney and mediator who cowrote the book *A Legal Guide for Lesbian and Gay Couples* and who has helped gay couples of all ages negotiate prenuptial agreements, told me that young gay men get the most impassioned when talk turns to monogamy. "A very common thing I hear them say in my office is 'If he has an affair, he's not getting any alimony!'" Hertz said. "That's just not something I hear among older gay men, who often make a distinction between emotional fidelity and sexual fidelity. There's an emerging rhetoric around monogamy among young gay couples. In that way, they're a lot more like married heterosexual couples than they are like older gay couples."

I SPENT THE following day with the Brandons. They'd met a year before on MySpace, although this was a source of some embarrassment for the couple, who instead told friends they'd met "at a concert." "I saw his MySpace profile and sort of e-mailed him as a joke," Brandon A. told me inside the sun-filled Boston apartment he shares with his fiancé and another roommate. "I was, like, 'We're both named Brandon. We're both skinny white boys from California. We're both gay. We both listen to indie rock. You must be my Doppelgänger. We have to hang out.'"

Like Marc and Vassili, the Brandons said they planned to pick and choose what elements of "traditional heteronormative married culture," as Brandon A. put it, to appropriate. (He loves using words like "heteronormative.") But the Brandons had different ideas from Marc and Vassili about what appealed to them about "traditional" marriage.

For one thing, the Brandons had eagerly told their families about the engagement and planned to incorporate them into their married lives. Their parents responded, in turn, with great enthusiasm. Brandon A.'s mother proudly accompanied her son and his fiancé to a monthly "queer" night at a Boston club (I was there, too, and couldn't quite get over the sight of mother and son on the dance floor), while Brandon L.'s mom, whom I met briefly at the couple's apartment, demanded to know the couple's "song."

"This is so weird," Brandon A. told me at the time. "I feel like I'm doing girl talk with my future mother-in-law!"

The young men's mothers were delighted to learn the details of how Brandon L., a Ph.D. candidate at MIT, had proposed—after a romantic dinner, on bended knee, by a roaring fire, their "song" ("This Modern Love," covered by Final Fantasy) playing on the stereo.

"I even got him a ring," Brandon L. told me.

"It was made of titanium," Brandon A. said, laughing. "He knew I would probably break or lose anything else."

The Brandons agreed that they would wait a year or two before marrying; they wanted to finish school before having a formal wedding ceremony. Unlike Marc and Vassili, the Brandons said a wedding ceremony was important—not as a "political statement" or "to get approval from anyone" but as a way to communicate their love to each other.

"Ever since I was nineteen or twenty, I knew that I would want to give myself over to one person in a formal way," said Brandon A., who had been in two previous gay relationships lasting more than a year before meeting Brandon L. "And it didn't even really matter to me if the politics of the world were going to bend in my favor so that my marriage was considered legal. Legal or not, I was going to have a commitment ceremony in front of the people who matter to me. I've always been oddly traditional about that."

But the Brandons suspected they were untraditional when it came to their thinking about monogamy. As they saw it, one enduring lesson of heterosexual marriage is that lifelong monogamy is unrealistic for most people—especially men. "Most straight people like to talk a great game about monogamy," Brandon A. said. "But what are they actually doing? Many of them have affairs at some point or break up because they want to sleep with somebody else. We're two guys, we're in our twenties, we haven't been sexual with that many people, and to pretend like we're never going to want to experience sex with another person until the day we die doesn't make sense to us. We're open to exploring our sexuality together in a way that makes us both comfortable."

• • •

NEGOTIATING QUESTIONS SURROUNDING monogamy was a critical issue for most of the young married and engaged couples I spent time with. But so, too, was the larger question of how they would fashion their social lives.

Several couples lamented the fact that they had never met another young gay married couple. This left them without a model to help them shape or understand their own relationship, and it seemingly left them without anyone who could relate to their unique circumstance.

"I sort of feel like we're on this island out here by ourselves," said Anthony Levin, a twenty-six-year-old account executive in Boston who met his husband, twenty-three-year-old Daniel Levin, while both were undergraduates at the University of Minnesota. (They legally married in August 2006 after moving to Boston, where Daniel was starting law school; Anthony took Daniel's last name. They were the only couple I spoke with in which one man took the other's name.) "That's probably the biggest difference between us and straight married couples," he continued. "They see other married people like them everywhere. We don't. It would be great to have young gay married couples who we could hang out with."

"I actually met one the other day," Daniel, who sat by Anthony on the couch in their apartment in Brookline, said matter-of-factly.

"You did?" Anthony said, nearly spilling his glass of wine. "Did you get their number?"

Daniel hadn't. This momentarily crushed Anthony, who

seemed to yearn to interact with other gay people—single or married—more than Daniel did. (Anthony had joined Boston's gay flag-football league the previous fall, partly in an effort to meet other gay people.)

Other couples, like Joshua and Benjamin, had an abundance of gay friends of all ages and clearly reveled in having their cake (marriage) and eating it too (a social life that rivaled that of many of their young single gay friends). It was hard to keep track of the many social engagements the couple invited me to. There was a fancy Oscar party. There were many dinner parties, including one attended by their friend David Cicilline, the openly gay mayor of Providence.

And there were nights out at gay bars. "No one assumes we're married when we're out at a club with our friends," Joshua said. "Maybe it's because I look like I'm twelve, but people see my wedding ring and are, like, 'What? Is that a *fashion statement*?' They just hit on us anyway, which, really, is kind of fun. I'll flirt right back, and I'll say to Ben, 'Oh, look at the butt on that one!'"

For Joshua and Benjamin (and for several of the couples I spent time with), there is no use pretending they aren't attracted to other people. "I think it's healthy that we don't have to lie about that like so many straight couples do," Joshua said. "We're also two gay guys in the couple, so we're attracted to the same gender. We can both appreciate a hot guy walking down the street."

But not all of the couples I spoke with were so open about men they noticed. "Pointing out a cute guy wouldn't fly with us," Anthony Levin said. Fortunately for him, Daniel has never had much of a wandering eye. "Flirting with guys, or trying to get attention from random guys, has honestly *never* appealed to me," Daniel told me. "I don't know why, but it's just not the way I'm built. It came as no surprise to people who knew me well that I would be the type to settle down in a relationship. And I've never been attracted to some of the drama that I've seen in the gay community."

WHEN I FIRST learned that some young gay men were marrying in Massachusetts, I wondered if their marriages might be a repudiation of the gay world fashioned by previous generations of men—men who had reacted to oppression and homophobia in the 1970s and '80s by rejecting heterosexual norms and "values," particularly around sex and relationships. Many older gay men would have scoffed at the idea of marrying and having kids. To many of them, their "family" was their network of close gay friends.

But most of the young married men I spent time with insisted that their marriages weren't a "reaction" to anything. They valued their connection to modern gay culture, and they weren't interested in choosing between being a married man and a young gay man. They could be both, and they could make it work.

Still, it wasn't always easy. "Joshua and I have had to do a lot of work around learning to communicate to each other what's okay and what makes each of us uncomfortable," Benjamin told me, adding that they have attended a couples' counselor. "I think that maybe we assumed that because we're two men, we would think the same way about things or know where the other was coming from. But the way we communicate is so different, so that's a challenge."

Jeffrey Chernin, the psychotherapist who works with both gay and straight couples, told me that gay couples tend to open up in therapy with less prompting. "Many of them are already used to talking honestly and openly about many issues," he said, "because there is no assumed model for how their marriage should function. Everything is on the table to be negotiated. Nothing is taken for granted. Everything is talked about—from monogamy to power dynamics to domestic responsibilities."

Most of the couples insisted they shared those responsibilities in "an egalitarian way." Though Joshua occasionally referred to himself as a "gay housewife," other young gay married men bristled at the notion that they would fashion their domestic lives around heterosexual stereotypes.

"It never ceases to amaze me how many people will say to us, 'So who's the woman and who's the man in your marriage?'" says Jason Shumaker, who lives in a Boston suburb with his husband, Paul McLoughlin II. They met eight years ago when they were twenty-five, and they legally married at twenty-nine (registering to wed on the first day gay couples could do so in Massachusetts). "I just think that's the dumbest question ever," he added. "Yes, we're married, but we're also two guys, so neither one of us has to be 'the woman.'" (And "with no ovaries drying up," as Paul put it, they don't need to rush into having children. They plan to adopt in the next five years, once Paul finishes his Ph.D. in higher education administration at Boston College.)

During a break from opening the door to trick-or-treat-ers at their home last Halloween, Jason and Paul—who wore matching lizard outfits—told me about the T-shirts they'd donned at the end of their reception. The front of Paul's shirt read I AM THE HUSBAND, while the back read I AM THE WIFE. (Jason's shirt had the opposite emblazoned on each side.) "It was fun to make a little bit of a social statement and poke fun at the idea that we would fit neatly into these heterosexual roles," Jason said.

AFTER A FEW months of barely hearing from Marc and Vassili, I was starting to worry: could they be having premarriage trouble? (I suspected the Brandons were fine. They regularly posted pictures of themselves together on their Facebook profiles and had even started a Facebook group, appropriately called "The Brandons.")

When I finally did hear from Marc and Vassili in February, they had good news: they had filled out the requisite forms at City Hall and were just waiting the three state-mandated days before collecting their marriage license. In the meantime, they were celebrating Valentine's Day by luxuriating for a night at a Boston hotel. They invited me to drop by.

When I did, I saw dozens of rose petals in the bathtub. Apparently, while they had been enjoying hourlong massages and a full-course meal, Vassili had arranged to have the hotel staff festoon the room with the petals.

"What are those doing in the bathtub?" I asked the couple.

"He moved them there," Vassili told me, rolling his eyes. "He's not very romantic, and he got embarrassed that you would see them."

"Yeah, yeah, I'm the bad guy," Marc said with a laugh.

A few minutes later, I asked the couple how their parents had reacted to the news that they would soon be married. Silence filled the room. "You *still* haven't told your parents?"

They offered many justifications, everything from "we haven't found an apartment yet" to "marriages become a dog-and-pony show when parents and families get involved." But in Marc's case, I really couldn't understand what the problem was. He had told me many times that his parents loved Vassili and that they would be supportive of the marriage. What was going on?

"I know my parents will be fine with it, but I want to do this myself," Marc told me. "If I tell my parents, they'll just want to get involved, and that will annoy me. I hate when people try to tell me how I should do something."

Vassili nodded and repeated something I had heard the couple tell me many times. "There's nothing conventional about gay marriage," he said, "so I don't feel like we need to do this in a certain accepted way."

Marc, who had been leaning back on a sofa, suddenly sat up in protest. "Hold on," he said. "I think it's conventional. Why do you say it's not conventional?"

"I mean, there are more complications because we're gay," Vassili told him. "But the most important thing is that we love each other. We don't need to have a big fancy wedding to prove anything to anyone."

"I hear you," Marc said, "but I think we're kidding ourselves if we say that we absolutely wouldn't want a ceremony where our families and friends were there and totally on board. I'm not going to lie. It would be nice."

I had never heard Marc talk this way. Neither, apparently, had Vassili, who seemed perplexed by the sudden change to the couple's longtime narrative, which they had used to justify not telling their parents and not having a wedding ceremony. "You would hate that," Vassili insisted. "Wouldn't you? You wouldn't get up in front of everyone and give vows."

"Maybe," Marc said, "but it would still be nice to have the option. And I'd still like to have a *party*. It would be cool to get the coffee machine, the blender, all the stuff that straight couples get when they start their marriages."

IN 2004, MTV broadcast a documentary chronicling the lives of two gay couples—one male, one female—as they prepared to marry in Massachusetts. The male couple, Aaron Pike Shainwald and Stephen Schonberg, were both twenty-two when America watched them become the forty-fourth same-sex couple to wed in the state.

Aaron and Stephen had met two years before at Axis, a Boston nightclub (since closed) with a popular weekly gay night. Their first date had lasted "three days," Aaron told me, and nine months later they moved in together. They were both still college students at the time (Aaron at Brandeis, Stephen at Boston University), but as their relationship deepened, they were equally eager to formalize it. "We both wanted to get married and commit our lives to each other," Aaron said.

A year and a half into the marriage, though, Aaron said they started growing apart. They went to couples' therapy for a year, but soon Stephen asked for a divorce. "We really, really worked hard to save the marriage," Aaron told me, "but he decided to move on. And it's hard not to feel like a complete failure sometimes. People who saw the show still stop me on the street and ask how the marriage is going. Most of the time I just lie and say: 'Great! Wonderful!' Let me tell you, being twenty-six and gay and already divorced is *soooo* much fun."

I met up with Aaron at Joshua and Benjamin's house party in November. He arrived with his new boyfriend, an affable fifty-year-old ("I'm done with the young ones!" Aaron joked) who also happened to be divorced. "But I suppose I went the more conventional route," Aaron's boyfriend told me. "I was married to a woman." (As he spoke, I couldn't help thinking of what Jason Stuart, a gay comic, once said: "Come on, straight people . . . if you let us marry each other, we will stop marrying you!")

Aaron lamented that he didn't know any other young gay divorced men, so he seemed delighted when I called a few months later to tell him about George—twenty-six, gay, and recently divorced from his husband. (He asked that his first and last name not be used to protect his privacy; George is his middle name.) I suggested to George that he, Aaron, and I meet to talk.

At a Boston coffee shop, Aaron and George bonded over

their unique experience—"I thought I was the only one." "Me too!"—and apologized for having a negative impact on Massachusetts' divorce rate, which is one of the lowest in the nation. (The state doesn't yet have divorce statistics for gay and lesbian couples, though I'm not sure the numbers would tell us much. Many of the first wave of same-sex marriages involved couples who had been together for ten, twenty, or even thirty years, presumably making them less likely to divorce than heterosexual couples who hadn't been together as long before marrying.)

"The ironic thing is that I really don't believe in divorce," George told us at the coffee shop. Tall and handsome, with dark hair and angular features, he sat by a corner window and was still dressed in his work clothes—black dress pants and a dark blue vest over a light blue dress shirt. "I was raised Catholic, went to Catholic school, and my parents stuck it out. I tried my best to make my marriage work, but we both decided it couldn't be saved."

George was still struggling to understand where his marriage had gone wrong. He had met his ex four years before, when George was twenty-two and living what he called "a carefree postcollege life" in northern California. George said he hadn't been looking for a serious relationship, but he fell in love with his ex (who was several years older) after meeting him through mutual friends.

"At the time I was thinking, Wow, I really wish I had met you eight years from now," George recalled. "But I met him when I met him, and I wanted to be with him. I knew I had a lot of growing up to do if I wanted to make the relationship work, and I did. I grew up pretty fast."

The couple registered as domestic partners in California (partly for the health insurance) and then, a year later, moved to Massachusetts, where they were married in 2006 in front of a couple hundred people in a church in the suburb where George was raised. Most of the attendees were family members and friends—some of his ex's extended family, George said, weren't supportive of the marriage.

"And in a million other ways we were constantly reminded that our relationship wasn't equal to a straight relationship, even though we were legally married," George told me. "Whether it was doing our federal taxes or hearing that most states weren't going to recognize our marriage or just not being able to walk down the street and hold hands without getting snickers or comments. Like many gay couples, I think we brought unresolved shame and deep-rooted feelings of unworthiness into the relationship. You don't even realize it's there sometimes, but it definitely affected us."

Both George and Aaron said they'd also felt an added pressure in their marriages to "prove to the world," as George put it, that gay relationships can last. "My ex and I really wanted to be an example to our families and straight friends that a gay marriage can work," he said.

Dan Savage, the sex advice columnist, told me he worried that some young gay men in Massachusetts might rush into marriage as a way to have their relationships validated by their families. "Once, our relationships were only respected if we had remained together for a long, long time," Savage said. "Only longevity earned us some modicum of respect. Straight couples could always rush that validity by getting married. Now I just worry that some gay kids, desperate to have their gay love taken seriously, will wield their new marriage licenses and say: 'See how *real* our love is? We've only been together five months, but we're already married. You better respect us now!'"

George said he hadn't been looking for respect when he told his grandfather about his marriage. "When I first got engaged, everyone told me that he would 'just die' if I told him about it," George said. "But one day I walked over to his house and said, 'Listen, I'm getting married to a man that I love, and it's going to be your choice if you're going to be in our lives. I'm not going to make that choice for you.' He sat back in his chair and said, 'Well, I don't really understand, but do you love him?' I told him I did. To that he said, 'Well, I know love, so I want to meet him and learn all about you guys.' I still can't bring myself to tell him about the divorce."

The day we met at the coffee shop was a particularly trying one for George. Hours earlier, he had signed papers giving his soon-to-be-ex-husband sole ownership of the house they had owned. "In return," he said, "I got some debt, a car, and a painting."

"Wow, and all I lost in my divorce was my cat," Aaron said. "We hardly had anything, so it wasn't difficult to decide who got what. The cat's living with my ex on Long Island now."

IT WAS A blustery weekday morning in February when I tagged along with Marc and Vassili to pick up their marriage license at City Hall. Marc pulled the couple's

Honda Accord to a stop at a red light in the city's South End neighborhood. Vassili sat in the passenger seat, sipping an iced coffee.

"We really wanted a BMW," Marc explained, but they had settled on the Honda as an exercise in premarriage fiscal responsibility. "It seemed like the right thing to do."

"We did a budget the other day," Vassili said. "That was really scary."

"We definitely need to reel in our spending," Marc told me. "We need to stop going out so often. I mean, we're getting married today!"

After parking, we trudged through the snow toward City Hall, a mammoth nine-level concrete bunker. Marc and Vassili often dress alike, and that morning was no different. Each wore stylish jeans, black dress shoes, and a peacoat (Marc's was brown; Vassili's black) over a T-shirt. "We're the same height and have kind of a similar style," Marc explained as we passed through the building's metal detector, "so we're always wearing each other's clothes."

On our escalator ride downstairs to the marriage license office, Vassili leaned in to Marc and kissed him on the lips. Marc didn't fight it, but he smiled awkwardly when it was over. "Marc's actually gotten a lot better about not freaking out over public displays of affection," Vassili told me. "The first fight we ever had was because I leaned up against him a little too close at Starbucks!"

"Vassili is just so comfortable with himself, much more so than I am or probably ever will be," Marc said. "He's really comfortable in his skin. That's so endearing about him. It's probably one of the reasons I love him so much."

In the basement, Marc and Vassili approached the marriage license counter.

"I'll be right with you," the clerk told the couple. "You picking up something?"

"Our marriage license," Vassili said proudly.

"Gays here!" Marc quipped. The clerk smiled, and Marc turned to me. "This is so weird," he whispered. "We're actually doing this. It's starting to hit me that we're actually getting married."

The clerk eventually brought Marc and Vassili a copy of the marriage license application they had filled out on their last trip here. Vassili beamed as he looked over the form, which had a column for "Party A" (Vassili) and "Party B" (Marc). (Before gay marriage was legalized in the state, the form listed "Bride" and "Groom.")

Feigning outrage, Marc grabbed the form from Vassili's hand. "Hey, why are you Party A?" he demanded to know.

"Because I'm the man, of course," Vassili said with a laugh.

"We decided to combine our last names," Marc explained, pointing to his typed name on the form: Marc Harrington Brent-Shields. "We thought about Shields-Brent, but that didn't sound right."

"Shields-Brent sounds like a verb," Vassili said. "It sounds like I'm trying to shield Brent from something."

When the clerk finished typing up the marriage license, she walked back to the counter. "Are you going upstairs?" she asked the couple.

"What's upstairs?" Marc asked.

"The city clerk. She can marry you."

"Does she like gay people?" Marc said.

"She loves gay people," the woman assured them. She looked at the document in her hand.

"Is that our marriage license?" Vassili asked excitedly.

"Yes, it is. Do you want it?" She started to hand it to him and then stopped, toying with him. "Are you sure?"

"Yes, please!" he said.

"Wait!" Marc said dramatically. "I think I'm having second thoughts."

The woman froze.

"He's kidding," Vassili said.

"Totally kidding!" Marc assured her.

The woman laughed, handed Vassili the license, and wished the couple well. As we walked away from the counter, Marc, who had tried to mask his nervousness with humor, looked as if he might pass out. "I need to go to the bathroom," he said. "I'm feeling light-headed. Don't get me wrong—this is very cool. But it's actually happening. I'm actually getting married—to a man!"

We searched for the men's room while Vassili accosted random people in the hallway and shared the news. "We're married! We just got our license!" he said breathlessly.

While Marc splashed water on his face in the bathroom, Vassili told me that he hoped to persuade Marc to go upstairs and make it official. "That lady really wanted us to go upstairs," he said. "I kind of want to make Marc do it. I mean, we're already here!"

But Marc was adamant that he wanted to wait. "I just

want to be sure we find the right person to marry us," he said once he was out of the bathroom. "I don't want to rush into this."

What Marc wanted instead was something to eat, and he was relieved when we came upon a Girl Scout selling cookies near the building's exit. He and Vassili bought five boxes and began devouring the cookies as we walked back to their car.

"You know what I figure?" Marc told me. "I figure that now that I'm practically married, I can start letting myself go. Isn't that, like, the main advantage of marriage? I'm definitely not going to the gym anymore!" He looked at Vassili and laughed. "Will you still love me if I'm fat?"

Regular Guys

They follow sports, wear flannel shirts, smoke, drink, belch, and make gay jokes. Oh, one other thing. They're gay.

MIKE SCHAEFER IS HAVING problems *getting some.* He admits this early during a night baseball game at Pacific Bell Park in San Francisco, right about the time Barry Bonds takes a called third strike on the inside corner. Bonds looks aghast. Schaefer, seated in the right-field bleachers and holding a Coke and two hot dogs, says he wouldn't mind having a date sometime this decade. Preferably with a regular guy.

Schaefer likes regular guys. He likes them so much, in fact, that he started a group just for them. He named it and he built it, not entirely sure that anyone would come. He put an ad in a local paper. He rented out a room to hold meetings. And, lo and behold, they came! Regular guys from the city and the suburbs, all hoping they weren't the only regular guys in the Bay Area. They couldn't be, could they?

His mind wandering from the baseball game before him, Schaefer tells me what his dream regular guy would look like. First and foremost, he would be both tall and built. Schaeffer wants natural, God-given mass, the kind that gets produced with some regularity on farms in Nebraska. Schaefer wants big arms, big shoulders, big hands (with big, veiny fingers), big thighs, a big neck, and big feet. And on all of these things, he wants lots of hair.

When this ideal regular guy came upon a game of baseball or football, he would know exactly what to say and do. If the ball were thrown toward him, he would not run away shrieking. He would wait for it knowingly, and then he would catch it with jockish, perfunctory ease. He would play with the ball for a moment, and when he was good and ready, he would throw it back, high into the air, and it would land pretty much where it was supposed to land. This is called "throwing the ball like a man," as opposed to "throwing the ball like a fag." "Not that there's anything *wrong* with that," Schaefer jokes.

Schaefer can joke about that, because he's a fag, too. And still, in this city that's never short on fags, Schaefer—forty-five and counting—is having problems finding one who would like to settle down with him and raise some regular kids. This could have something to do with the fact that Schaefer is (in his own words) not a beautiful man. He is short and pudgy and has an oddly shaped head. Whereas most human heads are squares or rectangles, Schaefer's is wider at the cheeks than it is at both the crown and the jaw. It is also unusually long, with most of the surface space concentrated between the eyes and the chin. On top of it all is a tightly trimmed crew cut.

On this night, Schaefer wears tight jeans, an orange T-shirt, and a black-and-orange Giants jacket. He doesn't talk much, except to make light of his dating woes and to confess that he prefers going to Oakland Athletics games, because their roster is packed with big, beefy guys with goatees.

Mostly, though, Schaefer sits quietly in his seat. He has been shy for as long as he can remember. Back in grade school, he was a nerd who hung out with other nerds in a social group on the very low end of the adolescent pecking order. This trend continued in high school and even into college at Fordham, but things changed for the better when Schaefer worked up the nerve to walk into the campus radio station his junior year. His radio gig got him talking, which brought him out of his shell, which allowed his long-dormant sense of humor to make an appearance.

Schaefer likes to be funny. He also likes to say things that he knows might get him into a whole heap of trouble. Like the time he said this, referring to what he calls gay culture's "masculinity paradox": "It's funny, because gay culture likes to ridicule guys who are into traditionally 'masculine' things, but at the same time, masculine guys are everyone's jerk-off fantasy," he tells me. "It's like we have a whole gay culture that says, 'Nudge-nudge, wink-wink, we all know we really want to have sex with masculine guys, but we have to ridicule them, too, because everyone knows they can't dress, and those are the guys who beat us up and made fun of us in high school.' But you know what? In the twenty-two years I've been reading personal ads, I've never once read one that says, 'Gay White Male seeks bitchy queen for long-term relationship.'"

ON A WARM, breezy, blue-sky day in late May, thirty Regular Guys—all sporting shorts and T-shirts—are warming up for a game of softball in Golden Gate Park. As they take batting practice and shag fly balls, it quickly becomes clear that few of these men (most are in their twenties, thirties, and forties) were members of their high school's jock elite. In fact, when Chris Sorensen, the group's director of sports activities (and master barbecuer), asks the men how many played baseball in high school, not a single hand goes up.

Later, while tending to the barbecue during a Regular Guys' picnic, Sorensen explains the kinds of athletes you'll find in this group for self-identified masculine gay men: "A lot of them were picked on in high school, and now that they are older and successful and go to the gym to get all buff, they think they're *athletes*. But if you throw them a real fastball, they pee themselves. So we play softball. It's less scary."

Sorensen is twenty-seven and, arguably, the most regular of the Regular Guys. He is overweight. He smokes. He drinks beer. He eats big slabs of beef and makes beef/sausage jokes. When he is tired or bored or feeling silly, he rolls around in the grass like a dog and plays dead. When he barbecues, he holds the slab of beef in one hand and a bottle of tequila in the other. He calls people "pussies." He reads sports magazines and says things like "Yeah, I read *ESPN* magazine. *Sports Illustrated*'s for *fags*."

Sorensen joined Regular Guys a year ago and has quickly improved the group's athletic activities. He organizes monthly football games, softball games, and trips to the batting cages. Today, he's firmly in charge of the softball game, barking out instructions and threatening to castrate those who goof off.

"Come on, *ladies*," he says. "Let's get with it!"

Eric Sweigard, a thirty-four-year-old Catholic boy from Nebraska who is often mistaken for a New York City Jew ("It's my wonderful attitude," he suspects), steps up to the plate. Sweigard may be short (five-foot-five), but what he lacks in size he makes up for in ego. In high school, when, he says, he wasn't shoplifting for school supplies or setting things on fire, he played on the wrestling and golf teams. He always knew he was different ("I was smarter and funnier than the other guys, so I guess that should have been a *clue*," he says), but it wasn't until much later that it dawned on him that he might be gay.

Sweigard waves the bat back and forth, waiting for Sorensen to lob a pitch. Just as Sorensen starts his motion, a Regular Guy in the outfield yells, "Hit it, munchkin!" to which Sweigard responds by waving the bat toward him and yelling "You fuck! You little *bitch*!"

Sorensen finds the exchange so funny that he stops mid-motion. "Throw the ball, jerky," Sweigard yells. Laughing, Sorensen lobs a pitch. Sweigard takes a mighty rip, nailing the ball over the head of the smack-talker in the outfield. "Yeah, chase it you *fuck*! Run!"

Sorensen lobs another pitch, which Sweigard smacks about a foot away from Sorensen's head. "Yeah, you laughing now, baby?" Sweigard says.

"You did *not* just call me baby," Sorensen says in mock exasperation.

"Yes I did, *sweetie,*" Sweigard says. "You got a problem with that?"

Grinning, Sorensen dramatically throws his glove on the ground and begins a full-frontal assault. Sweigard, the high school wrestler, stands his ground. Sorensen bowls into him. They fall over. They roll around. They curse. The bigger Sorensen pins Sweigard by the legs, causing Sweigard's butt to see the light of day.

Mark Terrell, a thirty-four-year-old Regular Guy from Oakland, points excitedly toward Sweigard's butt: "Hold him there and we'll all take turns!"

1) Which would you rather spend a Saturday afternoon doing?
   a) Catching the White Sale at Macy's.
   b) Catching the playoffs of any sport.
2) You meet a cute guy at a party. You start the conversation talking about . . .
   a) Your favorite quiche recipe.
   b) Why the 49ers sucked this year.

—Two questions from the Regular Guys' Web site, www.RegularGuys.org

If you answered (b) to both of the above questions, it is possible that you could be Regular Guy material. This is exciting news. Regular Guys get to go on hikes, play football, go whitewater rafting, ski in Tahoe, cruise the delta on houseboats, attend rodeos, watch movies, sample local brewpubs, and even take in a play or museum. ("We aren't *total* barbarians," Schaefer insists.)

Regular Guys also attend a monthly social meeting, where they introduce new members and listen to guest speakers. (Former ones have included Gay Games athletes, a gay Air Force officer, a representative from the StopAIDS project, and a leader of the Log Cabin Republicans, a gay Republican political group.)

Schaefer says there are more than a hundred dues-paying members of Regular Guys in the Bay Area, although only about forty are what he calls "regulars," which means they actually show up to events. Most members are openly gay, although many didn't come out until their late twenties or even later. Several are fathers. Some, like Sweigard and Sorensen, act straighter than most straight guys. Others are painfully shy and joined the group, jokes one Regular Guy, "because they had no friends." A few couldn't care less about sports and can queen out on occasion, a fact the Regular Guys ironically point to as their collective "feminine side."

Some people hear about Regular Guys through word of mouth or the group's long-standing listing in the *Bay Times*, but most find the group through its Web site, regularguys.org. Schaefer says he regularly gets calls and e-mails from married men who mistake the group for a sex club for closet cases or bicurious married men. Schaefer politely e-mails them back ("They're not big about giving out their home numbers," he says), informing them that their unsuspecting wives may pose some logistical problems and that Regular Guys is not about sex. He rarely hears from them again.

On the site, Schaefer makes clear the kinds of guys who make quality Regular Guys. "Regular Guys is a group for SF Bay Area gay and bisexual men who identify as masculine," he writes. "We're not sitting here with a checklist, and our definition of masculinity isn't rigid. But this is a group with a point of view, and guys who identify with what we're saying about masculinity and male bonding tend to have a much better time than guys who take issue with the concept."

In a nutshell, the concept is that it's okay to want to socialize with gay guys who don't like "gay stuff." Furthermore, it's acceptable to call yourself a Regular Guy, even though you know full well that this could be perceived (and usually is) as insinuating that gay guys who like "gay stuff"—musicals, bubble baths, Judy Garland, figure skating—are somehow "not regular."

"Yeah, the name 'Regular Guys' is a huge hurdle we have to deal with," concedes Sweigard. "But for the reason alone that it pisses people off and gets people talking, you kind of have to go with it. People who are self-identified as gay early in their lives or who have known for a long time that they're gay and have to go through a lot of shit, their reaction can be very angry. It's, like, 'Never again are you going to put me in a fucking box!' So even if you come near them with a box that you're putting over yourself, they freak out, because they think you're trying to put that box over them, or they think your box is saying that their box is second-class."

San Francisco State University sociology professor Christopher Carrington, who studies gay groups and subcultures, says that whether gay men find the group's name insulting depends entirely on their take on the word "regular." "I don't find the group's name bothersome, mostly because I am not moved by the idea that we should hope to achieve regularity," says Carrington, the author of *No Place like Home—Relationships and Family Lives Among Gays and Lesbians*. "But because so many gay men have grown up feeling terribly irregular and deviant, I can understand why a group of gay men claiming to be 'regular' would be threatening. But it's important to remember that this controversy and debate about appearing 'regular' is nothing new. Gay men and women have been arguing about it for decades. Should we act like straight people act? Should we reject everything that straight people stand for? Harvey Milk said he had to wear a tie because he had to look like a regular guy."

The Regular Guys insist that they aren't interested in "dressing up" to look masculine. Their goal, instead, is to offer naturally masculine gay and bisexual men an alternative to what Schaefer calls the "deceptively small tent of mainstream gay culture." "Everything in San Francisco's gay culture is aimed at a stereotypical notion of what gay men are supposed to like and what gay men are supposed to do and how gay men are supposed to think," Schaefer tells me. "We come out of a straight society based on rules and regulations, and then when we come out into this gay culture, we learn that, oops, now we have to learn more rules and regulations about what it means to be an openly gay man. The assumption is that we all like the same stuff, or at least we can all be pigeonholed into one traditional gay subculture. . . . So what do we do as a community? We show *All About Eve*. Again."

To Sweigard and many of the Regular Guys, gay culture still means the boring, superficial, sometimes mean-spirited world of the bar and club scene, where gay men play by a short list of acceptable, predictable roles: drag, bear, leather, circuit, fem. "Regular Guys is not about "Okay, what costume am I putting on today?'" says Caesar Walker, a forty-seven-year-old Regular Guy from Concord who came out of the closet when he was thirty-seven. "The great thing about Regular Guys is that you just have to be yourself. I liken it to *Seinfeld* in a lot of ways. That's a show about nothing, and Regular Guys is kind of a group about nothing too serious, either. We're just gay guys who want to hang out with other gay guys and go to movies or ballgames. And we don't feel a part of mainstream gay culture."

And in so being, University of Windsor sociologist Barry Adam says, the Regular Guys might not be as unique as they think. "I don't know many gay men who *would* say they have a strong connection to 'gay culture,' whatever that is," Adam says. "So few people seem to like it, so they are all running off to other identities and forming all these other specific groups that combine being gay with other social activities. There has been a real evolution over the last twenty-five years toward a multiplication and fragmentation of gay groups. If you look in the gay papers of any big city, the listings get longer and longer. Does anyone still believe in the dream of a single unitary gay identity? I don't think so."

As Carrington (an admirer of baseball *and* circuit parties) says, "There is no booming gay voice of God in San Francisco telling gay people, 'Go to Macy's!'"

SEATED AT THE Jumpin' Java Coffee House in San Francisco, Eric Sweigard—a funny, deceptively intellectual man prone to rambling tangents—is enjoying a mildly homoerotic recollection/tangent about his high school wrestling days.

"Wrestling is so fuckin' bizarre," Sweigard tells me, munching on the last bite of a turkey sandwich. "There are three periods in wrestling, right? If you win the first, you get to get on top of the other guy. The other guy is down on all fours, *doggie style*, and you get on top of him, and you literally grind your groin into his ass, taking control of one wrist with one hand and wrapping your other hand around his stomach. You get to break him down. So all of this grinding and touching, and not *once* did I have a sexual feeling! Not once! I got to grind my groin against some of the finest sixteen- and seventeen-year-old ass in the tristate area and never once got a boner. And I look back now, and I'm, like, 'Doh!'" (He smacks himself in the head.)

The youngest of four children in what he calls an "obnoxiously" gregarious family, Sweigard has been a loudmouth wiseass for as long as he can remember. As a teenager, Sweigard attended an all-boys Catholic high school and lived a fairly naive existence when it came to sex. "I didn't even know two guys could do it until I was probably fifteen," he says. "Seems crazy now, but it just wasn't talked about in Omaha. And everyone has all these crazy stories about sexual escapades at *their* all-boys Catholic schools, but I swear there wasn't any cornholing going on at mine."

In college at Chicago's Loyola University, Sweigard says he had no strong sexual feelings toward men but did have several largely anticlimactic homosexual experiences. The first, in the bathroom at the Loyola University library, began when Sweigard noticed that the man standing in the neighboring urinal was playing with his erect penis, which Sweigard remembers as being "truly fucking unbelievably large. Then the guy looked at me and said, 'You wanna touch it?'"

Experience number two happened on a couch at the Carmelite dorm after an evening of collegiate drunken debauchery. (Although not all that religious, Sweigard briefly entertained the thought of becoming a priest.) Sweigard says the instigator was the only openly gay student among the Carmelites—a persistent young man who did not take Sweigard's "No thanks, man" for an answer. Highly inebriated, Sweigard says he finally gave in to a blow job.

After college, Sweigard—then a proud Reagan Republican—dated women, only rarely feeling any same-sex attractions. That changed when Sweigard was twenty-six. "My girlfriend at the time and I were sitting at a café, and I remember not being able to take my eyes off the waiter's ass," he says. "He had these two melons for an ass. He was so cute, not too femmy. That night, I remember going home with my girlfriend and just fucking the hell out of her, thinking about him the whole time. The next morning she looked at me and said, 'Wow, you were amazing last night!'"

A year later, Sweigard met a guy at the side of Chicago's gay pride parade route. They went back to his place and argued about who was going to get fucked. Neither gave in ("I still had *issues* with being a 'man' and getting fucked at that point," he says), so they settled on oral sex.

Sweigard, who moved to San Francisco two years ago and is now a proud Democrat, considers himself comfortably "out" these days. Still, being openly gay doesn't mean he relates to San Francisco gay culture. "If it wasn't for my gym affectation and my true love of staying fit, I'm not sure how I would meet homos," he says. "And it's so funny, because people at the gym and other places will say, 'Oh, you're so *butch*,' and the condescending assumption is that because I like sports and don't like going to bars, that I must not have accepted or come to terms with my true *gay soul*. And I'm, like, 'How many cocks do I need to stuff down my throat before people will believe that I am totally cool and in tune with my gayness?'"

MIKE SCHAEFER E-MAILS me with a link to a Web site that he finds quite funny. Straightacting.com, he says, is the place to test just how "masculine" you really are. He suggests I take the quiz and let him know how I fare.

I sense that I am off to a nonmasculine start when I admit to enjoying "receiving flowers" on Question 1, but I hope to make up for it on Question 2, when I answer that I do not enjoy "being tickled."

For Question 3, I shamefully admit to occasionally using the word "pee-pee," but I am feeling masculine again on Question 7, when I answer that my apartment has "less than two candles." (Is it *gay* of me to want to correct the site's grammar? It should be *fewer* than two candles.)

Question 9 goes right to the heart of my sex life, asking if I prefer top, bottom, versatile, or cuddling. Since multiple answers are encouraged, I check all four and move on. For Question 11, I categorically deny having ever purchased "any article of clothing or accessories for myself from a woman's department store."

When I'm done, I click the results button and learn that on a scale from 1 to 10, with 1 being "The Ultimate in Straight Acting" and 10 being "Queen Status," I am a 3, which is to say I am "Mostly Straight Acting." For those of us at this level of masculinity, we lead, according to the results, "A normal everyday life, and it's 'no questions asked,' as people assume you are straight. Every once and a while a very aware person might notice something that causes them to think 'fem,' but it's a fleeting thought because you turn around and surprise them with more masculine traits."

Relieved (and amused) to know that I can pass for straight, I check my e-mail again a few hours later. Schaefer—who, incidentally, does not like the expression "straight acting"—writes to tell me that he is also a 3, a level he deems fairly accurate. "I had to admit to owning *Donna Summer's Greatest Hits,*" he says. Sweigard e-mails me to say he is a 2. "I do like musical theatre, in *theory,*" he writes. "And I'm neat."

• • •

IT IS 6 p.m. on a Sunday night, and the Regular Guys are hungry. Standing in the lobby of a local mall, five Regular Guys have two hours to kill before enjoying a screening of *Gladiator*.

Right now, though, the Regular Guys need to eat. "Should we go to the food court or the sports bar?" Schaefer asks.

"Oh, I'm flexible," says thirty-year-old Regular Guy Joe Delehanty from San Francisco.

"Yeah, we've heard!" Schaefer says.

Just then a balding, beer-bellied, fiftysomething man walks by the group with a younger, cuter companion. Delehanty, a self-described lover of "daddy types," doesn't look twice at the twentysomething, instead eyeing the older man. "Oh, I'll take that one home right now!" he says.

"Man, when did [this place] become cruise central?" asks Russ Meyer, a Regular Guy from Rockford.

"Duh," says Delehanty. "The second they built it!"

The Regular Guys finally decide on the food court. Delehanty orders chicken strips and fries off a children's menu, then goes on to explain what makes a movie a Regular Guys' movie. "There's gotta be death, destruction, real *guy* stuff," he says. "Someone's gotta die. Lotsa guns. Or it's gotta be a sports movie." In the past months, the Regular Guys have seen *Fight Club, Mission to Mars, Any Given Sunday,* and *End of Days*.

Delehanty excuses himself to go to the bathroom, after which the conversation turns slightly more serious. Everyone at the table is intrigued by Meyer's job at a company that creates brand names and logos, and the Regular Guys wonder about alternate names for Regular Guys.

"The Assholes," Delehanty says, having returned from the bathroom and forgotten to zip up his pants. "We could call each other The Assholes. That would be about right."

Meyer points to Delehanty's zipper: "Um, that much action in the bathroom?"

After a brief discussion about past bathroom sexual experiences, talk turns to the best city gyms. Delehanty fondly tells the group about the YMCA in Atlanta, where he used to live. "There are plenty of gyms with backroom action, but this one, I swear, it doubled as a bathhouse for 'straight' guys," he says, playing with his fries. "Their wives would be working their little hearts out on the treadmill, and meantime, the husbands are in the locker room jerking each other off."

The gym story leads to a debate about bisexuality and sexual labeling, and Delehanty listens in amazement as one Regular Guy mentions that he still likes girls, and another offers a graphic reenactment of a past experience eating out a woman. "Okay, I just lost my appetite!" Delehanty says. "Call me a big old queen, but I don't have *any* bisexual tendencies whatsoever. None at all."

Meyer raises his arms in mock victory. "And women the world over are celebrating! They're dancing in the streets!"

THE TASK IS simple, really. After the Giants game, Schaefer and I must cross from one side of the Embarcadero to the other. I choose the most direct route, which requires that we cross the Muni tracks, jump up on a three-foot-high platform, then jump down again. Two athletic-looking ladies in their forties (lesbians, perhaps?) have just chosen the same path, executing the simple exercise without incident.

I jump up on the platform, then jump down again, turning to wait for Schaefer, who is having some difficulty with the jumping down part. He eyes the three-foot drop with trepidation. He gets on one knee, hoping he can avoid the jump altogether by simply lowering himself down. He can't. He eyes me eyeing him and smiles bashfully, finally deciding to take the big plunge and jump. He stumbles slightly on impact.

"I guess I didn't look like much of a Regular Guy there, did I?" Schaefer says, shaking his head. "And I bet you're going to put that in the story, aren't you? The founder of Regular Guys is too chicken to cross the street! What a girl!"